Periods of European Literature

EDITED BY

PROFESSOR SAINTSBURY

III.

THE FOURTEENTH CENTURY

PERIODS OF EUROPEAN LITERATURE.

EDITED BY PROFESSOR SAINTSBURY.

" The criticism which alone can much help us for the future is a criticism which regards Europe as being, for intellectual and spiritual purposes, one great confederation, bound to a joint action and working to a common result."

—MATTHEW ARNOLD.

In 12 Crown 8vo Volumes.   Price 5s. net each.

The DARK AGES . . . . . Professor W. P. KER.

The FLOURISHING OF ROMANCE
    AND THE RISE OF ALLEGORY . THE EDITOR.   [*Ready.*

The FOURTEENTH CENTURY . . F. J. SNELL.   [*Ready.*

The TRANSITION PERIOD . . . G. GREGORY SMITH.

The EARLIER RENAISSANCE . . THE EDITOR.

The LATER RENAISSANCE . . . DAVID HANNAY.   [*Ready.*

The FIRST HALF OF 17TH CENTURY . Professor H. J. C. GRIERSON.

The AUGUSTAN AGES . . . . OLIVER ELTON.   [*Shortly.*

The MID-EIGHTEENTH CENTURY . J. HEPBURN MILLAR.

The ROMANTIC REVOLT . . . Professor C. E. VAUGHAN.

The ROMANTIC TRIUMPH . . . T. S. OMOND.

The LATER NINETEENTH CENTURY THE EDITOR.

WILLIAM BLACKWOOD & SONS, EDINBURGH AND LONDON.

THE

FOURTEENTH CENTURY

BY

F. J. SNELL

WILLIAM BLACKWOOD AND SONS
EDINBURGH AND LONDON
MDCCCXCIX

PREFACE.

THE range and difficulty of the task essayed in the following pages render explanation unavoidable. The writer entered on the undertaking, not only with much trepidation, but with some amount of misapprehension. When at last the real nature of the enterprise dawned upon him, he was already too deeply committed to withdraw from it. He determined therefore to do his best, consoling himself with the thought that the work was worth accomplishing, were the workman unworthy. It is evident that a book of this sort must depend, in a larger measure than is entirely agreeable, on compilation. The only alternative is to ignore the claims of whole literatures with which one possesses no large first-hand acquaintance. To be precise, the writer, though he once knew a little Swedish, is exceedingly backward in Icelandic, whilst his Welsh is even more elementary, being almost

non-existent.   It is hardly necessary perhaps to inflict
on the reader an exact statement of literary and
linguistic limitations in respect of other European
tongues.   Enough that these limitations are felt and
confessed ; but they do not affect, in any serious degree,
the vitals of the work.

From an author's point of view, the making of such
a book, though it has its advantages, especially in
deepening his insight into the various subject-matters,
has also its disadvantages.   If personal reputation
were the object at stake, then he must needs lament
the mingling of results attained by his own thought
and industry with those accepted on authority, though
he recognises, with all sensible judges, that only in
that way can a work of this kind be satisfactorily
carried through.   If there be a danger of the author
receiving more credit than his due, there is also a
danger of his receiving considerably less.   Neither
event, however, is of much public importance, if the
object of the series be overtaken, or, at any rate,
approached, in the broadening of literary study, in
the breaking down of artificial barriers of race, and
language, and country.

Long before he contemplated the possibility of such
an honour as that which has now fallen to his lot, the
writer had studied practically on the lines now suggested for imitation.   On the right-hand side of the
fireplace in the library of Balliol there was, and may
still be, a set of Italian classics, for inopportune

attention to which he was reproved by the illustrious scholar who then presided over the fortunes of the college. The reproof was strictly conditional. That sagacious and kind-hearted man would, I am confident, have been foremost in sympathising with the attempt here made to deal with literature, not indeed "scientifically," but still as an organism, as a whole in relation to its parts. Pursued by isolated readers, the study of European Literature too often becomes irregular—wanting in cohesiveness and wanting in aim. Apart from the guidance of a series like the present, a way to avoid a fatiguing and demoralising discursiveness is to take some great writer—Dante or Shakespeare—and then to *work outwards*, studying other writings and literatures in relation to the central subject. But, if this be done, it will still be desirable to gain, as it were, a "bird's-eye view" of the intellectual conditions of the age in which the great writer flourished, even though, as will often be the case, we can trace no immediate connection between particular "stars"—say, Dante and Froissart. To learn all of Dante and nothing of Froissart would be, at best, an imperfect education.

Most of the works that I have used, and some that I have not (*e.g.*, translations), have been mentioned either in the text or in the footnotes; but I desire especially to record the obligations under which I rest, in common with all students of mediæval literature, to the famous publishing house of Herr Karl J.

Trübner, whose services to learning, and especially to
this branch of learning, are simply incalculable.   If
only on account of their bibliographies, I may cite his
Grundrisse of Germanic and Romance philology, to
which the most eminent scholars have contributed,
and which are now almost completed, as monumental
additions to the scientific side of literary study.
Among scholars generally no one perhaps ever
covered so wide a field as Herr Karl Bartsch, from
whose shadow I found it at one time not easy to
emancipate myself.

As the drama of the fourteenth and fifteenth
centuries is very difficult to apportion and separate
exactly, it has, in accordance with the general plan
of the series, been left for consecutive treatment in
the ensuing volume.

CONTENTS.

CHAPTER I.

THE END OF COURT-POETRY.

CHAPTER II.

TOWN-VERSE AND FOLK-SONG.

CHAPTER III.

RISE OF A NEW LYRIC.

CHAPTER IV.

DANTE.

CHAPTER V.

DAWN OF THE RENAISSANCE.

CHAPTER VI.

THE WELL OF ENGLISH.

CHAPTER VII.

TIME AND SPACE.

CHAPTER VIII.

ALLEGORY, MYSTICISM, AND REFORM.

CHAPTER IX.

THE FOURTEENTH CENTURY.

CHAPTER I.

THE END OF COURT-POETRY.

CAUSES OF DECLINE—'ENFANCES'—REVOLUTIONARY SPIRIT—CYCLICAL
POEMS—FRANCO-ITALIAN EPICS—FRENCH PATRIOTIC VERSE—ROMANS
D'AVENTURE — 'CENTO NOVELLE ANTICHE' — THE 'AVVENTUROSO
CICILIANO'—THE 'REALI DI FRANCIA'—GERMAN EPICS—ICELANDIC
RÍMUR — FORNSÖGUR AND LÝGISÖGUR — ENGLISH ROMANCES — AL-
LITERATIVE POETRY—SCOTTISH ROMANCES—THE 'BRUCE'—LAURENCE
MINOT.

How came the old poetry—epic, romance, minnesong
—to die out as it did in the fourteenth century ? Was
Who killed it suffocated by adverse outward conditions,
court-poetry? or had it completed its natural term of
life ? Perhaps it is not necessary to choose between
these solutions. It seems probable that more than
one cause was at work. That there were hostile
agencies abroad cannot be doubted. In this task of

A

destruction, this intellectual vandalism, the clergy, the
traditional and bitter foes of the secular poet, were
more or less conscious tools, while the master-singers
contributed to the same result by their ineptitude.
Then there was the rise, both economic and political,
of the middle class.   The importance of this factor in
the overthrow of court-verse [1] cannot well be over-
estimated.   Already in the reign of Frederick II. a
wandering gleeman, Freidank, had scented the offence
and revenged it in advance.   His antipathy found
vent in opprobrious terms.   The knights, the clergy,
and the peasants were the orders created by God.
The fourth, or trading, class was of the Devil.

Over and above these external enemies, however,
it is possible to detect in the court-poetry of the fourteenth and concluding portion of the thir-

Internal decay.

teenth century many signs of decay —
signs that are strictly parallel with evidences of old
age in the individual.   " The gay poets of the Middle
Age," remarks M. Dinaux,[2] " began with singing love
and its delights ; later they turned into verse the tales,
the histories, and the *fabliaux* of the country ; then,
when age and infirmities overtook them, they fell back
on sacred and philosophic subjects."   He adds that the

---

[1] The words " court-verse," " court-poetry," &c., though in universal use on the Continent, have been adopted not without misgivings.
The terms are new, and have been censured as exaggerating the influence of courts on the poetry in question.   The diminution of this
influence, however, was of capital importance in the transformations
poetry was now to undergo.

[2] *Trouvères du Nord de la France et du Midi de la Belgique*, vol. iv.
p. 51.

gay poets did not always observe these "time-limits,"
and that, in general, their compositions exhibit a fine
medley of the worldly and other-worldly. The speech
and confession of a typical *trouvère,* Hugues de Bersil,
explain this apparent contradiction by the real contradiction of preaching and practice:—

> "Hugues de Bersil qui tant a
> Cerchié le siecle çà et là
> Qu'il a veu qu'il ne vaut rien,
> Préesche ore de fere bien :
> Et si sait bien que li plusor
> Tenront mes sermons à folor ;
> Qar il ont veu que j'avoie
> Plus que nus d'aus solaz et joie,
> Et que j'ai aussi grant mestier
> Que nus d'aus de moi préeschier."

M. Dinaux refers to a tendency only; and in these
lines the tendency is clear enough. We also have to
do with a tendency, and another French writer, quite
independently, sums up the character of the fourteenth
century in the words: "Every discourse is practically
a sermon. To speak is to preach. In the art of
preaching lies the whole art of speaking." True, on
the whole; and yet, in its inconsistencies, the period
resembles the gay poets. Outstanding inconsistencies
are the futile attempts of epic and romance to survive
and thrive in this uncongenial atmosphere; and convenience suggests that these failures be noted first.
To the decadent lyric, naturally more capable of adaptation, will be consecrated the ensuing chapter.

One striking feature of the "death-struck" epic is

the quality of inventiveness.   In the cavalier handling

Enfances.
of the various *matières*, whether of France, or Britain, or "Rome la grant," the later poets do on a large scale what their precursors had only ventured to do piecemeal and apologetically. Even the *Chanson de Geste*, supposed to be strongly based on the bed-rock of historical fact, manifests this caprice.   Doubtless the fiction of veracity had still to be maintained, but a compromise was not difficult of attainment, and lay in the direction of *enfances* (*i.e.*, first exploits) and genealogy.   A well-known name like that of the rather mysterious William is made the pivot of a whole cycle of poems more or less "contaminated."   To this particular cycle — the *Geste of Garin de Montglane*, as it was called in mediæval times —belong about twenty epics, assonanced or rhymed, ranging from the commencement of the twelfth to the end of the thirteenth century, and recounting the feats of seven or eight generations of heroes, in which are commonly included the taking of a town and the winning of a Saracen princess.   Of these the *Enfances Guillaume*, the *Département des Enfants Aimeri*, and the *Enfances Vivien* are wholly outside tradition.   The *Enfances Garin de Montglane*, perhaps the last of the series, pertains to the fourteenth century.

The lack of reverence already implied in the tampering with history or legend, the ascription of imagin-

Revolution-
ary spirit.
ary doings to traditional names, comes to a head in works like *Hugues Capet, le Bastard de Bouillon, Baudouin de Sebourc, Tristan de Nanteuil*, and *Charles le Chauve*, none of them attached

to the conventional cycles. These are not true epics, but parodies.[1] How little they are animated by the spirit of chivalry may be inferred from the circumstance that in them sentiments are avowed that would have ravished the heart of Cobbler Simon. Thus *Baudouin de Sebourc* explains:—

> " Car trestous venons d'Eve, notre père fu Adans.
> Il n'est nul gentis ; nul homme n'est vilain."

It is the same with *Hugues Capet :—*

> " Dieu est tout rassotis qu'ainsi avance un homme."

Nor do morals fare better than religion. In *Tristan de Nanteuil*[2] Blanchardine, Tristan's mistress, accompanies her lover disguised as a knight — " par jour est chevalier, par nuit la mariée." A Mohammedan princess falls in love with the pretended knight, who is already a mother, and Blanchardine, spite of all attempts at evasion, is compelled to wed the lady now converted to Christianity. Naturally she falls into sore perplexity as to how to discharge her marital duties, but, ere it is too late, is miraculously transformed into a man. Instead of Blanchardine she becomes Blanchardin, and lives happily with her wife Clarinde, by whom she has several children.

The best of the set is *Baudouin de Sebourc,*[3] and the

---

[1] On this point critics are not absolutely at one. *Hugues Capet*, at any rate, is open to grave suspicion.

[2] See *Jahrbuch für rom. und eng. Literatur*, ix. p. 366.

[3] *Li Romans de Baudouin de Sebourc*, Valenciennes, 1841.

best thing in *Baudouin de Sebourc* is the episode of the
The Old Man of Old Man of the Mountain, which is full
the Mountain. of delightful irony. "Would you see won-
ders?" he says to the kings, Baudouin, Polibans, and
the Khalif of Baudas, who visit him, and calling up one
of his subjects, signs to him to fling himself down.
The Hautassis complies, and is dashed to pieces. Five
others immolate themselves in like manner, to the
dismay of Baudouin. The Khalif, however, expresses
becoming admiration, and the guests are then conducted to a garden flowing with wine and honey. In
the midst sits Ivorine, the Old Man's daughter, in a
baldachin; and with her are two hundred damsels
singing melodiously. Ivorine has never yet smiled
on mortal man, waiting indeed for the flower of
knighthood. Her father, who has his eye on one of
the Saracen visitors, tries to coax her:—

> " Dame, vechi trois prinches corageus et hardis :
>   En i a nul des trois, doche fille gentis,
>   Par coi vos coers puist estre de joie rasouffis ?"

The lovely creature allows that this is so, and
Baudouin, who could not have held his tongue for
all the gold of Paris, inquires if he is the lucky man.
Ivorine, smiling on him, replies that he is her friend.
" Par Dieu," quoth Baudouin, " s'ai bel joëil conquis."
The Old Man, however, is not so well pleased, regarding Baudouin as the least worthy of the three. But
worse is to follow. Ivorine, the reverse of dutiful,
pours scorn on her father for having begotten her,
seeing that she was to be the cause of his ruin. More-

over, he is a heretic and believes in the Devil, while she has been soundly converted to the faith. Finally, she offers him the choice of two things, either to believe or to be slain. The Old Man, very wroth, orders the Khalif to kill his daughter, but the Khalif, despising his threats, draws a large knife and stabs the Old Man in the belly.

Old men's tales are not only genealogical, redounding to the credit, or otherwise, of somebody's father or grandfather, but they are wont to be in-
Cyclical poems. ordinately spun out. This frailty is reflected in the last state of the mediæval epic. Literary old age, unable to produce fresh masterpieces, revels in encyclopædic compilations. The *Entrée de Spagne*, for instance, is a hash of *Roland, Ferragus,* and the *Prise de Nobles,* very long (especially if we include the sequel), but by no means deficient in imagination or power of expression. This epic belongs to a class of poems composed in the north of Italy rather as rivals than as reproductions of native French verse, and merits, if only for this reason, particular attention.

Intellectually, Northern or " High " Italy was the " Italia irredenta " of the close of the Middle Age.
Franco-Italian The long array of *trovatori*, with Sordello
epics. at their head, poetising in the Provençal tongue, found in Lombardy their chief home and sphere. There also flourished a learned Latin literature which, in several not unimportant points, forestalled the classical revival inaugurated by Petrarch and Boccaccio. The North-French epic was transferred,

not merely as *matière*, but organically, to the same hospitable region, where, it is hardly too much to say, it enjoyed a second summer. The cultivation of this art takes different forms, and presents in the various specimens different degrees of perfection, but in all are discoverable native elements, not always of the same kind, attesting the nationality of the cultivators. In the Italian MSS. of *Aliscans* and *Aspremont*, preserved in the Biblioteca Marciana at Venice, the text is disfigured by Italian dialectal peculiarities, while *Gui de Nanteuil* contains an introduction of a thousand lines, for which the responsibility rests entirely with the copyist.

The *Entrée de Spagne*[1] belongs to the later type of French *chansons*, of which *Huon de Bordeaux* may be *The* Entrée de taken as a sample, and which exhibits a *Spagne.* blending of the spirit of the Crusades with the Arthurian legends. Roland, without his uncle's knowledge, storms the city of Nobles, and on his return is cuffed by the indignant Charlemagne. Stung by this insult, Roland quits the camp and travels in Persia and the Holy Land. He performs all manner of doughty deeds, and converts heathen Soldans to Christianity. In the desert he is warned by a hermit, whom an angel has inspired to this effect, that he has seven years yet to live, that he is destined to conquer Spain, and finally to die by the hand of a traitor. The

[1] A full account of the *Entrée de Spagne* is given by Gautier in *Bibliothèque de l'Ecole des Chartes*, 4th series, vol. iv. p. 217, &c. ; the *Prise de Pampelune* has been published by Mussafia in *Altfranzösische Gedichte aus Venetian.* HSS., Vienna, 1864.

Italian authorship is betrayed in the episode of Roland's visit to Rome, where he receives from the Pope an army of twenty thousand warriors; and these he leads in battle as a Roman senator.

Turning to the sister epic, the *Prise de Pampelune,* the title is not very happily chosen, inasmuch as only *The* Prise de the commencement of the poem is occupied Pampelune. with this incident, and the commencement, it happens, has been lost. The propriety of the title may be debated the more freely, as it was bestowed in quite modern times by Michelant. Although not by the same hand, it is practically a continuation of the *Entrée de Spagne,* and its theme is the capture of several towns, not merely that of Pampeluña. The work is much inferior to its predecessor. Very wordy, and altogether lacking in freshness, artistically it is little better than a rhyming chronicle, while of no value as a record of facts. The prominence of Desirier (Desiderio), who in the purely French *chansons* has no share in the conquest of Spain, is an evidence of the writer's Lombard origin. Desirier is the hero of the *Prise de Pampelune;* and when he comes to ask a favour of the emperor, he craves that the Lombards may ever retain their freedom, and that any Lombard, irrespective of birth, may have power to become a knight.

The same actors figure in both poems, and of these one now assumes an importance destined to be per-*Estout.* petuated in Italian epics of chivalry. This is Estout, the wag or humorist of the companionship of Charlemagne. Whimsical as he is,

Estout wants neither courage nor prudence. On one occasion he captures a town on his own account, and as a huge jest refuses admittance to the Christian host. Charlemagne pleads to be let in:—

> " Bieus sire Hestous, pour amour vous prion
> Che vous nous hostalies dedens vetre maison."

Estout curtly rejects his entreaty, and it is only through Roland's diplomacy that the rogue is induced to yield. When affairs are critical, however, this bizarre campaigner is the soul of caution.

Naturalised in Tuscan folk-tale, Estout reappears in the poems of Boiardo and Ariosto as Astolfo the Englishman. How did Astolfo become English ? In the purely French narratives he is Duke of Langres, and nothing is said as to his English extraction. The answer to the question witnesses to the influence of these Franco-Italian compositions on the development of the Carlovingian epic. The Anglicising of Astolfo is due to error or forgetfulness on the part of the author or transcriber of the *Entrée de Spagne.* At first Estout appears as de Lengres and Lengrois. Then he is designated de Lengles and Lenglois; and Lenglois, by psychological necessity, is improved into L'Englois, as more striking and intelligible.

It has been stated that the *Entrée de Spagne* and the *Prise de Pampelune* are distinct in their origin. *Authorship of the poems.* The precise relations between the poems seem to be as follows. The last hundred and thirty - one lines of MS. xxi. of the *Entrée de*

Spagne are probably by the author of the *Prise de Pampelune*. All that is known of the author of the *Entrée de Spagne* is his own statement that he was a Paduan. The writer of the postscript calls himself Nicola, and it is not unlikely that he is the same with one Nicola di Verona, who, in a Franco-Italian poem on the Passion, alludes to narrative verse written by him in the French language. Both epics are in mono-rhymed tirades. A shorter composition, the *Roman d'Hector*, like the more famous *Roman de Troie* of Benoit de Sainte-More, is in rhymed couplets of eight syllables, and, being concerned with the early exploits of the hero, may be cited as an instance of *enfances* in Franco-Italian verse.

It is necessary to insist on the Italian element, as it is by no means represented solely by the writers' nativity, or their natural predilection for *The language.* the land of their birth. By these circumstances the language is more or less modified — the *Entrée* less, the *Prise* more—and the degree of modification was no doubt determined by the status and education of author and audience. In general, it is safe to assume that the epic-writers never attained to the distinction of the Italian *trovatori*, and often were little, if at all, superior to the common ballad-singer. Two citations, one from a cyclical Franco-Italian *Bueve de Hanstone*, and the other from a *Bovo d'Antona* in the Venetian dialect slightly tinctured with French, will serve to illustrate the possible variations. On the score of art both must be condemned to the same Inferno of insignificance.

Bueve de Hanstone.

"Qe un çubler [*i.e.*, jongleur] qe è qui arrivé
Por veoir questa cort e la nobilité,
Tuto li son afaire el m'a dito e conté
Qe in la dama no è la falsité,
Salvo q' ela oit un poco grandi li pé ;
Nian por ço non vo' je qe stagé
Qi la po avoir, qe non la demandé."

Bovo d'Antona.

"'Fiolo,' disse Synibaldo, 'porestu çivalçer
Palafren o destrer ? A San Simon voio ander ;
Che quelo castelo me dona to per ;
Per quelo castelo me faço clamer ;
Ed è ben trenta ani ch' el me l'à doner.
Se a quel castelo te posso mener,
Io faro guera po' a sta citta.'
Respoxe Bovolin : 'Io porò ben çivalçer
Destrer e cavalo chi me possa porter ;
Infin a San Simon avero ander.'"

A similar comparison might have been instituted between a Franco-Italian *Huon d'Auvergne* and the Venetian *Ugo d'Alvernia*, but, as *Huon d'Auvergne* survives only in a rough Italian translation, this is no longer feasible. The fact of this translation, however, may be taken as proving that *Huon* was written in the same kind of "pigeon" French as *Bueve d'Hanstone*. These poems, *Huon* and *Ugo*, narrate a journey to Hell, and — a matter of exceptional interest—in both Dante's influence is discernible. The last product of Franco-Italian

Other Franco-Italian compositions.

literature is a prose romance, *Aquilon de Bavière*. Written by Rafaele Marmora of Verona at the close of the fourteenth century, it begins and ends with Italian *ottave*—a sure sign that the spell of French literary art was at last broken.

Closely allied with compilation as a symptom of decay are the *remaniements*, to which some ancient *Chansons de Geste*, like popular hymns in
Remaniements. our own day, were compelled to submit. Rehandling in these cases denotes several things. The verse may be changed. For the decasyllabic may be substituted the Alexandrine metre. The style and spelling are modernised. Old racy words like *entière, naïf, chétif* are supplanted by learned terms, *intègre, natif, captif*. Finally, by the insertion of new episodes and endless descriptions, the bulk of the poems is enormously increased. *Ogier le Danois*, in its latest form, numbers twenty-five thousand lines; *Huon de Bordeaux* thirty thousand; and others, it is said, forty, and even sixty, thousand lines. These totals are suggestive. The *Chanson de Geste* — may we not certify that it succumbed to fatty degeneration?

A predisposing cause of the decline of the French epic was the decline of the French nobility. French *The French* society, with a growing distrust of its own *nobility.* pretensions, and sensible that it could no longer sustain them, found small inducement to encourage the production of poems in which those pretensions were magnified. Clearly, in such circumstances, it was a problem not more difficult than unpleasant to determine at what point panegyric

shaded off into intentional, or unintentional, irony.
Here are verses depicting the actual state at which
the barons had arrived, and which is held to account
for the disaster of Poitiers :—

> "Bombanz et vaine gloire, vesture deshonnête,
> Les ceintures dorées, la plume sur la tête,
> La grant barbe de bouc, qui est une orde beste,
> Les vous font estordiz, comme fouldre et tempeste. . . .
> La très-grant traïson qu'ils ont longtemps covée
> Fut, en l'ost dessus dit, très-clèrement provée."

But there was still left in France a remnant of true
knights untainted by treason and capable of acquitting
themselves like heroes.   Their valour would almost
persuade us to reject the foregoing citation as libel-
lous, only that Crécy and Poitiers were facts.   But
such also was the Combat of the Thirty.   Froissart
bears witness to its reality, and the tidings must have
been inexpressibly consoling to gallant hearts jealous
for French honour.

The Combat, " memorised " in a brief poem of three
hundred lines [1]—"the last echo of the *Chansons de
Geste*"—is on a par with the famous duel
between the Chesapeake and Shannon.
The English were disposed to make the most of
their conquests, and the roar of the British lion
sounded very harshly in the ear of the brave Beaumanoir.   But he is even more afflicted at the woes of
the country-folk.   These poor caitiffs are bound with
gyves and fetters—two and two, and three and three

The Combat
des Trente.

---

[1] Crapelet, Paris, 1835 ; Bartsch, *Chrestomathie*, p. 403.

—and driven as one drives cattle to market. First, with great humility, Beaumanoir expostulates with the English commander Brambroc. He points out the folly of oppressing the peasantry. If they didn't work, the nobles would have to handle hoe and flail, and suffer poverty—a dreadful thing for any one not accustomed to it. In reply, Brambroc rudely boasts of the power and authority of his nation, where-upon Messire Jehan, changing his tone, challenges him to fight, sixty, eighty, or a hundred a-side. Bram-broc, for all his boasting, was but a false knight, and had failed to keep an appointment with "the valiant nobleman, the gentle bachelor," Pierre Angier. Beaumanoir reminds him of this, and expresses the hope that he will not play him the same trick. Brambroc begs him to desist, and assures him that he will be the first in the field with thirty men, the least of whom shall be a squire. "Never will I bring villein thither, so help me God!" When the time comes, however, Brambroc arms a huge ruffian "with a sackful of beans on his shoulders and a belly bigger than a courser's," trusting that he will carry all before him by sheer weight. The poet, whoever he may have been, does not belittle the English as a race. They are "bold as lions," as is proved by the event. The Bretons are equally brave, and win. The Combat took place in 1350, and the poem, which is in *laisses monorimes*, was probably composed soon after.

Later, the exploits of Bertrand du Guesclin pro-vided another opportunity, by which a *trouvère* named Cuvelier profited to the tune of twenty-three

thousand lines;[1] and in 1376 the glories of the Black
Prince were enshrined in a poem com-
posed in not very good French by one
Chandos, herald of Sir John Chandos, then Constable
of Aquitaine.[2] These writings, though possessing little
or no literary merit, are of considerable historical value,
since it is possible to glean from them many out-of-
the-way particulars respecting an exceptionally interesting time.

Historical Poems.

Romance showed itself even more impatient of
restraint than the *Chanson de Geste*, and there sprang
into existence a class of poems known as
Romans d'Aventure. The term is some-
what elastic ; definitions vary as to its scope, but all
definitions are at one in recognising as the core and
kernel of the matter the prevalence of the fictitious as
compared with the traditional element.   Outwardly,
the *Roman d'Aventure* is attached to the Breton cycle
—*i.e.*, its metre is the octosyllabic couplet.   Yet a
third characteristic may be noted : the tale, as it unfolds, often sheds light on contemporary manners.
Thus this species of verse has much affinity with the
modern novel ; and, to heighten the resemblance, the
material of these poems was worked up later into
miracles, many of which are merely dramatised versions of *Romans d'Aventure*.

Romans d'Aventure.

[1] *La Chanson de Bertrand du Guesclin,* par Cuvelier.   E. Charrière.
Paris, 1839.

[2] *Chandos Herald, The Life and Feats of Arms of Edward the Black
Prince.*   A Metrical Chronicle in Old French, with an English translation and notes by Francisque Michel.   London, 1888.

At first this might seem to intimate a long step in advance, but, in actual fact, the imagination of *romanciers* was "cribb'd, cabin'd, and confined." Whatever originality may have been theirs, the demands of their audience could not be ignored, and set bounds that they dared not pass. One class of romances devoted itself to celebrating "la fine et loyale amour," a very elevated attachment of which the royal poet had predicated that "of it comes sense and goodness," but which, in romance at least, is conspicuous rather for the latter than the former quality. A young vassal lifts his eyes to his lord's daughter, who not unnaturally despises him, but relents on his falling sick. Or perchance, as in *Blancandin*, to prove his worth, he sets forth in search of adventures. Sometimes, however, these "traverseurs de voies perilleuses" are merely plain folk, a husband looking for his wife, a father looking for a son, and, oddest of all, some infatuated person seeking the answer to a riddle. Also, pilgrims to Rome, the Holy Land, and St James of Compostella.

A pathetic figure often encountered in these romances —notably in the *Manekine* of Philippe de Beaumanoir and the rather later *Comte d'Anjou* of Jean Maillart— is the innocent wife on whose fair fame a rival has cast a blot. Driven from her husband, we find her in a frail boat on the open sea, or wandering in the forest, until Providence is pleased to vindicate her character. In *Guillaume de Palerne*, on the contrary, it is the knight that suffers. Through the felony of his step-mother he is turned into a wolf. Here and

B

there may be traced the influence of the *Romance
of the Rose*.   In *La Poire*,[1] for instance, a tale of
two thousand eight hundred lines, the actors are
allegorical personages — Franchise, Simplesse, Doux-
Regard, Beauté, Raison, and Curtoisie.   Finally, the
Christian idea of penitence, or penance, supplies a
motive.   A career of crime is atoned for by voluntary pains of the severest kind, borne without falter-
ing.   Thus the epic, whether it was originally Breton
or Carlovingian, ended by becoming a mere story designed to gratify idle readers.

The last stage was reached when poetry ceased, even
in the outward sense, to be poetry at all.   The great
Prose Romances.   age of the prose versions was the fifteenth
century, by which time the writings of
Froissart had given to prose a vogue, an air of distinction.   Some, however, are earlier.   In 1858 MM.
Moland and d'Héricault published three romances,
mutually distinct, though each is interesting — *Asseneth, Foulques Fitzwarin*, and *Troilus*.[2]   Concerning
Asseneth something may be said here.

Of the story of Joseph, as recorded in the Book
of Genesis, Voltaire remarked that in the
Asseneth.   whole range of Arabian fiction he could
not find its equal in beauty and pathos.   It is

---

[1] *Li Romanz de la Poire.*   Ed. Stehlich, Halle, 1881.

[2] *Nouvelles françaises en prose du xiv⁰ siècle.*   Paris, Janet.   *Fitzwarin*, which is in very interesting Norman, or rather English-
French, had been previously published by Thomas Wright for the
Warton Club (1855).   It has probably been "disrhymed" from an
earlier poem, and is a family history of an outlaw baron, full of
spirit.

evident, however, that somebody, less convinced of its unapproachable perfection, had ere this attempted an improvement, possibly for the benefit of the young. The credit of the idea has been conjecturally assigned to Jewish converts in the first ages of Christianity. After floating about for many centuries, the revised account found a haven in a Latin compilation which served as a sort of commonplace-book for writers in the "dialects"—Vincent de Beauvais' *Mirror of History*. Somewhere between 1317 and 1327 the tale was translated into French by Jean de Vignay, who succeeded in investing it with much of the charm of the old metrical romances.

Asseneth, the daughter of Potiphar, Pharaoh's chief counsellor, dwelt in the topmost storey of a tower adjoining her father's house, and rising in the midst of a magnificent orchard, watered by living streams. Her chamber, formed of coloured marble, incrusted with precious stones, and hung with cloth-of-gold, contained a gilt bed lined with purple woven with gold and jacinths. There slept Asseneth alone, and no man had ever sat on that bed. Asseneth was tall like Sarah, graceful like Rebecca, and fair like Rachel. One day Joseph came to the tower on an errand from Potiphar. Joseph was arrayed in a white coat, very splendid, and a purple cloak woven with gold. He bore on his head a gilt crown, and in this crown were twelve very fine stones, and over these stones were twelve stars of gold; and he held in his hand a royal wand and an olive branch very full of fruit.

When Asseneth beheld him approaching in a fair

chariot drawn by four snow-white steeds, she cried,
"Lo, here is the sun coming to us in his chariot. I
knew not that Joseph was a son of God. Who can
beget so great beauty, and what woman's womb can
bear such light?" Joseph agrees to marry her on
condition that she will cast away her idols. So Asseneth, sick with fear and joy, renounces her gods, and
does penance. For seven days, in black apparel and
ashes on her brow, she weeps bitterly. She has
thrown her idols out of the window, and given all
her royal food to the dogs. Then a light gleams in
the east; an angel, his face all aflame, comes down
from heaven into her chamber. He lays his hand on
her head and blesses her. " Asseneth! Asseneth!
rejoice and be comforted, for thy virgin's name is
written in the book of the living, and I have given
thee to Joseph to wife." On the morrow Joseph
returns to the tower. Pharaoh sets on their heads
crowns of gold, the best that he has, makes a great
wedding and great feasts that last seven days, and
commands that none do any work during the
interval.

It would be pleasant to give some account of
Perceforest, which, according to M. Gaston Paris, belongs to the fourteenth century. Un-
luckily, the composition as a whole exists
only in black-letter. Some notion of its character,
however, may be gleaned from a liberal excerpt in
Bartsch's *Chrestomathie* describing in considerable
detail the knighting of a young "damoysel." It is
tempting to compare this narrative with the over-

Perceforest.

ture to *Don Quixote:* here, a handsome youth, at the outset of his career, arrayed by fair ladies and gallant knights; there, the old, lean, crack-brained, but withal magnanimous, adventurer of La Mancha, who essays the same part amidst solitude and ridicule. In *Perceforest* is no jarring note of the mad, the mundane, and the modern. All is sweet, and serious, and serene. Each garment, each armour-piece wherewith the lad is attired, has its mystical meaning; and, while the rites and ceremonies remind us of freemasonry, the doctrinal exposition accompanying each act, and the pious responses of the novice, compel us to see in chivalry a type of the Church militant.

The first part of the programme is undertaken by three ladies. They enter a little pavilion and seat the candidate, " tout nud fors les brayes," on a chair. His white and tender flesh excites the admiration of Queen Fezonas, who slaps him on the shoulder, saying, " Sire damoyseau, bien vous a nourry celle, qui vous a eu en garde jusques à ores." However, there is no suspicion of impropriety, and the investiture is at once begun. First they put on him a white shirt, which, the ladies explain, is a symbol of purity. Over this they place a red silk tunic, which signifies an ardent desire for all knightly virtues and graces. Lastly, one of them fastens a belt—symbol of retention, this—round his waist. Fourteen knights then receive the youth, and dress him in armour, while Perceforest gives him the accolade with the words, " Chevalier, soyés hardi et preux."

With romances like *Perceforest*, instinct with the spirit of the past, it is natural to associate the *dits* of *Baudouin and Jean de Condé.* [1]   The *dit*, a very loose sort of poem, and first cousin to "debates" and "disputes," professed to sum up the qualities of an object.   Later, it became tinged with satire, and was hardly distinguishable from the *fabliau*. (The *fabliau*, it should be observed, disappeared in the course of this century, and was represented in the next, on the one hand, by the prose "novel," and, on the other, by the farce.)   Baudouin de Condé, who lived towards the close of the thirteenth century, wrote many *dits* in "equivocal verses"—*i.e.*, with rhymes formed of the same words in two or three different senses.   That on *Gentillece* anticipates Tennyson's sentiment:—

> "Nul n'est vilains si de cuer non ;
> Nul n'est gentils hom ensement,
> S'il n'uevre de cuer gentement."

These lines, however, it must be confessed, are somewhat delusive, for, taken generally, the *dits* are by no means "popular."   They are extremely finished compositions addressed to high society, of which they reflect the tone.   This remark is especially applicable to those of Jean.

In the sweet merry season when every creature is gay by right of nature, and joyous, and the flowers

---

[1] A. Scheler, *Dits et contes de Baudouin de Condé et de son fils, Jean de Condé*.   3 vols., Brussels, 1866.

spring in the meadow, and the birds sing morn and
Dit *of the*   night, and lead a glorious life — in this
Two Lovers. delicious time, coveting the joy of love, and
being, moreover, intent on making a new song, Jean
de Condé entered a very beautiful orchard, where he
met two ladies of high degree.   Immediately he
saluted them, and one of them said to the other,
"Here is Jean, who will tell us his opinion of our
debate."   Jean consents to be umpire, all three sit
down in a part of the orchard remote from passers-by,
and the discussion is resumed.   The problem agitating
these dear creatures is, Whether of the two loves
better, the bold or the timorous wooer ?   One supports
the claim of the bold suitor who speaks out—" couars
n'ara ja bielle amie "—while the other doubts if such
boldness consists with true passion.   Each in turn
defends her own view, and at length they call upon
Jean, whose heart is grounded in love-lore, to enlighten
them.   Jean, without pretending to universal knowledge, feels himself equal to the task, and decides in
favour of the timorous wooer, though, to flatter the
other side, he says that a lover should be bold in
serving :—

> " Je di, u qu'il ait finne amour,
>   Ce ne poet iestre sans cremour ;
>   C'est d'amours li plus ciertains signes."

One source of this fear is the possibility of rejection.
Another is the risk of displeasing the lady.   Nay, the
very force of love robs a man of nerve, of self-posses-

sion, when he is in his lady's presence.   So Jean concludes:—

> "Ne croi c'onques hons bien amast
> Qui hardiëment s'en clamast."

In his *dit* of the *Magnificat* Jean is more sombre. His subject is the legend of the Proud Emperor, of which there are other versions, and the story is not unlike that of Nebuchadnezzar.   The emperor, fancying himself above the power of heaven, sees an angel or demon take possession of his throne, and it is only after a severe penance that he is allowed to regain it. Other *dits* teach other lessons; and, indeed, though a court-poet, Jean de Condé is also undeniably a preacher.

The romance was but sparsely cultivated by the Troubadours.[1]   The best specimen is *Jaufre*, an *Troubadour Romances.* Arthurian romance composed in Aragon between 1222 and 1232.   To the scanty total, amounting to less than a dozen, the fourteenth century contributed two *romans d'aventures*, in themselves of no great mark or likelihood.   *Blandin de Cornoalha et Guilhot Ardit de Miramur*[2] describes the achievements of these heroes, who traverse the world in search of adventures, fight with giants, serpents, and dragons, and emerge victorious from their conflicts. Blandin is lucky enough to awake a lady called Brianda from a trance, and she rewards him by becoming his wife.   Her friend Irlanda confers her

[1] Compare a remark of Raimon Vidal : "La parladura francesca val mais et es plus avinenz a far romanz e pastorellas, mas cella de Lemosin val mais per far vers et cansons et serventes."

[2] Paul Meyer, *Romania*, ii. 170-202.

hand on Guilhot. The authorship of the poem is unknown, but there are reasons for surmising that it was written in Catalonia.

The other romance is *Guilhem de la Barra*.[1] The author was Arnaut Vidal de Castelnaudary, leader in a

Guilhem de la Barra.

movement, hereinafter to be mentioned, for the restoration of Troubadour verse; and the poem was finished in May 1318. The "plot" is as follows: The King of Serra sets out for the wars, and during his absence appoints Guilhem de la Barra his vicegerent. The young queen falls in love with him, but Guilhem rejects her overtures. Thereupon he is calumniated *à la* Joseph. He escapes with his son and daughter, and the latter marries the Count of Terramada. Fifteen years pass, and Guilhem, unrecognised by his daughter, acts as governor to his children. Meanwhile his son, adopted by the King of Armenia, is on the point of fighting a duel with Guilhem, who enters the lists as champion for the Count of Terramada. The same battle-cry "Barra! Barra!" unmasks their relations, and this is followed by a similar scene between father and daughter. The Queen of Serra confesses her guilt, and all ends satisfactorily.

There is a close resemblance between this romance

Origin of the Romance.

and Boccaccio's novel (ii. 8), *The Count of Antwerp*. It is hard to say whether the romance was the source of the novel, or whether they had a common origin. It is conceivable at least that

---

[1] *Guillaume de la Barra*, Roman d'aventure. Par Paul Meyer. Paris, 1868.

both were based on an historical incident, to which
Dante alludes in the *Purgatorio* (vi. 22):—

> " I saw Count Orso ; and the soul divided
>   By hatred and by envy from its body,
>   As it declared, and not for crime committed,
>   Pierre de la Brosse I say ; and here provide
>   While still on earth the Lady of Brabant,
>   So that for this she be of no worse flock." [1]

Pierre was, in fact, accused by Marie of Brabant, wife
of Philippe le Bel, of having written love-letters to
her, and condemned to death.

Whatever may be the case with the *Decameron*,
there can be no question as to the influence of Pro-
The Cento No- vençal life and literature on the *Cento*
velle Antiche. *Novelle Antiche.* Thus in N. 61, which
presents so vivid a picture of Provençal manners, the
sonorous *langue d'oc* involuntarily supplants the Italian
prose. Sometimes single words, sometimes whole sentences, thrust themselves in, and at length we are
brought full in view of a Provençal ode. The knight
begins his complaint in pure Tuscan (" altresi come
il leofante quando cade non si puo levare "), then he
gets mixed, and, finally, he drops into pure Provençal
(" per tos temps las non cantar "). It looks very much
as though the author had sought to translate the poem,
and afterwards, finding the task too irksome for him,
had abandoned the attempt.

The identity of the author is profoundly ob-

[1] Translated by Longfellow. Opinions vary as to the merits of
this translation. The rhythm is good, and it is extremely literal.
Mainly for its fidelity it has been adopted, for purposes of citation,
throughout.

scure. Signor D'Ancona conjectures that he was a
Florentine merchant and a Ghibelline; but this is
mere guesswork. The traditional belief is that the
Cento Novelle Antiche were the work of more than
one author, and the great variety of the tales may be
considered in some measure confirmatory of this belief.
The collection probably dates from the middle or
latter half of the fourteenth century, as mention is
made in the sixteenth novel of Ricciardo de' Manfredi,
who died in 1340. The title by which it is now most
generally known is that of the first edition, printed
in 1525 at Bologna; but it is also (since 1835) referred to as the *Novellino*, while Borghini's edition
(Florence, 1572) was published under the title of
Libro di novelle e di bel parlar gentile. The matter
is of some importance, as it is certain that the fourteenth-century MSS. do not contain exactly a hundred
tales. Some have more, some less; and it is not improbable that the number 100 was fixed on in imitation of the *Decameron*. It is to be observed, also, that
the work does not consist only of tales. It says of
itself, " This book treats of certain flowers of speech,
and of beautiful courtesies, and of beautiful answers,
and of beautiful deeds of valour "; in other words,
anecdotes, witticisms, puns, in addition to the novels,
help to fill its pages. Thus Borghini's more ample
title corresponds better with the facts.[1]

[1] The best edition, however, is not that of Borghini, who " edited "
in favour of the Catholic reaction, but Michele Colombo's, whose text
has been reprinted by Tosi (Milan, 1825), and by Mazzini and Gaston
(Florence, 1867).

The date of the collection, then, is comparatively late ; but as regards their spirit the *Cento Novelle Antiche* belong to an earlier time, to which, indeed, some of them must be referred chronologically. The Greeks and the Romans are pictured, after the manner of the Middle Age, as knights, and this is the best evidence for the age of the tales in question. The anecdotes and tales about the *giovane rè*, about Lancelot and Queen Ginevra, might have sprung up when chivalry was already declining ; but this false portrayal, this " knighting " of antiquity, could only have occurred at the time of its highest bloom. In Italy chivalry never attained to full development, and therefore the tales penetrated by its spirit have probably been imported from France.

The *Cento Novelle Antiche* show very little art, and this, their artlessness, constitutes their main charm. Insensibly we are reminded of the old simple Florentine days when, as Dante records, the women lightened their toils with such stories :—

> " One o'er the cradle kept her studious watch,
>   And in her lullaby the language used
>   That first delights the fathers and the mothers ;
>   Another, drawing tresses from her distaff,
>   Told o'er among her family the tales
>   Of Trojans and Fesole and Rome."
>
> —*Paradiso*, xv. 121.

There is a close connection between N. 51 of the *Cento Novelle Antiche* and book iii. of *L'Avventuroso Ciciliano*, a romance composed quite early in the fourteenth century—probably about

The Avventuroso Ciciliano.

1311 — by Busone de' Rafaelli da Gubbio, a friend and admirer of Dante. In both cases the proximate source was undoubtedly the French poem *L'Ordene de Chevalerie* by Hue de Tabarie; and a comparison of the two writings suggests that the novel was either written by Busone da Gubbio, or, as is more probable, that he had at some earlier date translated the poem, and that his translation, with the omission of certain parts, was received into the *Novellino*.

The *Adventurous Sicilian* is a very tedious work. It has neither the naïve simplicity of the old style of fiction, nor the studied elegance of the new. It was written for a moral object—" for the instruction of all those who shall be stricken by the Fortune of the world, to give them comfort that they may not despair." The word " instruction " has an ugly sound, and prepares us for a total absence of inspiration. On an examination of the romance it will be found that the great inspirations of chivalry—honour, ladies' favour, and zeal for the Christian faith—have receded into the background. The noble knights are by no means indifferent to lucre. They are in truth soldiers of fortune and precursors of the *condottieri* who, at this period, broke up the city-republics and established personal lordships in their room. The following is an outline of the story.

After the famous Vespers (A.D. 1282) Sicily was in an unsettled condition, and five barons found themselves constrained to seek their fortunes elsewhere. Three of them—Gianni, Olinborgo, and Simonetto—

enter the service of the King of Tunis, and Gianni
and Olinborgo fall in the war with the Arabs. The
fourth, Antonio, is employed by Pope Nicholas III.
in a mission to England for the recovery of tithes.
In England, his errand having been successfully accomplished, he takes service with King Edward, becomes his trusty adviser, and assists to quell the
insurrection of one Brundisburgo, a personage, it is
needless to say, unknown to English history. He is
likewise appointed tutor to Prince Polinoro, but ultimately returns to Sicily. The fifth knight, Olivo,
hires himself to the King of Servia (Rascia in Ischia-
vonia), marches with five hundred French knights to
the aid of the King of Armenia against the Saracens,
is taken prisoner, and conveyed to Babylon. His
valour and address having mightily pleased the Sultan
—whom, by the way, he dubs a knight—he and his
comrades are released. Finally, he wends his way
back to Messina, where he lights on his old friends,
Gianni and Antonio.

The three survivors, it is recorded, make a "good
thing" out of the adventures, "netting" between them
no less than 430,000 ducats; and this ingredient in
the romance adapted it for the consumption of the
bourgeois magnates, now the dominant factor in Italian
politics. The adventures, however—chiefly imaginary
—are in reality little more than a skeleton or frame-
work for long-winded speeches, which latter are either
translations or resettings of Cicero and Sallust. The
myth that Florence owed its origin to the Catilinarian

conspiracy enthralled Busone, as it enthralled Villani and the early Italian chroniclers.[1]

Lastly may be mentioned that vast reservoir of chivalrous legends, the *Reali di Francia*.[2] The com-
The Reali di *Francia.* pilation, which stretches from Constantine to the birth and boyhood of Roland, is due to a certain Andrea da Barberino, a *cantatore in panca* and "romancer"—*i.e.*, a translator and compiler of French romances of chivalry. For example, chapters 1-4 of book vi. are based on the romance *De Berte au gran pié*. Andrea's French was not French of Paris, for, in explaining the name Roland, he observes, "in francioso a dire rotolare eglino dicono *roolar*." Not much is known about him, but he was probably born after 1370, and he made his will in 1431. The date of his death has not been ascertained. Andrea's industry, inspired, perhaps, by the "sixth sense," seems to have been untiring, and, besides the *Reali di Francia*, he has bequeathed a *Guerrin Meschino ;* a *Storia di Ajolfo dal Barbicone ; Storie Nerbonesi ;* a *Storia di Ugone d'Alvernia*, to which is to be added *La Discesa di Ugone d'Alvernia allo inferno*, after the Franco-Italian before-mentioned ; and an *Aspromonte*, only parts of which have been edited. All these works are of the same character. So prolific a writer could not in the nature of things be a great master

[1] *L'Avventuroso Ciciliano* has been published by G. F. Nott in two editions—Florence, 1832, and Milan. A third edition, including the *Capitolo sopra la divina Commedia*, appeared at Florence in 1867.

[2] First edition, Modena, 1491. Professor Vandelli has undertaken a new edition for the *Collezione dei testi di lingua*.

of style; but Andrea writes, at least, good "journalese," and his *Reali di Francia* is certainly an improvement on a somewhat similar attempt, the wretched *Table Round* of Rusticiano da Pisa, of a century previous. The latter, however, was in French.

In Germany there is not much to arrest attention. The most striking phenomenon is the persist-
German Epics. ent influence of Wolfram von Eschenbach, tokens of which meet us at every turn. Not that the disciples inherited aught of the master's genius—his mantle fell upon none of them—but there is abundant evidence to prove that it was the great illiterate rather than his more polished contemporaries that the "epigoni" were for the most part ambitious of emulating. Coleridge, speaking in relation to *Faust,* gives it almost as an axiom that continuations are foredoomed to failure. If this be true of labours undertaken by the original author, how much more likely is it to be true of mere *nachwerk* or imitation? No such reflection, however, deterred Claus Wisse and Philipp Colin from entering on an *Erweiterung* of Wolfram's *Parzival.* Colin had been a goldsmith at Strassburg, and in an epilogue addressed to his patron, Herr Ulrich von Rappolstein, expresses the hope that the profits of the work will enable him to resume business! The *Erweiterung* was executed between 1331 and 1336. It was based on continuations of Chrestien's poem by Gautier de Dourdans, Manessier, and other French writers, and the chief addition, comprising 30,000 lines, is interpolated between the thirteenth and fourteenth book of Wolfram's

Parzival, the last two books being also materially enlarged. The translation, completed with the help of a Jewish interpreter, Samuel Pine, is remarkable for nothing but its fidelity. The verse is scandalous. Many lines exceed their proper tale of syllables, and the rhymes are often of the sorriest description.

Another example of the epic-aftermath is *Friedrich von Schwaben*, of which the first portion is grounded on Konrad von Würzburg's *Partonopier und Meliur*, while names and motives have been borrowed, slightly altered, from Gottfried and Veldeke. Far more important than even these coincidences is the fact that the later adventure is taken direct from the Wieland saga. This conjunction of popular legend and court-epic is a veritable sign of the times. We meet with it again in Albrecht von Scharfenberg's *Seitfried von Ardemont*, which, however, is known to us only by an excerpt in Ulrich Fütrer's *Book of Adventures*. These late epics are invariably long, invariably dry, and invariably clumsy, and those which exist in print would certainly not repay analysis. The MSS. are not all of equal merit. Those of *Friedrich* are faulty and fragmentary, while in the case of the *Erweiterung*— such, at least, is the belief—the original text has been preserved.

More in accord with the spirit of the age is the coarse realism of the epic in the countries adjoining the Rhine. This realism is undoubtedly *Dutch influence.* due to the influence of the Netherlands, which served as a halting-place for French *chansons de geste*, especially those relating to Charlemagne, in

C

their passage to Germany. The tendency before observed to pile up Pelion on Ossa, and Ossa on Olympus once more discloses itself in a gigantic compilation which, unlike Fütrer's rather similar work in the next century, makes no pretence to recast the material. Apart from verbal alterations— by no means consistent or complete—adapting them to his own dialect, the Franconian editor simply reproduces various Dutch and German poems, his own additions being relatively unimportant. The title *Karlmeinet* (*i.e.*, " little Charles ") is appropriate only to the commencement.

Lastly, the allegorical romance is represented by *Die Jagd*, the work of a distinguished Bavarian knight, Hadamar von Laber. The chase in question is courtship, and the hunter, preceded by his heart as by a hound, pursues after the quarry —*i.e.*, the beloved object. Other hounds are Happiness, Pleasure, Love, Consolation, Fidelity, while spies, as endangering the success of the quest, are symbolised by wolves. The poem is open to all the objections to which all allegory is exposed. It is childish and unreal; and yet, as an expression of the chivalrous spirit—especially in its reverence for woman—it is far above the average epic of the time. Allegory was not a novel feature in German literature. It had been used by Konrad in his *Klage der Kunst*, and by Heinzelin von Constanz in the introduction to *Der Minne Lêre*. Isolated examples occur also in *Tristan* and other chivalrous poems, while, in the religious sphere, a notable instance is the allegorico-mystical poetry of Bruder Lamprecht von Regensburg, where, *e.g.*, the soul is figured as a lady who looks after her lover from the battlements. *Die Jagd* is written, not in the ordinary epic verse, the couplet, but in the *Titurel* or four-lined stanza.

In Iceland the art of the Scalds died, as it were, in the odour of sanctity. An important work, compar-
Icelandic able in breadth and fulness to the *Heliand*, *rímur.* was the *Lilja* of the Augustinian monk Eystein Ásgrímsson († 1360)—a poem respecting the life, death, and sufferings of Christ. Two *drápur* on Bishop Guðmund, by Arngrím Brandsson and Abbot Arni Jónson, are composed in the octosyllabic *drott-kvaett* stanza. A third on the same subject, by Einar Gilsson, marked the transition to a new sort of verse, the *rímur*, which appear to have been connected with the Low German *rimels*. This poetry, like that of the Scalds, is alliterative, while it preserves also the pictorial style of the *kenningar* (periphrases). But the interior rhyme, owing apparently to foreign influence, is replaced by the end - rhyme, and the four-lined *vísur* or stanzas resemble, from a metrical standpoint, not so much the old Scald-verse as the Danish *kämpevisen*. It is rarely, and only in the older poems, that we meet with a single *ríma* forming a complete whole. The later examples are in sets or sequences. The *ríma* is introduced by a *mänsongr*, or love-ditty, usually the poet's complaint on his ill-success. This furnishes the lyrical element in the composition. The *ríma* proper is epic in character, and its subjects are drawn from existing *sögur*. In

essence the *rima* was a dance-song, and this circumstance suggests what its epic quality confirms—a certain likeness to the English ballad. The majority of *rímur* still only exist in manuscript, a goodly number in the library at Wolfenbüttel. As, however, the first complete specimen—Einar's *Ólafsríma*—dates from 1398, it is clear that the matter is not fully within our jurisdiction.

The decline of the *frásaga*, that peculiarly northern institution, is marked by the coexistence of *fornsögur* and *lýgisögur*. The former are based on sagas and myths, while the latter, as is implied by their not too complimentary description, are inventions, and so correspond in a sense to *romans d'aventure*. In practice, it is not always easy to discriminate between them, as the mythical *sögur* often contain much ill-authenticated episodical matter, while the *lýgisögur*, as is often the way with writings of the *aventure* class, have a substratum of myth vaguely present to the mind of the narrator.

Fornsögur and lýgisögur.

Two sagas of about this period are particularly interesting, inasmuch as they connect with an earlier branch of Icelandic literature—the Edda-songs, to which they stand related much as do French prose-romances to the more ancient metrical versions. These are the *Hervararsaga ok Heiðreks Konungs* and the *Örvar Oddssaga*. The former is named from the elder Hervör, daughter of Argantýr, and her son Heiðrek; and the pivotal idea is the curse-laden sword Tyrfing, to possess which means death. This fatal gift Hervör receives from her

The Saga of Hervör.

father, to whose grave at Samsey she steals by night on purpose to crave it; and afterwards it passes to her son. There are two versions of the *Hervararsaga*, both very imperfect. One, contained in the *Hauksbók*, ended probably with the death of Heidrek, while the other, composed in Norway, included an account of a terrible battle between the Goths and the Huns. Hlöd, who had been brought up at the court of Humli of Húnaland, demands from his half-brother Argantýr, Heidrek's son, the half of his father's kingdom, but, being a bastard, he is contumeliously rejected. Thereupon Humli collects his Huns and prepares to revenge his fosterling in battle. The fight lasts eight days, and ends in victory for the Goths.

Closely related to that of Hervör is the *Örvar Oddssaga*, the *vísur* being many of them practically the same. Odd, who gets his name "Örvar Odd" from a giant on account of his wonderful arrows, travels for three hundred years in search of adventures, and dies at last, in accordance with an old prophecy, from the bite of a serpent. Ere he expires he sings an *erfidrápa*, or dirge, on himself, in which he reviews his life; and this dirge forms the conclusion of the saga. The song has no artistic merit. It is, in fact, one of the last offshoots of the ancient *thulir* or popular poetry, and represents an older song which celebrated Odd's achievements in the same way that the songs of the *Herverarsaga* do those of its heroes.

Örvar Odd.

In general, Örvar Odd much resembles a personage of wide popularity in the North—Starkad Storverks-

son, stated by Saxo Grammaticus to have composed
the magnificent song on the Battle of Bravalla, in
which he, Starkað, took part. This song is known
to us from the *Sögubrot af Fornkonungum,* which preserves the relics of a great saga formed out of a series
of ancient writings in honour of the mythical Kings of
Denmark and Sweden. Of Starkað's youthful exploits
something is told us in the second part of the *Gaut-
rekssaga.*

The most noticeable thing about Icelandic literature
in its prime is its independence of other literatures.

*Foreign
elements.*   In the fourteenth century this insularity is
no longer maintained. Romantic traits are
to be found in the *Hervararsaga,* the *Örvar Oddssaga,*
and the *Sögubrot af Fornkonungum,* in the last of
which there are tournaments. This circumstance prepares us for the statement that during the thirteenth
and fourteenth centuries there arose a complete set
of *Fornsögur Suðrlanda—i.e.,* free translations of
"south-country" epics and romances, which, in point
of style, have been thoroughly naturalised. From
Germany came the *Thiðrekssaga,* or, as it was formerly
called, *Vilkinasaga,* and, according to the Norwegian
author, his information was derived orally from Low
German traders. The central and dominant figure
is Thiðrik,[1] but there are included in the work stories
of King Samson, Wieland the Smith, Kriemhild,
Sigurd and the Volsungs, &c.

About the year 1250, in which this saga was
produced, a Norwegian *Karlamagnussaga* was com-

---

[1] German, *Dietrich* (Theodoric).

posed, although in its complete form it is found
only in Icelandic versions some fifty years later.
This translation-literature was greatly encouraged by
Hákon Hákonarson (1217-63), his chief agent being
a mysterious Abbot Robert, to whom were due the
Elissaga ok Rosamundu, perhaps also the *Iventsaga*
(the saga of Iwein), the *Möttulssaga* (the story of the
enchanted mantle), and, above all, the *Strengleikar*
or *Ljoðabók*, a translation of at least nineteen North
French *lais* of Marie of France. Even this enumera-
tion conveys only an imperfect idea of the wealth
and variety of the *fornsögur* which (many of them by
way of England) wandered northwards to the land of
snows and much leisure. Germany is represented by
the *Konradssaga* and the *Magussaga* (story of the
children of Haimon, &c.); France, by the *Florents-
saga* (obtained through a Latin medium) and a whole
row of Arthurian romances not yet published. Ire-
land furnishes a *Duggalsleizla;* and England, a *Bevers-
saga*, as well as *Bretasögur* based on Geoffrey of
Monmouth's *Historia Britonum*. The Icelanders possessed also a rich store of tales and legends, which in
the *Islendzk Aeventýri* of the learned and travelled
Bishop of Skálholt, Jon Halldórsson, attained to the
dignity of a distinct branch of literature.

We come now to the *Eufemiavisor*—i.e., metrical
renderings named after Queen Eufemia, wife of Hákon
The Euphemia Magnússon (1299) and daughter of a Ger-
Visor. man count, who, for the pleasure of her
stepson, Duke Eric, is stated to have caused three
poems to be translated into Swedish. The first, *Ivan*

Lejonriddaren, was written probably in 1303, and at the conclusion the translator observes that it was rendered into "our speech" out of the French. From this it has been supposed that the immediate model was a version, now lost, of Chrestien de Troyes' well-known *Ivain* or the *Chevalier au Lion.* On the other hand, *Ivan* already existed in Norwegian prose, and certain features contained in the Swedish poem occur in the saga, but in no hitherto discovered French text. The second poem, *Hertig Fredrik af Normandie,* was written about 1308. The story is that the Emperor Otto had it translated from French into German, and Queen Eufemia from German into Swedish. Here, again, matters are not free from difficulty. The difficulty consists in this, that no French original can be traced, and, consequently or inconsequently, no German translation can be found. It may be that *Hertig Fredrik* was first composed in Low German, and thence translated into Swedish. The third poem is the universally popular *Flores och Blanzeflor,* which dates from the year 1312, and is based directly on a Norwegian prose romance.

Lastly, as to the *lýgisögur,* or lying sagas. This term, it is said, was employed by King Sverrir of the *Sturlungasaga* (a history of Iceland written in the early part of the thirteenth century), and in different senses might be employed, perhaps, all round. As between this and that class of writing, it is a question of comparative lying, and the distinction is largely artificial. Bound up with the *Örvar Odds-saga,* a canonical work, is the *Ketilssaga Haengs,* which treats of the hero's grandfather, and describes a number of mythical adventures, such as fights with giants. As a further illustration of the overlapping of *fornsögur* and *lýgisögur*, it may be mentioned that the journey to Ódainsakr, the Land of the Immortals, which occurs in the *Hervararsaga*, is reproduced in the *Eirikssaga Vídförla*. Finally, the *Króka Refssaga*, of which the scene is partly in Greenland, is a kind of historical novel, and, as with other more celebrated novels, the history is shaky.

English romances differ from those of France, and Germany, and Iceland during this period, in that they

English Re- do not pale by comparison with a more glori-
vival. ous past. They may be looked upon rather
as the school-exercises of youth than the laboured efforts of age, as a sort of preparation for Chaucer. This reawakening of the English speech to dignity and recognition was due partly to internal causes, partly to the wars with France. The various elements of society, glowing with resentment against the common foe, were fused by patriotic ardour into a single nation. The adoption of the English language as the medium of intercourse was sure to follow. For a while French might continue to be spoken, as Robert of Gloucester testifies that it was, by "heie men," but even in respect of them, before the century was out, a revolution was accomplished, for, says John of Trevisa, "gentil men haveth now mych ylefte for to teche her children Frensch."

It is natural to suppose that complete recognition and triumph, as in the days of Chaucer and Gower,

was preceded by a phase of toleration. Great noblemen, like Humphrey de Bohun, though retaining
French as a badge of their rank, may have been well
pleased to listen to itinerant "seggers," who visited
their halls primed with adaptations of favourite French
poems, and even to encourage such adaptations by
substantial rewards. Thus while some, indeed most,
English romances bear the impress of the middle-class
spirit, others—notably *Iwain and Gawain*, based on
the *Chevalier au Lion* of Chrestien de Troyes—preserve the old knightly tone unimpaired.

The term "adaptation" expresses much better than
"translation" the actual relation between French
"'*Convey*,' *the* and English romances. "Translation" has
wise it call." a suggestion of Bohn, but the real parallel
is the adaptation of French plays to the London stage.
The adapter seldom approaches his models with the
reverence, the loving and conscientious devotion, of a
disciple. He was a man of business anxious to meet
the tastes of his customers; and, speaking generally,
he regarded the whole body of romances as raw
material to be exploited in any way he deemed proper.
Who were the adapters? The question cannot be
answered with certainty. Anyhow, they were not
always identical with the persons reciting the poems.
Often they were degenerate clerks who thus provided
the minstrel with means of livelihood. But the
most ignorant "segger" could not remain unaffected
by the schooling his occupation afforded. If he were
intelligent and something of a poet, what more natural
than that he should throw in, here and there, a touch

of his own?   The "segger," however, tended rather to
curtail than to add.   And his alterations were not
rated as improvements.   Robert Manning says of
Tristrem—

> " Over gestes it has the steem,
>
> .   .   .   .
>
> If men it sayd as made Thomas."

Lapses of memory and misconception were account-
able for many of these disfigurements.

It was in the Arthurian cycle, as an ideal represen-
tation of high life, that the French court-epic attained
its highest technical perfection.   In the
Word-painting.   English imitations this art is, for the most
part, ignored; and instead of heightening the court-
liness of his version by all the resources he might
have learned from Chrestien de Troyes, the adapter
makes shift with some long-winded prose romance,
and churns it into poetry by the light of nature.
Arthour and Merlin [1] contains a feature which is highly characteristic of the Old English romance, and, in
more skilful hands, might have signalised a positive
advance.   This is the landscape, specimens of which
are to be found also in *Alisaunder*. [2]   Here is one.

> " Whan corn ripeth in every steode,
>   Mury it is in feld and hyde ;
>   Synne hit is and shame to chide.
>   Knyghtis wolleth on huntyng ride,
>   The deor galopith by wodis side.
>   He that can his tyme abyde,
>   Al his wille him schal betyde."

---

[1] Ed. Kölbing, Leipzig, 1890.
[2] See Weber's *Metrical Romances.*   3 vols., Edinburgh, 1810.

Such pictures—reinforced, and indeed, as will be seen, rather incongruously and miscellaneously, by pithy sayings—have frequently no organic connection with the narrative, and are in this way out of place. They are used to stimulate the attention of the audience, as well as to mark divisions in the narrative, and correspond to what we find in the later popular ballad. This romance *Alisaunder*, based on the *Roman de Toute Chevalerie* of Eustace (or Thomas) de Kent, brings before us the mediæval ideal of a king. *Richard Cœur de Lion* [1] reveals to us a coarser type, but much more alive—that of a rough knight of enormous frame and overbearing temper. There is something peculiarly felicitous in Ten Brink's comparison of him with John Bull, for by this time Richard was everywhere regarded as the representative national hero.

A striking trait of the English romance is the way it seeks to link itself with glorious epochs of the national life in the far distant past. This is seen in *Arthour and Merlin*. The Franklin in his tale speaks of

Patriotism.

> " Engelond, that cleped eke was Bretayne."

But the romancer goes further, and boldly identifies Britons and Englishmen—

> " The Bretouns that beth Inglisse now."

That this is not a mere gloss may be inferred from the general tone of the writer. English, he says, shall be my speech, no longer French or Latin. He who is

[1] Also in Weber.

born in the land, to him also English is known. The
gentleman speaks French, but every Englishman
knows English.

The tendency to retrospect is even more marked
in two romances dating from the first quarter of the
fourteenth century—*Guy of Warwick* and
Looking back. *Bevis of Hampton.* Arthur, never really
an Englishman, had been divested of his local attributes, but Athelstan and Edgar could only be
thought of as members of a race which was now,
after centuries of oppression, reassuming its rightful
place both at home and in the eyes of the world.
The story of *Guy of Warwick* is closely allied with
the legends of Eutachius and Alexius. Of humble
origin—the son of a steward—he rises by his own
merit and wins the hand of an earl's daughter. One
day after hunting he feels a sudden compunction,
leaves his castle and his blooming bride, and sets
out for the Holy Land. On his return he finds things
in a sorry plight. King Athelstan is besieged in
Winchester by the Danes, and lacks a champion to
contend with the gigantic Colbrand. The monarch
receives supernatural directions to apply to the first
pilgrim that knocks at his door. This happens to be
Guy, who is prevailed upon to do battle. Victory
smiles on him, but, indifferent to worldly honours,
he again takes his pilgrim's cloak and journeys to
his home. Here, unrecognised, he finds his wife all
that he could desire — pious and given to good
works — and, after some stay, departs once more
and lives the life of a hermit. Finally, he sends for

her, and dies in her arms. This poem is written in short couplets. A second version in twelve-lined stanzas, indited "ful fer in the north cuntre," contains an account of Guy's son Rembrun.

The Carlovingian cycle is represented by two versions of *Otinel*, of which the scene is principally in Lombardy. These versions are of very different merit. The first, *Sir Otuel*, is a tolerably close translation of the French *chanson de geste*; and, technically, the substitution of the short couplet for the monorhymed tirade is an improvement, as harmonising better with the non-epic character of the poem. As regards its rival, the versifier had no great skill in his art, though he was not to seek in Charlemagne-lore, and probably aimed at producing an extensive compilation, of which *Sir Otuel* was an instalment. Even as it is, the title is plainly inadequate, and French criticism has proposed as an amendment *Charlemagne and Roland*.

Sir Otuel.

Another poem founded on a *chanson de geste* is *Amis and Amiloun*. In France this legend had been drawn within the Carlovingian cycle, from which, in the English version, it is again divorced. Instead of Charlemagne we meet with a Duke of Lombardy, whose daughter Belisant is an exact counterpart of her imperial namesake. Her mission is to seduce Amis, and she does seduce him. Amis, not Amiloun, for the English romancer, despite the precautionary "n," has succeeded in confounding the pair so as to attribute to Amis the grisly devotion of Amiles. Practically, it does not much matter; in either case

Amis and Amiloun.

the moral is the same.   David forswears himself for
Jonathan, and is punished with leprosy.   In return,
Jonathan, warned by an angel, sacrifices his own
children, and heals David with their blood.   Such
love is indeed wonderful, passing the love of women.

Nor, as "sensation," is *Amis and Amiloun* in any
way unique.   In *Sir Degare* (*l'égaré*) the hero, born of
an erring princess, and bred by a hermit, has the
misfortune, in sheer ignorance, to marry his mother,
though the mistake is discovered in time.   From such
Œdipean horrors it is a relief to turn to *Floriz and
Blancheflur*, apparently the first English version of
one of the most widely known of French romances,
dealing with a youthful pair whose innocent love
so moves the heart of the fierce Sultan that he
not only spares their lives, but actually becomes a
Christian.

Before going further it will be well to say something
as to the metres in which these romances were written.

Metre.
Until late in the reign of Edward III. the
short couplet maintained its position as the
prevailing form of the romance, but even under Edward
I. another form had appeared whose rivalry grew more
and more formidable.   In the religious lyric of the
last-named period we light on a strophe evolved from
the *versus tripertiter caudati* of the Latin sequences, but
the metre, instead of being trochaic, is iambic.   This
ryme couee, as it was called, perhaps first became popular in the North, and usually took the shape of a six-
or twelve-lined stanza.   This latter consists of four
triplets.   In each triplet the two first lines contain

eight syllables, the third six, and the short lines keep the same rhyme throughout.

The transition from the short couplet to the twelve-lined stanza may perhaps have taken place in this way. In reciting French romances in English the " seggers " employed the stanza for their proems, and for single passages especially appealing to their fancy or that of their audience. Gradually the custom spread over England, and a number of romances originally translated in rhymed couplets were wholly or partially recast in *ryme couee.*

A good deal is implied in the metre—much more than the satisfaction of the ear. The short couplet lent itself to the old artistic handling, the gradual unfolding of the theme in its causal and psychological bearings. The stanza, on the other hand, tends to resolve itself into a single picture in which only the results are shown, just as in modern hymn-tunes there is a straining after vivid effects in harmony to the exclusion of the flowing counterpoint which conferred such grace and dignity on the old chorale. In other words, the narrative is disjointed, inconsequent, abrupt. For more select circles the short couplet appears to have kept its charm until in Chaucer's time the twelve-lined stanza had become the sole property of the ballad-singers.

The revival of national feeling was marked by a curious phenomenon—namely, a return to the alliter-

Alliterative ative verse of pre - Norman times. This *Verse.*   fashion, which set in about the middle of the fourteenth century, especially in Northern and

West Midland districts, at first strikes us as a deliberate assertion of independence, and, in view of the growing ascendancy of rhyme during many previous decades, as altogether novel. Probably, however, alliterative composition had never wholly died out,— the patriotism referred to above no doubt consciously or unconsciously favoured what seemed national,— and, as for independence, it is confined to rhythm and language. The colour, the atmosphere, of the alliterative epic is still chivalrous and romantic. Its ideas and inspirations are those, not of Beowulf, but of Chrestien de Troyes.

With regard to the language, it is distinctly, and no doubt deliberately, archaic, and includes a rather larger proportion of Germanic terms than average contemporary rhymed verse. On the other hand, the principles of Anglo-Saxon alliteration are obeyed only imperfectly. To be correct, a line should consist of two parts, of which the first should have two words, and the second one, commencing with the same letter ; and the words thus alliterated should be those on which, in reading, the accent would properly fall. In the later academic examples a tendency is shown to alliterate unaccented syllables, sometimes in lieu, more generally in excess, of the accented ones. Moreover, the rhythm is burdened by groups of three or four " feminine " syllables, and by minor or secondary accents interposed between the so-called " loud " syllables. The most important, as well as best known, work in this style of alliteration is, of course, *Piers the Plowman*, but there are also a number of alliterative romances,

D

some of which exhibit a blending of alliteration and rhyme, and most a decided stanza arrangement. The normal type of the alliterative rhymed stanza is that of the *Adventures of Arthur at the Tarn Watheling*. As will be seen by the annexed example, it consists of nine full lines, followed by four half lines—

" In King Arthure tyme ane awntir by-tide.
By the Tern Wathelyne, als the buke telles,
Als he to Carelele was commene, that conqueroure kyde,
With dukes, and with duchiperes, that with that dere duellys,
For to hunt at the herdys, that lange hase bene hyde ;
And one a daye they tham dighte to the depe dellis
To felle of the femmales, in foreste wele fryde,
Faire in the fernysome tyme, by frythis and fellis.
Thus to the wode are thay wente, the wlonkeste in wedys.

　　　　　Both the kynge and the qwene
　　　　　And alle the doghety by-dene ;
　　　　　Sir Gawan, gayeste one grene,
　　　　　Dame Gayenoure he ledis."

In *Sir Gawayne and the Green Knight* the full or long lines are alliterative, but unrhymed. The concluding short lines are introduced by a link similar to that in *Sir Tristrem*, and are always four in number. No limit is prescribed to the number of long lines. In the *Pearl* — a tender allegorical poem on a dead infant—the stanza consists of twelve lines each with four accents, and the rhyme-scheme is : *ababababbcbc*.

The masterpiece among English romances, whether alliterative or in rhyme, is by general admission *Sir Gawayne and the Green Knight*. Although founded on *Perceval*, the English poem shows considerable independence, and the

Sir Gawayne and the Green Knight.

story is told with excellent skill and address. The romance is divided into four "fyttes," representing as many acts of the drama, which opens with a Yule-tide scene in King Arthur's days at Camelot. Just ere the feast begins, the company are surprised by the entrance of a portentous knight in green, and he proffers a request not less portentous than his aspect. It is that a Knight of the Round Table shall do him the favour to cut off his head—only, if any consent thereto, he must abide a like stroke at the Green Knight's hands in a year and a day. Nobody being in a hurry to take up this challenge, the stranger falls to jibing, as though the glory of the Round Table had departed. The king, unable to brook such insult, leaps from his seat, but his nephew, Sir Gawayne, craves the privilege of the blow. Thereupon, at one swoop, the devoted head sinks to the ground, but not its owner, who unconcernedly picks up his belonging, and merely reminding his opponent of the compact, goes his way. In due time Gawayne sets out on his travel to the place of meeting—a certain Green Chapel in the north. It is dismal travel, combined with foul weather, rough roads, robbers, and giants, but at length the knight arrives at a castle. The lord of the castle, who is elderly, treats him kindly, and the lady, young and fair, is more than kind. And now host and guest make a strange bargain. The old knight is to go a-hunting, while the young knight stays at home with the ladies. At the close of each day, each is to "swap" with the other the day's gains. The young dame kisses Gawayne more than hospitality requires, and Gawayne, mindful of his promise, gives the knight her kiss, without any explanation, in exchange for the game. But this Vivien, though she cannot conquer his virtue so as to win from him an embrace, corrupts his faith by inducing him to accept a green girdle which has the marvellous property of warding off death from the wearer; and Gawayne, wishing to keep the same, withholds the gift and all mention of it when the host again comes back from his hunting.

It is now time for Gawayne to quit the castle for the Green Chapel, said to be but two miles distant. No chapel can he find, only a hollow hill, but, lo! the Green Knight appears, and calls on Gawayne to bare his neck to the blow. He feigns to strike; Gawayne swerves. The Green Knight prepares a second stroke, and this time the victim remains firm. Then the axe descends again, but very gently, and the blood trickles down Gawayne's neck. The ordeal is over, and anon the mummery is explained. The first feint was intended to complete the original bargain. The second stroke was bloodless, because Gawayne had honourably rejected the lady's overtures, while the third stroke had punished the slight breach of honour involved in the keeping of the girdle. Gawayne is stung with remorse at his own cowardice and treachery; but the old knight makes light of the matter, and invites him to return with him to the castle. The courtesy having been declined, the young adventurer hastens back to Camelot, and recounts his adventures to his welcoming friends.

The subject of English romances is so large and has so many sides that any attempt to deal with it in full would be hopeless.[1] Yet it may not be amiss to exhibit in some detail the relations between a French *A Comparison.* original and an English adaptation, selecting for the purpose *William of Palermo.* As regards the matter, the chief distinction between the French and the English version is that the adapter, a much truer poet, curtails reflections and accounts of

---

[1] Nearly a hundred, ranging in date from the late thirteenth to the late fifteenth or earliest sixteenth century, have been enumerated, nor is there yet any single book which gives a complete account of them. Ellis's well-known *Specimens* is still the best introduction. Nearly, but not quite, all the most interesting will be found in the collections of which a detailed list has been appended below, or in the publications of the Early English Text Society. The dates of the romances are usually guesswork, but those certainly belonging to our present period may be ascertained from the contents of the famous Auchinleck MS. (middle fourteenth century), which contains, among other things, *Guy, Bevis,* the *King of Tars, Amis and Amiloun, Sir Degaré, The Seven Wise Masters, Florice and Blancefloure, Arthour and Merlin, Roland and Vernagu, Otuel, Alisaunder, Tristrem, Orfeo, Horn-Child,* and *Richard Cœur-de-Lion.* References in the extremely interesting religious poem of the *Cursor Mundi* show us some of these, and others, as existing still earlier ; but it is improbable that many date before 1300.

The principal collections are—

(a) Ritson (J.) *Ancient English Metrical Romances.* 3 vols. London, 1802.

(b) Weber (H.) *Metrical Romances of the 13th, 14th, and 15th Centuries.* 3 vols. Edinburgh, 1810.

(c) Utterson (R.) *Select Pieces of Popular Poetry.* 2 vols. London, 1817.

(d) Hartshorne (C. H.) *Ancient Metrical Tales.*

(e) Halliwell (J. O.) *The Thornton Romances.* Camden Society, 1844.

(f) Hazlitt, (W. C.) *Early Popular Poetry of England.* 4 vols. London, 1864.

(g) Hales (J. W.), and Furnivall (F. J.) *Bishop Percy's Folio MS.* 3 vols. London, 1867.

feasts, while, as compensation, he gives free scope to descriptions of Nature. This is seen, not only in long passages wholly interpolated, but in incidental touches. For instance, the lines—

> " En ceste forest le trouvai,
>   Asses pres dont nous somes ore "

are represented in the translation by

> " How he him fond in that forest here fast bi-side,
>   Clothed in comly clothing for any kinges sone,
>   Under an holw ok thurgh help of his dogge."

The length of the line and the needs of alliteration help to explain the particularity, but such picturesque accessories, when not too obtrusive, certainly enhance the interest of the narrative. On the other hand, when motives are in question, the English version is less lucky. The emperor asks William what his father is called, and the boy declines to satisfy him.

> " ' Nay, sire, bi God,' quath the barn, ' be ye right sure,
>   By Christ that is krowned heye King of heuen,
>   For me non harm schal he haue neuer in his life.' "

The French William is more precise.

> " Non ferai, sire, et por coi,
>   Car je ne sai que vos voles,
>   Qui vos estes, ne que queres ;
>   Ne se voles riens, se bien non,
>   Ja ne me face Dix pardon."

Alliterative poetry took an even stronger hold of Scotland.[1] The writer curiously designated by Wyn-

---

[1] See *Scottish Alliterative Poems*, S.T.S., ed. Amours, Edinburgh,

toun the chronicler, from whom alone we hear
of him, as "Huchown of the awle ryale" has been
Scottish Romances. identified by some with Sir Hugh Eglin-
toun of Ayrshire, brother-in-law of Robert
II., but this is mere guesswork. Of the three works
attributed to him, the *Epistle of Susanna*, the *Adventure of Gawain*, and the *Great Geste of Arthur*, the
first alone has come down to us with a fair degree
of certainty. The poem—especially in the *dénouement*,
where God sends Daniel to deliver the chaste and
harassed matron—has many suggestions of the *Pearl*.
The metre is the thirteen-lined stanza, combining
alliteration and rhyme in the style of the *Adventures
of Arthur at the Tarn Watheling*. With respect
to the *Great Geste of Arthur*, the main question
is whether it is one and the same with the still
extant alliterative *Morte Arthure*, a poem characterised by a high sense of the glory of knighthood joined to an intense feeling for the beauty of
Nature.

The note of originality, and the national spirit,
never more active and awake than in this the heroic
John Barbour. age of the Scottish people, are shown by
a contemporary poet with whom Huchown
—if Sir Hugh Eglintoune were he—was associated in

1897, where the best account of "Huchown" and the guesses about
him will be found. It contains *Susanna* and *The Adventures of
Arthur*, with others. Most, if not all, of these alliterative romances
have been edited for the Early English and the Scottish Text Societies,
and many of them have attracted the attention of German scholars—
e.g., Herr Hans Köster, who has published a critical edition of the
Pistel of Swete Susan (Trübner, Strassburg).

the audit of public accounts. The name Barbour, or
Barber, suggests a plebeian origin, but impenetrable
gloom surrounds the parentage and youth of the bard.
According to some, he was born as early as 1317,
while by others the event is postponed to the year
1330. For some time he studied at Oxford. Entering
the Church, he attained to the dignity of Archdeacon
of Aberdeen, and in 1357 was appointed by his bishop
a member of the commission for deciding the ransom
of King David. He died in 1395.

Barbour's first achievement appears to have been his
Trojan War, but whether the fragments attributed to
him by a fifteenth-century copyist, and recently brought
to light, are genuine, may well be doubted. If they
are, all that can be said is that they do not serve to
convey any lofty idea of Barbour's talents at this
stage of their development, being neither more nor
less than a slavish translation of the columnar Guido's
History of Troy.

A very different verdict must be passed on his *Bruce.*
There is nothing in English literature exactly resem-
bling this work. To call it an epic might
be misleading, for the term inevitably suggests a free exercise of the imagination, whereas it was
Barbour's intention to hand down the actual memory
of events. The theory has been mooted that the *Bruce*
was manufactured, as it were, out of folk-songs, of the
existence of which Barbour was certainly aware, current at the period. That these racy and spontaneous
effusions influenced him on his poetic side hardly admits of question; but there, it is likely, his obligations

The Bruce.

ended. Barbour was a scholar and a statesman; he
possessed both aptitude and opportunity for research,
and it is probable that he had sources of information
fuller and more authentic than mere popular ballads.
Anyhow, no topic could have been chosen more accept-
able to Scotsmen, and the comparative nearness of
the transactions has no bearing on their essentially
romantic character.

It is unnecessary to trace in detail the career of the
chivalrous Bruce. Barbour launches his poem with
the murder on consecrated soil of the traitor Comyn.
This violation of Divine prerogative the writer, a man
of religion and learning, well knew could not go un-
punished, and accordingly it is his melancholy task to
follow the champion of Scotland over moor and mountain, hunted by John of Lorne with his sleuthhound,
and in hourly peril of ignominious arrest. But the
king, though often sore bestead, always contrives to
"win through," and, indeed, inspires the enemy with
a wholesome respect for his prowess. Sir Aymer de
Valence, on learning how five men had been slain in
the bootless chase—

> "Sanyt hym for the ferly,
> And said, 'He is greatly to priss,
> For I knaw nane that liffand is
> That at myscheif can help hym swa;
> I trow he suld be hard to sla,
> And he war bodyn all evenly."

Bruce, however, is much more than a formidable
antagonist. His form has the soft hues of genuine
knightly grace; and in his demeanour towards

females, even the humblest, he is the pink of courtesy.

Only passing allusion can be made to the Legends of the Saints,[1] ascribed to Barbour, and received by Professor Horstmann in his edition of 1881 as genuine, though doubted by others. The legends are an extensive compilation, amounting to thirty-three thousand lines, compared with the thirteen thousand lines of *The Bruce*.[2]

The English side in the quarrel is represented in the political lyric of a Northumbrian minstrel, Laurence *Laurence Minot.* Minot, a bitter enemy of the Scots, and a scarcely less bitter enemy of the French. Minot always believes in the justice of King Edward's (the *Third* Edward's) cause, and a strain of piety, mingling with his enthusiastic loyalty and patriotism, leads him to invoke the divine blessing on that monarch's arms. The songs are in various metres, and some of them share a peculiarity found also in the *Pearl*[3]—namely, the linking of consecutive stanzas by the repetition of a word—

> Fader, and Son, and Haly Gaste
> Haly Gaste, thou gif him grace.

> And thare he dightes him forto dwell.
> He dwelled thare, the suth to tell.

---

[1] Altenglische Legendensammlung, nebst den Fragmenten seines Trojanerkrieges (Heilbronn, 1881.) Also S.T.S. ed.

[2] *The Bruce* has been edited for both the Societies above-named by the Rev. W. W. Skeat. Other editions are those of Pinkerton (Edinburgh, 1790) and Jamieson (London, 1824).

[3] Ed. Gollancz, London, 1891.

This artifice occurs in Provençal, as, indeed, in most
poetry pretty advanced on the formal side, and was
employed either as an aid to memory or as an orna-
ment pure and simple.   It is in technical points that
this writer displays his skill, and he half succeeds in
elevating popular verse into a fine art.   Minot is
something of a court-minstrel, something of a ballad-
singer, but he was not strong enough to do what
Chaucer might have done in his place—transfigure
this combination in the *rôle* of a great national
poet.[1]

[1] The Poems of Laurence Minot.   Edited, with Introduction and
Notes, by Joseph Hall, M.A.   Oxford, The Clarendon Press.   See
also, Thomas Wright, Political Poems and Songs relating to English
History.   London, 1859.

CHAPTER II.

TOWN-VERSE AND FOLK-SONG.

DECLINE OF THE TROUBADOUR ART—THE 'LEYS D'AMORS'—LEGEND OF
CLEMENCE ISAURE—OLD PORTUGUESE POETRY—CATALONIAN VERSE
—GERMAN LOVE OF SONG—THE MEISTERSINGERS—VOLKSLIEDER—
MINNESINGERS IN LEGEND—REIMSPRECHER—THE LOW COUNTRIES—
ENGLISH MINSTRELS—WELSH BARDS—ROBIN HOOD—SCOTTISH BAL-
LADS—NORTH FRENCH 'PUIS'—ITALY.

I̲T̲ has been said that the decline of court-poetry and
the growth of middle-class culture are to be regarded,
*What "bour-
geois Litera-
ture" means.* not as independent phenomena, but as, on
the whole, the same thing contemplated
from different points of view. Much of the
literature already reviewed is unmistakably *bourgeois.*
What makes it *bourgeois* is not so much that its professors were men of humble station or plebeian origin
—that is a detail, in itself of no great importance—
but the triumph of matter over manner. The Germans
have a convenient phrase for expressing this trait—
I do not know that we have any quite so apt—*stoff-
interesse.* Regarding the tone of the new verse (and
the remark applies to both lyrical and narrative com-

positions) there is revealed a growing strictness, the working of a Puritanical spirit. The citizen was appreciably more serious than the knight, being not so much a social animal delighting in feast and song as a man of commerce to whom honesty was a thing of weight, and the father of a family responsible for its decent bringing-up. Possibly also a substantial householder—it was to such that the "masters" did most commonly resort—accustomed to impose his ideas on a circle of admirers and hangers-on. Morality, love of home, power of the purse—out of these three factors was evolved the awful notion of respectability, always and everywhere the middle-class fetich.

Let us turn in the first place to the smooth and polished art associated primarily with Provence. At *Fate of the langue d'oc.* the very outset we are confronted by a startling discovery. "Great Pan is dead!" Diez' *Poesie der Troubadours,* still perhaps the best introduction to the subject, closes with the year 1300, while the last of the Troubadours in general repute was Giraut Riquier, who flourished 1234-1292. The wonder is that the literature had lasted so long. Nearly a century before, the house of Anjou and the Pope had entered into an unholy alliance for the extirpation of the *langue d'oc,* tainted by the heresy of the Albigeois. The result was an exodus of the poets to foreign lands. The barons fared just as ill. Like the English nobility in the Wars of the Roses, they were engulfed in the national disasters—in other words, slain or disseized. The old order became a thing of the past.

So far as Provence itself is concerned, interest centres almost exclusively in the "sobregaya com-

The Over-gay Company. panhia dels VII. trobadors de Tholoza." We have now reached the stage of *meistergesang,* or co-operative authorship, and the efforts made to prolong the term of Troubadour verse issued in a night of lunar academic poetry. The form remained; the glory had departed. In the year 1323 seven of the principal inhabitants of Toulouse conceived the idea of a circular invitation bidding the poets in Languedoc to a contest on May-day 1324. The competition took place, and Arnaut Vidal de Castelnaudary (author of *Guilhem de la Barra*) won the prize — a violet of pure gold — for a hymn in honour of Mary. It was decided to repeat the event, and a constitution was drawn up, which included a chancellor and seven stewards (*mantenedors*), and could even boast of bedels. These expressions suggest, what was indeed the case, that the consistory was formed on the model of the universities. It conferred the degrees of bachelor and doctor "of the science of gay knowledge," and the laureate who had thrice gained the prize was entitled to rank as troubadour. The first prize, a golden violet, was given to the best *canso* or *descort*. The second prize, a silver eglantine, rewarded the best *sirventes, pastorella,* or hymns in honour of the Virgin. And the third prize, a silver marigold, was conferred on the best *balada* and *dansa,* and the less meritorious examples of the former classes.

The term "science" correctly defines the poetry as

an artificial product demanding no special inspiration, *The Leys d'Amors.* as an affair of rhyme and rhythm. But "*gay* science" is a misnomer. True to its *bourgeois* inception, the consistory encouraged, in the compositions submitted to it, a religious tone. The poets were to sing for the glory of God, and instead of earthly maiden were to eulogise Our Lady. And yet, in one sense, the adjective may be deemed in place, inasmuch as the assemblies formed part of the recreation of the people. In 1355 the society commissioned its chancellor, Guilhem Molinier, to draw up the rules of poetical composition, and this was the origin of the *Leys d'Amors*. In the metrical section the treatise enumerates, distinguishes, and illustrates all the ancient sorts of poetry, with the exception of the *tensos*, which had apparently fallen into disuse; and no doubt it exercised considerable influence on the later French, Spanish, and Portuguese technique, at the time of the Renaissance. On the other hand, the *Leys* themselves were indebted to Uc Faidit's *Donatz Proensals* and the *Rasos de Trobar* of Raimon Vidal de Besaudun. There are two versions of the *Leys d'Amors*. One, not yet printed and containing many erasures and corrections, probably represents the first draught. The other, which is at Barcelona, in the archives of the Crown of Aragon, is the work as finally approved.

The name which, more than any other, will always *Clemence Isaure.* be associated with the Floral Games of Toulouse is that of Clemence Isaure. The object of a local cult, it is by no means certain that she is anything but a symbol or a myth. In the Town Hall there is, or was, a small marble statue, and, beneath it, a brazen tablet recording that she was descended from an old and illustrious family; that she founded the Floral Games; that she built the Town Hall at her own cost; that she bequeathed to the city markets for corn, wine, fish, and vegetables; and that the residue of her fortune went to the said games. No dates are assigned, though it is known that the statue was erected in 1557; and a sceptic of the day celebrated the occasion in a sarcastic sonnet. At any rate, with sundry variations, such as the substitution of French for Provençal, the Floral Games continued to be held down to the time of the Revolution, and, as is well known, the present century has witnessed a revival of Provençal literature, mainly through the genius of Mistral.

The topic of old Portuguese poetry has a special interest for English readers, as it was through the *Old Portuguese* labours of a British diplomatist, Sir Charles *poetry.* Stuart, that the study was again brought into vogue. Having lighted on a collection of ancient inedited songs, he caused them to be transcribed, and, in 1823, a small edition—only twenty-five copies—was published in Paris, with the title: *Fragmentos de hum Cancioneiro inedito que se acha na livraria do Real Collegio dos Nobres de Lisboa.* Hence the codex is sometimes known as the *Cancioneiro do Collegio dos Nobres.* Since 1825 it has been lodged at the royal castle of Ayuda, near Lisbon. This circumstance has furnished it with a second title,

and it is now generally described as the *Cancioneiro
da Ayuda*.   A third appellation—for which not much
can be said, seeing that it is founded on a misapprehension—is *Livro das Cantigas do Conde de Barcellos*.
The codex dates from the first half of the fourteenth,
or the last of the thirteenth, century, and is certainly
the oldest in existence.   Besides this, there are two
Italian collections, the *Cancioneiro da Vaticana* and
the *Cancioneiro Colocci-Brancuti*, both of the sixteenth
century.

While epics were written in Castilian or Leonese,
the language of all peninsular (non-Catalan) trouba-
Supremacy of dours was Portuguese or Gallician.   The
Provence.   Portuguese poets frankly acknowledge their
dependence on Provençal models, and in the Vatican
song-book it is common to meet with such lines as

> " Proençaes soen muy ben trobar,"

or, by way of reproach,

> " Vos non trobades como proençal."

The "art de trobar," as practised in this western-
most kingdom, covers a space of more than a hundred
Royal patronage and fifty years, which may be divided into
and example.   four periods calculated with reference to
two kings of Portugal, Affonso III. and Dinis: Præ-
Alfonsine, 1200-1248; Alfonsine, 1248-1280; Diony-
sian, 1280-1325; and Post-Dionysian, 1325-1350.   It
is worthy of note that Affonso III. of Portugal married
Beatrix, daughter of Alfonso X., the "Alfred the
Great" of Castile.   Dinis's successor, Alfonso IV.,

E

nicknamed *o bravo,* or "the wild," was not poetically
inclined. His half-brothers, Dom Pedro Affonso, Count
of Barcellos, and Dom Affonso Sanches, were poets,
but had to flee their country. They took refuge at
the court of Alfonso XI. of Castile. Around this
monarch, son of the Portuguese Constance, and husband of the Portuguese Maria, gathered the last of
the troubadours.

Alfonso the Wise, though he did so much to pro-
mote the use of Castilian, himself *sang* in Portuguese,
possibly because that language is softer, or, not improbably, because the kings of Castile were brought
up in Gallicia as remote from the Moors. As many as
450 poems have been attributed to Alfonso X.; 138
to the "trobador de amor," as Dinis was called by his
contemporaries; 11 to the Count of Barcellos; and
Dom Affonso Sanches, also, is represented in the Vatican MS. There is a fairly long list of troubadours
belonging to each period, and the total number of
secular poems assigned to the 13th and 14th centuries,
and still preserved, is 1698.

With kings and kings' sons as authors, a discussion
of early Portuguese poetry may seem singularly out of
Classification. place in the present chapter; but "the wind
bloweth where it listeth," and you cannot
prescribe that the old lyric verse shall be everywhere
in the same hands. Moreover, this opinion, natural
at first, will be modified as the contents of the song-
books are more closely examined. Of these over a
thousand are love-songs, which may be classified in
two different ways. Either, with reference to sex, as

cantígas de amor and *cantígas de amigo*, or, on formal grounds, as *cantígas de maestria* and *cantígas de refran*.

In the *cantígas de amor* the lover—king, or count, or simple knight—serves as vassal of his lady, always throned afar, always incomparably wise and fair. Necessarily of noble birth, and often his own kin, she is sometimes married, more generally a maid; and he humbly sues for her favour. The *cantígas de amigo* are ladies' songs, and accordingly pendants to the first. They speak of blissful trysts, and mournful partings, and soft messages, and warm confidences, and angry mothers; and occasionally they resolve themselves into dialogues with *him*. In addition to these, there are some hundreds of mocking and abusive poems.

The whole *Cancioneiro* is separable into two groups —songs with, and songs without, a refrain. The former, constituting one-third, are those composed in the Provençal manner, and known as *cantígas de maestria*. The others, *cantígas de refran*, have been acclimatised to the court, but are really popular. A habit racy of the soil, and affecting even studied compositions *em maniera de proençal*, is the repetition of a thought with only a slight variation in the expression. This is best exemplified in a species of verse for which the Portuguese have strictly no name, or, it might be proper to say, no name coextensive with all its possible forms. It is written in parallel stanzas, of which one is the echo of the other, and which hardly differ except as to the vowels. The favourite assonances are *i-o* and *a-o ;* and the words most frequently interchanged are *amigo* and *amado,* as in the following instance :—

I.

> " Solo ramo verde e florido,
>   Vodas fazem ao meu amigo !
>   E choram olhos d' amor !

II.

> Solo florido e verde ramo,
>   Vodas fazem ao meu amado !
>   E choram olhos d' amor ! "

Of such songs in parallel stanzas the Vatican collection contains fifty-four, forty being quite pure, while the rest are mixed.   King Dinis wrote eight, and a ninth was written by Dom Affonso Sanches, his son.   One of the lyrics, originally a pure *volkslied,* of which two versions are given and assigned to the gifted clerk, Ayras Nunes, and a popular bard Joam Zorro respectively, is a dance-song, commencing—

> " Bailemos já todas, todas ay amigas
>   Sob aquestas avelaneyras floridas," &c.

Probably this was actually sung by a double chorus of young maidens round a budding hazel-bush on Mayday or at Eastertide.

In conclusion, this is not really a great period of Portuguese literature.   Its real blossoming time is the fifteenth century, the age of voyages, and discoveries, and surpassing national energy, to which, however, the poetry itself offers but faint resemblance, being rather tender and melancholy than vigorous and heroic.

The most salient fact in Catalan literature is the difference of language in artistic poetry and artistic *Catalan literature.* prose. Till the end of the thirteenth century poets wrote, not indeed without occasional solecisms, in the language of Provence. Even at a later period, when an apprenticeship in prose had rendered Catalan more fit for versifying purposes, the poets kept many words and phrases borrowed from the Troubadours or the academic verse of Toulouse. What they did was to simplify the technique, to exchange variety for certain unalterable forms. The intricacy and refinement of the art degenerate in their hands into clumsiness and obscurity, and Petrarch's influence was most pernicious, leading, as in his own country, to general affectation.

This description of Catalan literature, as it presents itself from the fourteenth to the sixteenth century, applies to artistic composition. Liturgical poems— poems in honour of God and the saints — were in the native speech; and the *goigs*, religious hymns to-day extraordinarily popular, are unquestionably of ancient origin. The visionary and philosophic Ramon Lull, though in complicated rhythm, employed the Catalan tongue.

Between the early Provençal epoch in Catalan and the founding of the Consistory at Barcelona, there *The favourite stanza.* was a period of transition in which writers display a marked reluctance to break with the old forms. Thus the chronicler, Ramon Muntaner, in his *Sermó* on the Sardinian expedition (1323), adopts a monorhymed strophe of twenty lines, each line consisting of twelve syllables. In the *cobles* (or strophes) addressed by Peter IV. of Aragon to his son, King Martin of Sicily, in 1378, we come upon a favourite and characteristic metre of the Catalan gay science— the *cobla croada unisonant*. A *cobla* is called *croada* when the rhymes cross: thus, *abba*. It is said to be *unisonant* when the same rhymes are continued through all the strophes of the poem. In the *cobles* referred to, the lines are decasyllabic and divided into two unequal halves of four and six (or seven) syllables respectively. The standing pause after the fourth syllable produces a monotonous effect, which, however, appears not to have been felt by the Catalans themselves, as even Auzias March, lauded by Santillana as "gran trovador é ome de assaz elevado espiritu," and one of their few distinguished poets, made no attempt to vary it.

Distinct from the "art de trobar," or representing only its most vulgar and prosaic side, are the poems in *bordons appariats* (couplets), already *Couplets.* designated in the *Leys d'Amors* as *novas rimadas*. This form was early adopted by the Catalans; indeed, according to Santillana, the *noves rimades* had preceded the *cobles*. In any case, this non-strophic variety, because much easier than *cobles croades* or *encadenades*, was bound to attract many versifiers too lazy or stupid to attack the more intricate forms.

> "Car ignorant suy del estil
> Dels trobadors del gay saber,"

says, unabashed, the writer of one of these poems.

The great master in this style was Jaume Roig, who
flourished about the middle of the fifteenth century, and whose *Libre de Consells* or *de les Dames*
is a satire against women, inspired by his own experiences and the confessions of similarly unlucky
wights.

The break-up of the aristocratic monopoly is nowhere more evident than in Germany, where the whole
German nation seems to have abandoned itself to
enthusiasm. song. This enthusiasm is strikingly at-
tested in the *Limburg Chronicle*, in which the appearance of a new song is hailed as an event, and something is said as to the author. "Item at this time [*i.e.*,
in 1356] people sang the matin ode of the Holy
Passion, and it was new, and a knight made it.

> " 'O starker Got,
>   Alle unse nôt
>   Befelen wir herre in dîn gebot,
>   Lass uns den dag mit gnâden oberschînen!
>   Di namen drî
>   Di stent uns bî.
>   In allen nôden wo wir sîn,
>   Di negel drî, das sper und ouch di krone.'

"Item in the same year 'dictamina' [*i.e.*, prose-
writings] and verses in German songs were transformed.
Whereas heretofore people had sung long odes with
five or six strophes, now the masters make new songs,
which they call *widersänge*, with three strophes. A
revolution has occurred also in pipes and piping, and
never were they so good heretofore as they have begun
now to be. For he who five or six years before was

called a good piper all over the land is now nothing
worth.   Item people sang then the *widersang*—

> " ' Hoffen heldet mir das leben,
>   Trûren dede mir anders wê.'

"Item at this time, five or six years before, there
was on the Main a monk of the barefoot order, who
was by the people rejected, and unclean [*i.e.*, he was
leprous].   He made the best songs and dances in the
world, both verse and melody, so that no man on the
river Rhine, or in this country, could match him.   And
what he sang, that sang the people right gladly, and
all masters, pipers and other minstrels, carried about
tune and words.   Item he sang the ode—

> " ' Des dîpans bin ich uss gezalt,
>   Man wîset mich armen vur di dure,
>   Untrûwe ich nu spure
>   Zu allen zîden.'

" Item he sang—

> " ' Mei mei mei, dîne wonnecliche zît
>   Menlîchen freude gît
>   An mir, was meinet das ? '

" Item he sang—

> " ' Der untrûwe ist mit mir gespelet,' &c.

"Of odes and *widersänge* made he very many, and
all was charming."

From this account it will be seen that poetry was
extremely popular among all classes of society, and

that the writers were persons of widely different station. It is often—quite accurately—stated that the minnesingers were succeeded by the meistersingers, but, as will shortly be seen more clearly, *minnesang* was perpetuated in the *volkslieder*, which everybody, irrespective of rank or calling, felt competent to indite, much to the indignation of the "masters," one of whom complained that there was not a peasant, no matter how common, but claimed to be a singer.

First, however, as to the "masters." This title was adopted in the thirteenth century by certain poets— *The Meistersingers.* such as the celebrated "Frauenlob"—in contradistinction to the ordinary peripatetic gleemen on the one hand, and the makers of *sprüche*, half-lyrical, half-gnomic compositions, on the other. The "masters" were professional poets, but as there had been professional poets before—notably Walther von der Vogelweide—the term expressed more than the mere vocation. It connoted pride both as to general culture and the technical side of poetry itself. Indeed, "Frauenlob," or, to give him his actual name, Heinrich von Meissen, deemed himself superior to the old poets, Reinmar, Walther, and Wolfram. They, said he, had extracted their song from the scum, while his own art had come from the bottom of the kettle.

The chief characteristics of this *meistergesang* were skill in the management of difficult rhythms, artifices of style, and a parade of scholastic and theological learning. It was cultivated exclusively by burgher poets, content, on the whole, to work up old material.

Marner, in a cynical vein, allows this lack of originality :—

> " Lihte vinde ich einen vunt,
> Den si vunden hant, die vor mir sint gewesen:
> Ich muos us ir garten, und ir spriuchen blumen lesen."

A noteworthy feature of this new verse is the *rôle*
the *joc partit* plays in it.   The so-called " Wartburg-
Krieg " is perhaps the most elaborate instance of the
sort, but quite as interesting is the contest wherein
Heinrich von Meissen acquired his romantic nickname.
Meissen propounded the question : Which is the more
honourable title for a woman, *Weib* or *Frau?* and
defended the latter alternative against the valiant
Meister Regenbogen.   Competitions like these excited
a petty litigious spirit, showing itself in personalities
and scurrilities.   Indeed, the rules of their art and
mystery—the " masters " had a strong bias for the
occult—were discussed and fought over with almost a
theological hatred.   The professors were tenacious of
their privileges.   A stranger claiming to be a " master "
was at once challenged with the inquiry, where he had
learnt his art ; and the title was only admitted in regard to those who had indited poems in the various
recognised sorts of verse.   Meetings were held for
practice, and, like other tradesmen, the " masters "
formed themselves into a guild.

In spite of their distinguishing vices, pedantry and
conceit, some of the " masters " found favour in the
halls of the nobility.   Hadlaub (*c.* 1302),
At Court.
for instance, whose love-story reminds us
of the *Vita Nuova*, warmly commends Herr Rüdiger

Maness of Zürich, an indefatigable collector of songs, and doubtless a good customer of Johann Hadlaub. Johann is a staunch believer in the ennobling influence of poetry, which he brackets, as a source of high feeling, with the charm of womanhood.

> "Swem ist mit edelem sange wol,
>   Des herze ist vol gar edeler sinne.
>   Sang ist ein sô gar edeles guot:
>   Er kumt von edelem sinne dar.
>   Dür frouwen clar, dür edel minne,
>   Von dien zwein kumt sô hôher muot.
>   Was waer diu welt, enwaern wîp niht sô schoene?
>   Dür sî wirt sô vil süessekeit,
>   Dür sî man wol singt unde seit
>   Sô guot gereit und süess gedoene:
>   Ir wunne sanc ûss herzen treit."

There is plenty of art here. The reader will notice especially the middle-rhymes, the recurrence of the key-words, and the long-drawn seventh line, which impart to the stanza its peculiar quality. The effect on the ear is very far from displeasing, and the pleasure is enhanced by the subdued alliteration. Moreover, the alternation of masculine and feminine rhymes attests a fine sense of harmony. Altogether, Hadlaub is a favourable specimen of his class, and coming so early, merits perhaps the name of "Minnesinger." Later "masters" also enjoyed the patronage of the great. For example, Heinrich von Mügeln lived in the service of Charles IV. at Prague, and was well known at other courts. In a great allegorical poem entitled *Kranz der Meide* he depicts twelve liberal arts as virgins, who appear before the emperor and crave his sentence, which among them is the most excellent. Besides this *capo d'opera*, Mügeln, who suffered grievously from an astronomical "fad," wrote many pieces on both secular and religious topics. The "masters" holding these court posts—always few in number—at length disappeared as a class, for the following reason. It appears from the *Limburg Chronicle* that the musical side of the art was as important as the poetical; and, in the sixteenth century, the "masters," with their airs for one voice, and very often old airs, found themselves eclipsed by a new race of court musicians competent to meet the then universal demand for part-songs.

In general the Meistersingers did better in the towns—Maintz, Worms, Nürnberg, and Strassburg—

In town. in which last, according to a document of the year 1598, "die uralte löbliche kunst des teutschen Meistergesanges wurde durch etliche kunstliebende, gottesfürchtige Personen vor ungefähr 105 Jahren aufgerichtet." This is precisely as might have been expected, for the art of the "masters," in spite of exceptions, was essentially democratic. Regenbogen, "Frauenlob's" opponent, who lived about 1300, was a smith; and Michel Beheim, a singer of the fifteenth century, a weaver. Such favourites of Apollo did not necessarily quit their employments, but followed the "laudable art" as a recreation. However, the rise of the drama drew away the minds of the multitude from artistic poetry, and left the Meistersingers in a double sense "high and dry."

The "masters" did not excel in the pure lyric. In treating the themes of their predecessors they in-
Court-lyric and folk-song. dulged a didactic tendency, issuing in the formation of a mixed kind of verse. This is notably the case with the odes of Meister Suchensinn († 1392). Probably, however, they did not always wear the gown. For their own profit divers of them may have thrown off verses conceived in a more popular vein—in other words, may have deigned to write *volkslieder*. Even the old court-lyric was not devoid of popular elements. In the songs of the "lower *minne*" the heroine is a humble maiden, while the *dorfspoesie* of Neidhart von Reuenthal, though tending to be satirical, furnishes a not wholly prejudiced picture of rural life and manners. A typical scene in Neidhart's summer-odes is a "row" between mother and daughter, when the girl is going to the dance. This scene is again depicted in the dance-songs of the Ditmarsch peasantry in the sixteenth century.

Artistically, the *volkslieder* are often debased minnesongs, and exhibit in relation to the "society" lyric
Volkslieder. the contrasts already pointed out as differentiating the popular from the court romance. The connection between the parts is looser, and more is left to the listener's imagination. More purely human than the minnesong, with its trammels of court-etiquette, the *volkslied* has frequently the character of an occasional poem. Sometimes it is an immediate reflection of experience, as, for example,

when it analyses, so to speak, at first hand the feelings
of a lover in the hour of dismissal.

> "My pretty love hath bid me go,
>   Yet care not I, and well 'tis so—
>   For that I'll not be dying ;
>   Let a fresh summer come along,
>   Another I'll be trying.
>
> My pretty love hath yellow hair,
>   And jet-black eyes—a radiant pair,
>   They burn serene and starry.
>   Whenever she abroad doth stir,
>   I see her, nowise sorry.
>
> And whenso she abroad doth stir,
>   If any man look after her,
>   That may not be endurèd ;
>   So many lying curs there be,
>   When love from me is lurèd.
>
> They'd have me in a cloister barr'd,
>   To win my pretty love's reward,
>   And so my hopes would smother;
>   Had Whitsuntide but longer been,
>   Lo, I had won another !"

The original stanzas were copied by Herr Karl Bartsch
from a manuscript in the library of the University of
Basle,[1] and it is not improbable that they were written
by a student, one of those "freie burschenknechte"
who, in their love-ditties and drinking-songs, parodied
the Bible and liturgy.

The *volkslied* is often hardly distinguishable from

[1] *Beiträge zur Quellenkunde der Altdeutschen Literatur.* Strassburg,
Trübner. The best collections of *volkslieder* are those of Uhland, *Alte
hoch-und niederdeutsche Volkslieder*, Stuttgart, 1844-46, and Böhme,
Altdeutsches Liederbuch, Leipzig, 1877.

the ballad. Either it arises out of a tale, or it is a tale
Minnesingers in legend. *sans façon.* Very interesting and remarkable is the fact that the names of four
prominent Minnesingers—Reinmar von Brennenberg,
Heinrich von Morungen, Gottfried von Neifen, and
Tannhäuser—are preserved in German folk-song.
The *volkslieder* do not remember them as poets, doubtless because the song-writers depended on tradition.
Let us take an example, included in Uhland's collection—that of the "noble Möringer." This song appears to have been based on a tale inserted by Cæsarius
of Heisterbach in his *Dialogus Miraculorum*, to the
following effect.

In the country of Hollenbach dwelt a knight, Gerhard by name, a great votary of St Thomas. A devil
Gerhard and the grateful devil. in human form accosts him, and in the
name of the saint bespeaks his hospitality.
Gerhard receives him kindly, and lends him
his own fur cloak ("cappam suam furratam bonam
satis"). The devil makes off with the cloak, where-
upon Gerhard's wife reproaches him for his folly. He,
however, consoles her by saying that St Thomas will
compensate their loss. Some time after, Gerhard
starts on a pilgrimage to the apostle's grave in India.
Ere he goes, he gives his wife one half of a ring. The
other half he takes with him; and he tells her that if
he does not return within five years she is free to
marry again. In India Gerhard enjoys himself so
well that it is only on the last day he remembers his
agreement with his wife. Recollecting this, he becomes very downcast, when suddenly the thief of a

devil appears, commissioned to fetch him back before
bedtime, as his wife is on the point of wedding.
Catching him up, the devil transports the pilgrim to
his home on the Rhine, and sets him down safe and
sound, in the twilight. While bride and groom sit at
the marriage-feast, Gerhard drops his half of the ring
into the goblet. His wife recognises him, and the
poor bridegroom would have gone away in disgrace,
but Gerhard, out of politeness, keeps him in the house
overnight. Cæsarius insists that the story of this
miracle was known to all the inhabitants of Hollenbach, and that Gerhard's grandchildren were, in his
day, still living there.

Now as to the *volkslied*. The precise date of its
composition cannot be fixed. It was certainly written
The noble before 1359, and may have been written as
Möringer. early as 1300. The tale of the "noble Möringer" is the tale of Gerhard, with the episode of the
devil and the stolen cloak left out. On the eve of a
pilgrimage to St Thomas, Möringer sets his wife a
term of seven years, after which she may do as she
lists ; and he commends her, during his absence, to
the protection of the young Herr von Neifen. The
seven years are up, but Möringer still tarries in the
land of St Thomas. In a dream an angel comes and
warns him that, unless he returns that very day, Von
Neifen will take his spouse. Möringer prays to the
saint, and falls asleep again. When he awakes he is
at home sitting before his mill. From the miller he
receives a confirmation of his dream. Everybody believes him dead. Feigning to be a pilgrim, he enters

the house, and just when the bride is to be bedded, he lifts up his voice in a song describing his own case. The bride orders a wine-cup to be passed to him. Möringer puts in the ring, and sends it back to his wife. At once she recognises him, and throwing herself on her knees pleads for forgiveness. Young Von Neifen, too, accuses himself of breaking faith. Möringer, very gracious, pardons them all, and gives his daughter to Von Neifen. " But," he exclaims, pathetically, " lass mir die alte Braut."

The songs of Heinrich the Lion belong to the same cycle; and in these also, though not as in Cæsarius, *"Since conjugal* the agency of a devil comes into play. *passion," &c.* It is worthy of note that in *The Noble Möringer* two genuine stanzas of Walther von der Vogelweide are put into the mouth of the hero. This suggests another remark—viz., that while the Minnesingers had complimented married ladies, the common poets bestow their praises, or dispraises, on young maidens. It is due, perhaps, to the stricter morals of the rising burgher-class that two noblemen, who may be termed the " last of the Minnesingers "—Count Hugo von Montfort and Oswald von Wolkenstein—in their later verse celebrate the virtues of their wives.

I have by no means exhausted all that might be said on the German *lieder*. The large part which *Rhyme-speakers.* nature plays in these songs, as in all popular poetry of the time, is specially deserving of recognition.[1] Again, the satirical verses aimed at

[1] See on this Scherer's *History of German Literature*, vol. i. p. 250 (English translation). Clarendon Press, Oxford.

different classes of society—the *schwänke*, in which patient Hodge and his clumsy attempts at merry-making are served up *à la* Neidhart for the amusement of the spruce townsman—would provide ample ground for expatiating, were expatiation possible. Some little room, however, must be reserved for a tribe of performers who went by the name of *reim-sprecher*, and whose forte was improvisation. Not that their rhymes—any more than modern obituary notices, parliamentary oratory, or colloquial witticisms —were always and purely extemporaneous; but the "occasional" character, which we have learnt to distinguish as the note of this late folk-song, is here accentuated and pronounced.

The chief exponents of the school were the King of the Odenwald, Teichner, and Peter Suchenwirt in the fourteenth, and Hans Schnepperer (nicknamed Rosen-plüt), and another Hans (surnamed Folz) in the fifteenth century. The three first represent in a curious way the ideas of the three orders into which it is usual to divide society. Suchenwirt made a special study of heraldry, and composed *ehrenreden* on dead princes and nobles. Teichner gives expression to middle-class sentiment. He is moral and religious, and cannot away with robber-chivalry, tourneys, serving of ladies, or any such trash. Lastly, the King of the Odenwald *The King of the Odenwald.* (so named apparently as head of the minstrels in that part of the world) glorifies the kailyard, and revels in such inspiring themes as the cock, the sheep, the cow, &c. In one of his poems he undertakes to show how far superior is the goose,

or gander—he is not particular which—to all other
feathered fowl.   He recapitulates its uses after being
converted into dead stock, and in his way is fairly
amusing.   The King of the Odenwald can also, as the
conclusion testifies, be exceedingly vulgar, though not
more so than many of his betters had been in bygone
days.[1]

The topic of vulgarity takes us straight to the Low
Countries.   There, as elsewhere, eminent moralists, of
The Low   whom Jan Boendale, author of *Der Leken-*
Countries.   *spegel*, may serve as a type, had varied and
enforced their teaching by the introduction of short
tales.   This custom suggested a " happy thought " to
the *sprekers* or *zeggers* who held forth now in the halls
of the gentry, now before town-audiences, and they
took to relating such tales for their own sakes.   The
tales, always in verse, are of two kinds, comic and
tragic, and consist, for the most part, of translations
of French *dits* and *fabliaux*.   The *boerden*, characterised by coarse wit, do not reach any high level of
excellence.   One of the best is the *Wise Counsel of
Women*, by Peter van Jersele ; it is identical in subject with a novel of Boccaccio (*Decameron*, iii. 3).   The
sproken, or serious poems, include a version of the
Pyramus and Thisbe story under the quaint title,
Van tween Kinderen die droeghen ene starcke Minne.
The names of several *sprekers* have been handed down,
the most famous being those of Augustijnken van
Dordt and Willem van Hildergaersberch.   The former,

---

[1] Many of these " reimereien " may be found in Lassburg's
Liedersaal.

who was in the service of the Count of Blois, composed, among other poems, an allegorical description of a young woman's head (*De Borch van Vroudenrijc*). The latter was a sort of poet-laureate to Albert and William IV. of Holland, and has bequeathed a hundred and twenty poems—historical, political, satirical —besides fables and *boerden*.

There is reason to surmise that the term "minstrel" (Anglo-French, *ménestrel*) was first used in this sense *English minstrels.* at the court of the Norman conquerors in England; and those to whom it was applied were not destitute of personal and social distinction. The stories of Taillefer and Blondel de Nesle, though not necessarily true in the letter, are conclusive as to the estimation of the order. It was not in the nature of things that the sayers and singers of the vanquished should enjoy similar advantages. If they existed as a class, they can only have practised their art under severe restrictions, not wholly unlike those enforced in more recent times against strolling players.

On the revival of English in the reign of Henry I., there emerge from the dimness native performers who, like their Norman predecessors, are called "minstrels." As was the case with the more general term "jongleur," the description covered many degrees of professional skill, as well as, perhaps, some inequality of rank. It is improbable, however, that the "harpours," "disours," and "gestours" attained to anything approaching fame or fortune. In the "prologus" of *Piers the Plowman*, Langland discriminates between the more reputable minstrels and a baser sort which he calls "japers and jangelers," who, like the hermits, were influenced in the choice of a vocation by idleness and love of dissipation. The making of a minstrel, in the less honourable sense, is described in another prologue —that of the *Cokes Tale*. Here we have an account of the progress of a certain victualler's apprentice, Perkyn Revellour. A handsome youth, and glad of any excuse to throw off the burden of business—

> " At every bridale wold he synge and hoppe,
> He lovede bette the tavern than the shoppe."

For these pleasant ways Perkyn's master had some-times to pay in the shape of an empty till.

> " For such a joly prentys revellour
> That haunteth dys, revel, or paramour,
> His master shal it in the shoppe abye,
> Al have he no part in the mynstralsye.
> For theft and ryote be convertible,
> Al can they pley on giterne or rubible."

This was manifestly unfair. Moreover, his "maister" was not without concern as to the influence of this scapegrace on his other apprentices. So—on the prin-ciple, "well bette is roten appul out of hord"—he gave Perkyn his discharge. Thereupon the reveller sent his bed and other appurtenances to a companion, who, fortunately, had a wife "that held for counte-nance a shoppe," and lived—God rest you merry !

It is interesting to compare the ambiguous lot of the English minstrel class with the elaborate organi-sation of the Welsh bards. The latter were *Welsh bards.* divided into three orders : the *teulüwr*, the family bard ; the *clerwr*, the vagabond bard, who sub-

sisted on charity ; and the *prydydd*, the honourable
bard, who sometimes claimed the monopoly of the
name. Over and above them all were the *priv-veirdd*,
or chief bards, who reckoned themselves Druids. The
massacre of the bards by Edward I. is, of course, a
popular error. All that he did was to order that the
"Westours, Bards, Rhymers, and other idlers and
vagabonds, who lived upon the gifts called Cymmortha,
be not supported, nor sanctioned in the country, lest
by their invectives and lies they lead the people to
mischief and burden the common people with their
impositions." The mandate was directed against dis-
orderly bards, and similar proclamations were issued
by Henry IV., Henry VIII., and Elizabeth.[1] With
regard to the English minstrels, so far as it is possible
to draw any distinction, it is natural to suppose a
difference between those who popularised romances
of chivalry, and the more patriotic, but perhaps also
more ignorant, "jangelers" who kept alive the memory
of Robin Hood, the traditional representative of English manhood.

The earliest mention of these ballads is found in
a passage of *Piers the Plowman*, where the outlaw
figures, in conjunction with Randolph, Earl of Chester,
as a hero of profane and popular rhymes. That such
rhymes were composed for "the vulgar," and merely
for "the vulgar," may be inferred from the absence
of contemporary MSS. It is only after the lapse of
a century that a glimpse can be obtained of the character of the poetry circulating among the common

[1] Stephens's *Literature of the Cymry*, p. 102.

people in the time of Chaucer, with the exclusion of those glimpses afforded by the poet himself. A detailed account of *The Gest of Robin Hood, John the Reeve,* and other outlaw ballads, might therefore be out of place. It is otherwise with the *Tale of Gamelyn,* which has been handed down as an appendix to Chaucer's poems, and may once have been copied by him for the purpose of adapting it for the *Canterbury Tales.*[1] This tale, the handiwork of some unknown minstrel, whose speech bewrayeth him as of the Eastern Midlands, occupies a place midway between the Anglicised romance and the popular ballad. On it is founded, indirectly and through Lodge, *As You Like It.*

A good old knight, a-dying, is much troubled about his property He has three sons, the eldest of whom The Tale of is a villain. In his need he sends for Gamelyn. certain wise knights to aid in dividing the estate, and he adjures them particularly not to forget his youngest son, Gamelyn. For some reason the advisers ignore this injunction ; but the old knight reproves them, and soon after gives up the ghost. The presentiments of the old man are now realised. The heir treats his brother scurvily. He gives him bad food to eat and wretched clothing to put on, and suffers his possessions to go to ruin. Gamelyn takes it all meekly, until one day he objects to be called

[1] In the *Poetical Works of Geoffrey Chaucer*, edited by Richard Morris, LL.D., and published by George Bell & Sons, it is printed as *The Cokes Tale of Gamelyn*, but Dr Skeat has decided that the title is a later addition. (Clarendon Press edition, iii. 399.)

"gadelyng." His brother orders him to be beaten,
but the boy espies a "pestel" or staff under a wall,
and seizing it, assumes the offensive against the
serving-men. The heir himself, a miserable coward,
flies for safety to a loft, whence he refuses to come
down whilst the staff remains in Gamelyn's hand.
Moreover, he promises to restore the land his father
bequeathed Gamelyn, and to put everything in order.
An apparent reconciliation follows, but the knight
meditates treason.

Not far from the castle a wrestling was cried, the
prize consisting of a ram and a ring. Gamelyn asks
permission to attend, and permission is granted in the
hope that he may get his neck broken. Instead of
that, the young man throws the champion, and on the
morrow returns with a great rout. His brother, seeing
this, tells the porter to lock the gate. Gamelyn forces
it open, kills the porter, and flings his body into a well
seven fathoms deep. He entertains his friends right
royally, emptying in the process his brother's cellar;
and on the eighth day the guests depart. The knight
now comes out of hiding, and declares he will be for-
sworn unless Gamelyn allows himself to be bound
hand and foot for throwing the porter into the well.
Gamelyn consents, and forthwith the knight pretends
that he is mad. After that the unnatural brother
makes a feast for high and low; and there arrive,
among others, abbots and priors, monks and canons.
Gamelyn appeals to them for help, but the reverend
guests answer him roughly. However, he wins over
Adam the cellarer; and the pair, having furnished

themselves with staves, serve the men of Holy Church much as Ulysses served the suitors. The monks conclude that it had been better for them had they dined at home on bread and water.

The sheriff, five miles away, is informed how Gamelyn and Adam have broken the king's peace, and sends a large party to arrest them. Forewarned, they betake themselves to the forest, where, hungry and thirsty, they light on a band of young outlaws dining. The "king" inquires their business, and Gamelyn explains

"He moste needes walke in woode that may not walke in towne."

He is made free of their company; and when the "king," having been pardoned, departs, Gamelyn succeeds to his place. Meanwhile the knight has been appointed sheriff, and Gamelyn is cried "wolf's head." Thereupon, outlaw as he is, he marches boldly into the moot-hall and reproaches his vile kinsman. For his pains he is cast into prison. But now another brother, Sir Ote, appears and goes bail for him. Gamelyn returns to the forest to see how his merry men fare, and, at the proper time, presents himself before the judge. The case, however, has been already heard, and Sir Ote sentenced to be hanged. But all is not over. With the help of his comrades, the outlaw-king seats himself in the judge's place, and the proceedings are reversed. Judge, jury, and sheriff are condemned and executed, no mercy being shown to the false knight, though he pleads hard for it. For love of Sir Ote, the real king forgives Gamelyn this outrage, and makes him chief justice of his forest.

English folk-song is cheerful and gay, answering to the prosperous condition of the rising middle-class.

Scottish ballads. Langland mentions the burden, *Trolliloli*, well known later, as sung "at the ale." Scottish minstrelsy, on the other hand, partakes of that "dour" quality which might else have been traced to Knox and the Reformation, and which certainly reached its acme in the Whigs. The earliest northern songs known to us, at any rate in writing, are those mocking ditties exchanged between Scot and Southron over the walls of Berwick, during the memorable siege, and preserved by the contemporary Pierre de Langtoft. Similar verses in disdain of the English, sung by the lassies after the battle of Bannockburn, have been handed down by Fabian. Seeing, however, that his chronicle was first published about 1500, absolute confidence cannot be placed in the text. Again, Barbour, about the year 1378, alludes to popular songs in honour of the Bruce. Considerations like these led Bishop Percy, and, after him, Sir Walter Scott, to fix on the Scottish border as the primitive home of the ballad; but the conjecture can only be endorsed with reference to the particular sort describing the warlike occupations and stirring deeds of the Border folk.

The original metre of the ballad seems to be, on the accentual system of scansion, a couplet consisting of two members, of which the first has four

Metre. and the second three accents, and exhibiting a mixture of alliteration and rhyme. The Carolingian romance, *Ferumbras*, is partly composed in this metre, with the addition of middle-

rhymes. This last innovation led to the two long
lines being broken up into four short ones, rhyming
abab. In some old ballads, however, like the *Battle
of Otterbourn*, recast in accordance with the later
fashion, the alteration was not consistently carried out,
and we get stanzas like the following :—

> "Sir Harry Perssy cam to the walles,
>   The Scottish oste for to se;
> And sayd, and thou has brent Northumberland,
>   Full sore it rewyth me."

Yet another variety evolved out of the septenarian
couplet is that which has two lines of four accents,
followed by one of three accents. This being repeated
produces the-six-lined stanza so common in romance
and parodied in *Sir Thopas*. The *Tale of Gamelyn* is
in lines of four accents arranged in pairs, but the
versification is extremely rough.

I have not been careful to distinguish between folk-
song and town-verse—as regards, at least, the inclusion
of both subjects in the same chapter —
Class-hatred. because the dividing line between gentry
and commons was much sharper than that between
any sections of the commons themselves. Indeed,
at this period the middle-class was, for literary purposes, only just coming into existence. Its nativity
was signalised, partly by the spoiling (in a twofold
sense) of the literary treasures of the gentlefolks, and
partly by the exhibition of hatred and jealousy towards
superiors. It was in northern France that these un-
amiable feelings obtained their fullest and most ran-
corous expression.

The explosion is quite intelligible when we remember that the townsman had shared with the clerk and the villein the obloquy of the preceding age. In the *fabliaux* he is commonly depicted as a cuckold or as tyrannised over by his wife, and though it would doubtless be inaccurate to think of *fabliaux* as designed exclusively for the noble, it is likely enough that the pieces in which the townsman is vilified were faithful reflections of aristocratic prejudice. The townsman was now to essay his revenge. The satirical turn, the sansculottism of certain *chansons de geste*, has already been noted. The same thing is visible, in a greatly exaggerated form, in an amazing production, entitled *Renart le Contrefait* (*i.e.*, copied from the old). This long poem is rich in scandals, and such episodes as that of Athis and Prophilias—we might style it " The Adventures of a Contented Wittol "—look uncommonly like an attempt to pay off old scores. Roman senators do duty for Christian knights, and high-flown chivalrous sentiments are parodied in a succession of scenes ridiculous and quaint, and serving as a mirror of actual topsy-turvydom. The work is in two parts, one of which was written by a grocer; and it comprehends a history of the world down to the year 1319.

Renart le Contrefait, however, is not the only verse in which the *bourgeois* spirit allies itself with history. *Rhyming Chronicles.* A title like *Branche des Royaux Lignages* naturally awakens an expectation of a courtier - like production, but that is precisely what Guillaume Guiart's memoir is not. It is occupied chiefly with the war of Philippe IV. in Flanders, where

Guiart had served as sergeant of artillery. The poem extends to 12,500 lines, nearly all of which have "leonine" rhymes. Of more vital concern is the fact that Guiart is a sworn enemy of the *chansons de geste*, whose marvels he rejects with scant ceremony. His aim is not to flatter, but to tell the truth; and this trait, in spite of eccentricities, renders his work precious. The style is past praying for. Either Guiart never read or foolishly put aside Cæsar's memorable caution against the *verbum inusitatum*, which exercises over the man of Orléans a fatal attraction. Thirdly, Godefroi de Paris, who wrote *Le Martyre de Saint Bacchus*, a witty parody of the *Lives of the Saints*, wrote also a by no means witty chronicle of Paris from 1300 to 1316. As poetry this is rubbish, but the composition deserves mention as describing contemporary events from the standpoint of a keen observant citizen.

Politically, Paris was conspicuous as the theatre of a conflict between the University and the mendicant orders. For purely *bourgeois* manifestations

Puis. it behoves us to turn aside to a thriving municipality of the North. To literary students Arras is interesting from its associations with Adam de la Halle. After his departure the taste for lyric poetry, which he had helped so much to foster, lived on in the citizens, and led to the establishment of *puis* or poetical contests. Like the consistories of the Gay Science, the *puis* allowed themselves to be absorbed by technical considerations, with the result that the matriculating verse was uniform and laboured. From this general censure may perhaps be excepted the *sottes chansons*, or burlesque poems, which, coarse as they sometimes are, have a positive value for the light which they throw on the life and language of the place and period.

In Italy vernacular verse may be said to have begun with the *Cantico del Sole* of St Francis of Assisi, while *Italian folk-song.* a prominent feature in the goings-on of the Flagellants (not, of course, in Italy only) was the chanting of a *lauda*, or hymn. The composition of *laude* was a favourite exercise of the half, or wholly, mad Jacopone da Todi ; and the fourteenth century produced a large crop of such poems, the best being those of Bianco da Siena. All this is very plain, but secular developments are proportionally obscure. A great and recurring difficulty with regard to all early popular poetry is that it was written down, for the most part, a century or two after the presumed date of its composition. The comfortable theory of one eminent critic that a poem roughly synchronises with the event which it celebrates is applicable only to the class of historical ballads, if there. Nevertheless, it seems certain that Italian folk in the thirteenth century, however they may have been inspired, ventured on poetical experiments of their own. The famous Sicilian *contrasto* of Ciullo d'Alcamo (or Cielo dal Camo) can hardly have stood alone, and in the opinion of some speaks for a lost world of kindred compositions, which always remained oral, or, committed to writing, perished from want of care. Again, the *strambotti* of southern Italy, though conceivably not preserved exactly in their original form, undoubtedly represent a very old tradition.

The specimens we possess of primitive Italian folk-song, some of which goes back to at least the thirteenth century, do not differ materially from the same class of poems elsewhere. Take, for example, what are perhaps the most characteristic of any, the Bologna ballades. In one of these a mother wrangles with her daughter, who has a mind to wed. Another is a dialogue between two sisters-in-law, who have been false to their respective spouses. The third " shows up " the ill-breeding of a couple of gossips. The verses are of the unbidden anonymous sort which, like fungi, spring up everywhere. In other words, they are typical folk-songs.

A century passes, and we meet with a self-conscious poetry produced, as the earlier was, in the bosom of the city-republics, and reflecting the life and conversation of the citizens. In the interim much has happened. A classic Italian literature has blossomed, and has struck its roots deep and wide among the Italian people; and, of course, this circumstance does not count for nothing. The precursors of the later town - verse were Cecco Angiolieri, Folgore di San Gemignano, and still more, Pieraccio Tedaldi and Pietro Faitinelli. These writers, who flourished during the first half of the fourteenth century, have been happily described in the words " poeti volgari famigliari, o giocosi, o umoristi, o borghesi, come si debbano chiamare " (Morpurgo). Concerning them more will be said in the following chapter.

The wit and play of fancy which characterised this older school are not altogether wanting in their successors. But in Italy, as in Germany, the distinctively middle - class lyric exhibits a strong moralising tendency. Its principal exponents are Antonio Beccari of Ferrara, and Antonio Pucci of Florence. Beccari, a physician and friend of Petrarch, was prolific enough; but he is too formal, too didactic, and too faulty a versifier to rank as an artistic poet, which was apparently his ambition. Far more richly endowed *The Trumpeter* was the Florentine trumpeter, Pucci,[1] who, *of Florence.* though he also teaches and preaches, preaches and teaches in a simpler, more natural style. Not improbably, the rhymes he composed on the leading events of the day were sung by himself in the *piazze.* Pucci's great achievement is to have turned Villani's chronicle into *terza rima.* This work he christened *Centiloquio,* which, it would seem, expressed his intention on commencing, for it is arithmetically a misnomer. These things — rhyme and title — show that Pucci, in a very humble way, followed in the footsteps of his great fellow-citizen, in the study of whose writings lay the best and chiefest part of his education. Accordingly, special interest attaches to that portion of his poem relating to Dante, for whom he displays boundless reverence and enthusiasm. It commences as follows :—

> " The mind that heretofore right bravely wrought
> So as to talk of precious things and high,
> At present standeth utterly distraught.

---

[1] See Morpurgo, *Antonio Pucci e Vito Biagi, banditori fiorentini del secolo,* xiv. Rome, 1881.

Coy are the rhymes become, and maiden-shy,
   That hitherward are wont to come with ease ;
   Now hardly do they come, with shamefast eye.

For knowing how their coarseness will displease,
   They have not heart to show themselves without
   On matter so sublime as Fate decrees.

Emperors and Popes I have discoursed about,
   Nought caring for my rude coarse intellect,
   And commonwealths and despots pictur'd out ;

But, above all, he's worthy, I suspect,
   Of being mention'd in a goodly style,
   That man to whom my talk I now direct.

And among speakers tho' I be more vile
   Than e'en among the dates would be the thorn,
   I'll speak just as I can, no trick nor guile."

G

CHAPTER III.

RISE OF A NEW LYRIC.

ITALY AND PROVENCE—ITALIAN VERSE-FORMS—CHILDHOOD OF ITALIAN
POETRY—PARTY SPIRIT—GUITTONE OF AREZZO—EARLY FLORENTINE
POETS—BRUNETTO LATINI—THE SWEET NEW STYLE—GUIDO CAVAL-
CANTI—CINO DA PISTOIA—MODISH AND REALISTIC POETRY—THE
'VITA NUOVA'—PROBLEMS—DANTE'S DREAM—PETRARCH—CHAR-
ACTER OF HIS PASSION—HIS STYLE AND INFLUENCE—WELSH VERSE
—NEW FRENCH SCHOOL—MACHAULT—DESCHAMPS—FROISSART—
CHRISTINE DE PISAN—THE 'LIVRE DES CENT BALLADES.'

THAT Italian literature stands in some kind of filial
relation to that of Provence, is a fact accepted on all
Italy and Provence. hands as absolutely certain. When, however, we come to define the exact nature
and degree of this relationship — daughter, step-
daughter, or merely god-daughter—the task is by no
means simple. Dante's testimony is conclusive that,
in his day, Provençal writers were read and admired
to the detriment of native poets. He speaks in one
place of the " sorry people of Italy," who praise the
vernacular of others and disparage their own. "These,"
he adds, " vilify the Italian speech and cherish that

of Provence." On the other hand, he himself is far from undervaluing Provençal literature. He introduces the Provençal language into his great poem, and in it institutes a comparison between two Provençal poets, Giraut de Bornelh and Arnaut Daniel, the latter of whom, in the opinion of most judges, he, as well as Petrarch, unduly exalts.

I shall be well within the mark in saying that Troubadour verse served the early Italian poets as a great inspiration. It may be, as Gaspary observes, that, in their case, imitation seldom extends to plagiarism, though certain parallels adduced by Diez seem to prove that even plagiarism was not unknown. Let the following suffice:—

Aimeric de Pegulhan.

"Si cum l' albres, que per sobrecargar
Fraing si mezeis e pert son fruig e se."

Amorozzo.

"Com' albore, ch' è troppo caricato,
Che frange e perde sene e lo suo frutto."

Folquet de Marseille.

"Co l' parpaillos, qu' a tan folla natura
Que's fer el foc."

Jacopo da Lentino.

"Si como 'l parpaglion, ch' ha tal natura,
Non si rancura di ferire al fuoco."

Here the verbal coincidences seem too close to permit of any other explanation than direct borrowing.

In other instances,   re the later poet merely repeats
the idea without the *ipsissima verba*, one cannot be
sure whether he copies a Troubadour model or draws
from a common source. While the parallels which
Diez cites would favour the former alternative, it were
absurd to pretend that observation and reflection are
the privilege of any one people. Moreover, there
were modes of thought in the air, which naturally
and unconsciously found expression, now here, now
there, without any question arising of direct communication.

Difference of technique is a strong argument for
the original character of the Italian lyric, which,
Evidence of however influenced by Provençal models, is
Originality. probably in its essence a higher development of native folk-song. Though the term occurs in
Provençal in the general sense of " ode," the sonnet as
a special artistic form is indigenous to Italy, while the
canzone has nothing in common with the *canson* but
the name. Again, the *ballata* differs from the *balada*
in having no refrain. These distinctions are important. They indicate, on the part of Italian poetry, considerable independence of the Troubadour art whether
in Sicily or High Italy.

With the exception of *terza rima*, these three forms,
the sonnet, the *canzone*, and the *ballata*, are the only
Hendeca- kinds of verse on which it is needful to
syllables. bestow particular attention ; and as the
sonnet, according to one theory, is nothing but a *canzone* of one strophe, it will be best to deal with the
canzone first. A *canzone*, strictly understood, is a poem

composed of several strophes, each of which is similarly constructed, save that there is sometimes added a shorter strophe variously known as *comiato, congedo, licenza, chiusa,* and *ritornello.* For several reasons the *canzone* is the typical form of the Italian lyric. In the first place the metre is decasyllabic, or, as the Italians, by virtue of the unalterable feminine ending, describe the lines, *endecasillabi.* Interposed at irregular intervals, and at the discretion of the poet, are *settenarj,* or lines of seven syllables. Where such a short line occurs, it may often be regarded as an echo of the preceding long one. Other metres were attempted, of which that of five syllables (*quinario*) was the most common, but the mixture of *endecasillabi* and *settenarj* was always the favourite, and after being adopted by Petrarch, to the exclusion of others, became, with few exceptions, invariable. This dominance of the *endecasillabi,* not only in lyric poetry but generally, points to something racy and national in their character, and throws doubt on Pio Rajna's conjecture that they were imported from the North of France, where, however, the *vers heroïque,* as Du Bellay named it, was the metre of the *Chanson de Roland* and by far the larger number of the assonanced *chansons de geste.*[1]

This doubt is countenanced by the fact that Italian differs from Old French poetry in some of its funda-

---

[1] It has been suggested that the predominance of the decasyllabic metre in all the modern languages depends on natural selection. It is the longest line possible to modern mouths, which does not tend to break into two. Even the French Alexandrine only escapes this tendency through the French faculty of sinking accent.

mental principles.   Metrically, both have a syllabic
Hiatus and caesura. basis; but whereas Old French prosody is,
broadly speaking, tolerant of hiatus, Italian
abhors them to such a degree that it is prepared to
elide almost any number of unaccented vowels—and
even an accented vowel if it constitutes a whole word
—rather than miss the satisfying consonant.   Ariosto
supplies an instance in which four vowels pertaining
to three distinct words compose only one syllable—

> " Di vera pudicizia è un paragone."

That is one difference.   Another is the circumstance
that, in passing from Old French and Provençal to
Italian versification, the cæsura ceases to be important.
Thirdly, notwithstanding what has been said, you may
occasionally come upon a masculine rhyme in Italian,
but in Provençal poetry there are many more, and
the sex of the rhymes is the chief formal distinction
between the *vers* and the *canson.*

The nature of the Italian *canzone,* a very different
and more complicated thing than its Troubadour
The Italian canzone. namesake, has been luminously expounded
in the tenth and succeeding chapters of
the *De Vulgari Eloquentia.*   From this invaluable
account we learn that certain rhymes must be
repeated.   If the repetition occurs before what is
called the *dieresis,* then the subdivisions, of which
there are commonly two (though there may be three),
are called *pedes;* and, in this case, the rest of the
stanza is styled the *cauda* or *syrma* (Gr. " train ").
If, on the other hand, the repetition takes place after

the *dieresis*, then the subdivisions are called *versus*,
and the first part of the stanza is known as the *frons*.
The tripartite division of the Italian *canzone* is generally regarded as, outwardly, its most striking and
significant feature, though it has its analogy in the
stollen and *abgesang* of German minnesong. But,
putting the matter another way, it may be said that
the strophe consists of two parts—the more regular
and highly organised, and the more simple and variable; and the separating—or, it might equally well
be termed, the conjoining—line is the *dieresis*. Instances, however, are to be found where a strophe
has both *pedes* and *versus;* and, in such cases, it is of
course composed of four parts. A single example
chosen at random will be useful in illustrating these
remarks, though it must be clearly understood that,
apart from the limitations above mentioned, and the
necessity of all the stanzas being alike, the poet is
a law unto himself, both as regards the length and
number of the lines, and the order of the rhymes:—

> " Cosi nel mio parlar voglio esser aspro,
> Com' è negli atti questa bella pietra,
> La quale ognora impetra
> Maggior durezza e più natura cruda :
> E veste sua persona d' un diaspro
> Tel, che per lui, o perch' ella s' arretra,
> Non esce di faretra
> Saetta, che giammai la colga ignuda
> Ed ella ancide, e non val ch' uom si chiuda,
> Nè si dilunghi da' colpi mortali ;
> Che, com' avesser ali,
> Giungono altri e spezzan ciascun arme :
> Perch' io non so da lui, nè posso aitarme."

In Troubadour verse it is usual to find the same rhymes recurring in all the stanzas of which the poem is composed, and which were named, therefore, *coblas unissonans*. The Italians, on the contrary, their rhyming vocabulary being less rich, almost always varied the rhymes in successive stanzas, which were accordingly, in Troubadour terminology, *coblas singulars*.

Besides *coblas unissonans* and *coblas singulars* the Provençals knew of *coblas esparsas*, or isolated stanzas, which were especially used for in-

The sonnet.

culcating moral lessons. Now one explanation of the sonnet is that it is really, morality apart, just such a *cobla esparsa*—that it was evolved out of the *canzone*-strophe, whose three-fold character it preserves. There is, however, a rival explanation. According to Biadene,[1] the sonnet sprang from the fusion of a *strambotto*, or catch, of eight lines with another *strambotto* of six. The original rhyme-scheme was *abababababcdcdcd*. Afterwards the second *strambotto* was remodelled on the principle of the two-fold division of the first *strambotto*, so as to consist of two tercets instead of six lines rhyming alternately. This, if historical, may be taken as a conscious and deliberate attempt at improvement. The next step was the adoption of the scheme *abba abba cde cde,* except that the tercets, like the tail of the *canzone,* are suffered to wag pretty much as they please. If this account be accepted, the theory of the isolated stanzas, or *cobla esparsa*, which till lately held the field, must be given

[1] Monaci, *Studj di Filol. Rom.*, fasc. 10 (Rome, 1888).

up. It is worthy of notice that the scheme of the supposed primitive sonnet approximates closely to that of the Shakespearian variety, though the final couplet imparts to the latter a pointed, epigrammatic ending, foreign to the spirit of the Italian sonnet.

The earliest sonnets known are those of Dante da Majano and Paul Lanfranc, which are written in Provençal. So far, however, the fact has been invested with no particular significance; and the specimens in question are looked upon as freaks more than anything else. The true home of the sonnet, or, at any rate, the region in which it attained fullest bloom, was Tuscany. Sonnets have been attributed to Sicilians, to Peter of the Vine, King Enzo, Mazzeo Ricco, and, above all, to Jacopo da Lentino; but in no instance is the attribution certain. As compensation, the Sicilians could boast of a *discordo* answering to the Provençal *descort*. The *discordo* was composed of long irregular strophes; the lines were very short, and the rhymes followed one after the other. In some cases the meaning was so obscure as to suggest the complete ascendancy of the musical element, and possibly that may account for the speedy disappearance of the *discordo*. This was the kind of thing:—

> " Si mi sdura
> Scura
> Figura
> Di quant' eo ne veio
> Gli occhi avere
> E vedere
> E volere
> E loro non disio."

To return to the sonnet. In Tuscany it underwent sundry transformations. *Settenarj* were interposed between the *endecasillabi*, the results being the so-called *sonetto doppio* and *sonetto rinterzato*, forms for which Guittone d'Arezzo had a special predilection. The fourteen lines were composed of mixed *endecasillabi* and *settenarj*, and instances occur of a sonnet being written wholly in *settenarj*. Other innovations affected the quatrains, which, to their perdition, Guittone raised from eight lines to ten. Monte Andrea did the same; and, in addition, he wrote real *sonetti doppj* of twenty-eight lines, arranged as four quatrains and four tercets. The most notable change, however, was the invention of a *coda* in the shape of two (sometimes three) *endecasillabi*, or of a *settenario* rhyming with the preceding line and two *endecasillabi* rhyming together. I say "most notable," because, while other experiments were short-lived, the sonnet with the tail survived as *the* form for verse that was witty and gay.

While the *canzone* was dedicated to lofty and serious subjects, and the sonnet was employed for all purposes, *The* Ballata. the *ballata* was a popular form designed to accompany the dance. Unlike the *balada*, the *ballata* had no refrain, but the last line of the strophe echoes the *ritornello* or *ripresa*. The *ripresa* is a kind of chorus prefixed to the poem, and the name suggests that it was taken up again after each strophe, the strophe itself being sung as a solo. As regards the structure of the *ballata*, it has been clearly affected by the laws of the *canzone*, since it consists of two

equal *pedes* and a *volta*—Dante mentions this term
as the popular equivalent for *dieresis*—agreeing with
the *ripresa*. At the close of the poem some verse-
writers substitute a new *ritornello,* which may almost
be regarded as an envoy. Three of Dante's *ballate*
are irregular.[1]

Lastly, with regard to the *sestina*. The inventor
of this form was Dante's great admiration, Arnaut
Daniel; the first to transplant it to Italian
soil, Dante himself. Its leading principle
was that the same "refrain-words"—not rhymes—
were repeated in each stanza, which consisted of six
lines. But though the words were the same, the order
of their succession was different, and the laws governing their succession in each of the six stanzas were
rigorous and precise. It was like change - ringing:
abcdef, faebdc, cfdabe, &c. At the close was an envoy
of three lines, in which three of the "refrain-words"
were re - introduced. Sidney's *Arcadia* contains a
"crown of sixtines," and the form has been tried also
in more recent English.

The Sestina.

Discussion of the formal side of the Italian lyric
is necessarily somewhat tedious, but will serve to
pave the way for a more intelligent consideration of
its material and spiritual aspects. It would have been
deplorable to leave the reader under the impression
that *canzoni, ballate,* and such things were purely
arbitrary creations, and still worse not to satisfy legiti-
mate curiosity concerning their structure, their prob-

[1] Carducci, *Intorno ad alcune Rime dei Secoli* xiii. *e* xiv. (Imola,
1876).

able origin, and their development. I shall now review the stages by which Italian poetry, from being a humble copy of the then famous, but essentially mediocre, literature of Provence, attained to greatness in the writings of Dante and Petrarch.

As is well known, the birthplace of this poetry was Sicily, and the periods of its infancy, childhood, and *Sicilian verse.* adolescence are all comprised within the brief space of about sixty years (1220-1283). This extraordinarily rapid growth is easily accounted for by the fact that the Italians had not to build up a literary organism by their own unaided efforts. They entered on a rich inheritance in the bodyings forth of other lands. This was not entirely an advantage, and the main interest of the first half-century of Italian verse centres in the gradual throwing-off of the shadow of Provence. At the outset Provençal influence may be described as absolute. What we see is Troubadour poetry masquerading in Italian dress. Troubadour poetry, in form as in content, was intensely artificial, but the Sicilian imitation was even more unreal. Whatever may be our opinion of the former, it is undeniable that it reflected an actual state of things. In Italy, it is notorious, the chivalrous idea had never taken root. The arch-patron of the new Sicilian verse was Frederick II., who, whilst singing in exalted strains the divinity of woman, himself lived the life of a sultan. Poetry was regarded as an intellectual pastime; and the place of real feeling was supplied by simulated passion expressing itself in conventional, stereotyped

modes. It is needless to furnish a detailed account
of Troubadour verse in what may be termed its
Sicilian phase. Suffice it to say that its general character is that of more or less refined compliment, of
which the fair sex in some imaginary person is the
object. In verse of this kind—uninspired art—metaphor and simile, which, properly applied, strengthen
thought and vivify emotion, sink into mere embellish-
ments, or even into "expletives." The commonest is
the likening of love to fire. The lover lives in fire,
like a salamander, without being burnt; or he would
willingly share the lot of the phœnix, if, rising from
his ashes, he could better please his mistress. Guido
of the Columns (not, perhaps, the Trojan historian)
has rather more independence than most of the school,
but Guido sought for independence in wrong directions. His similes tend to be prosaic, or, when not
prosaic, far-fetched.

From Sicily, probably through the agents of the
Imperial court, the Troubadour lyric passed over to
Mid-Italy. Mid-Italy, and took up its abode in Arezzo,
Siena, Pisa, and other towns. At Lucca
lived a poet, Buonagiunta Orbicciani degli Overardi,
who was accused of decking himself with the "plumes
of the Notary"—that is, with the plumes of Jacopo da
Lentino. This wretch of a fowl may be conceived as
spanning with his outstretched legs (or with his
mouth - filling tubular name) the at first not very
significant gap between the Sicilian and the Tuscan
schools of verse. On the material side he belongs
to the earlier school. His ideas and images are those

of the Troubadours.   In other respects, he shows himself in touch with the later developments—*e.g.*, in his adoption of the *ballata*-form, almost certainly unknown to the Sicilians.

Although the Sicilians so closely followed Troubadour precedent, it is remarkable that a class of writing possessing special attraction in the wane of Provençal literature—the political *sirventes*—was wholly, or almost wholly, neglected by them.   The pioneers were engrossed with the theme of knightly love.   In the democratic cities of Tuscany, where the thing itself was unknown, this exclusive attachment could not continue to hold.   It fell before the conditions of the age, and especially that spirit of faction which was as the breath of life in the nostrils of the Lapi and the Bindi.   It was the success of his party, not any female abstraction, that fascinated the citizen ; and the burning questions of the day, and the controversial fury that flashed and flamed in them, naturally found a mirror in contemporary verse. Bologna had its *Serventese dei Geremei e Lambertazzi.* But a caution is necessary.   A production like this is something totally different from the Provençal type, and at the commencement of the fourteenth century the misshapen, and to some extent misnamed, verse is laughed out of court by Francesco da Barberino as mere mountebank mummery, which artistic poetry disowns.

Party-spirit.

Politics, however, in the wider, international sense, laid hold of all, poets and lay-folk both.   Guittone of Arezzo wrote nothing better than his political ode on the defeat of the Florentines at Monteaperti. This blow to the "country party" was due in a measure to the presence of German horse—a circumstance more than once ironically alluded to—and Guittone, ardent Guelf, wishes the Ghibellines joy of the alliance:—

> "Pray, serve them well, and make them show the blades,
>   Wherewith your faces they have cleft in twain,
>   And sons and fathers slain."

The triumph of Charles of Anjou in 1266, which decided the supremacy of the Guelfs throughout Italy, and the ill-starred expedition of the young Conradin two years later, gave rise to a war of *sonetti a tenzone*, especially at Florence, where Monte Andrea, secure in the power of the French, gibes at the baffled Ghibellines, while Schiatta di Messer Albizzi Pallavillani espouses their cause and promises them good fortune. The day will come, says he, when it will be seen how the lamb can bite. Other versifiers who shared in the polemic were Orlanduccio Orafo, Palamidesse Belindore, Bernardo Notaio, and Ser Cione Notaio. This title "Ser," in Italian literary annals, is of evil omen, but it is bootless to make exceptions. The notary-people, one and all, are ciphers to the tough friar.

In Guittone's story there is much that reminds us of Dante. Converted "nel mezzo del cammin," he *Guittone of Arezzo.* left wife and children, and joined himse to the order of the Knights of Mary. This order was commonly known as that of the Joyous Brethren, because the knights, as a rule, gave them-

selves but little concern for the strict observance of
their vows.   Guittone, however, if the phrase may be
forgiven, "meant business."   He looked back with
something like horror on his past career, wherein he
had composed worldly Troubadour songs and prated
about love as the only source of excellence.

> "Then was I from my birth to middle-age
>   Pent in a foul, unhonour'd, noisome stye,
>   Where wholly wallow'd I."

He now regards Love as a sickness to be remedied
by prayer and fasting, and if he still writes poetry,
and poetry of an artistic kind, he has undoubtedly
changed his tone.   The Troubadours, in their repertory
of forms, had a verse for enumerating the things that
bring pleasure to the poet.   To Bertran de Born the
supreme bliss was the joy of battle, while the Monk
of Montaudan found his delight in founts and flowers,
in the song of birds, in maiden loveliness.   Far otherwise is it with the Aretine penitent, who confesses
himself pleased with the chaste and loving wife, with
the widow that minds her house, with the conscientious prelate, with the monk — is there a sly touch
here ?—that gads not about in a world on which he
is supposed to have turned his back.   Thus morals
and religion, as well as politics, furnish material for
poetry, and not only for poetry but for prose, since
Guittone practised both.

Fra Guittone, then, is an important link in the
evolutionary chain, but Heaven forbid the thought
that he is an attractive writer !   A dialectical manner,

an incessant baptism of Cicero and Aristotle, Boethius
and Seneca—if that be your liking, perhaps Guittone
may serve. But his borrowings of pagan sentiment
are not all. He of purpose confounds Latin and
Italian. In other words, he uses Latin and Italian
vocables *ad libitum;* and though Italian was a language barely able to lisp, insists on its adapting itself
to the complicated Latin period. This is one reason
of his obscurity, though other causes were contributory.
The Troubadours had what they called *rims cars,* or
"dear rhymes." These "dear rhymes" the Italians
imitated in their *canzoni equivoche,* so named because
words similar in sound, but dissimilar in sense, are
made to rhyme therein. Such rhymes have always
been permissible in Italian,—they may be found, for
instance, in Tasso,—but the employment of them was
a fixed principle with Guittone, Chiaro Davanzati,
Monte Andrea, and others affecting the "chiuso par-
lare" or "oscura rima." [1]

An intermedi-
iate group.
The passage in which Dante alludes to
Guittone may be termed classical:—

> " 'O brother, now I see,' he said, 'the knot
> Which me, the Notary, and Guittone held
> Short of the sweet new style that now I hear.' " [2]

The words are put into the mouth of Buonagiunta
of Lucca; and the originator of the "sweet new style"

[1] For further information respecting Guittone, the reader may be
referred to L. Romanelli, *Di Guittone d' Arezzo e delle sue opere,*
Campo-basso, 1875 ; and W. Koken, *Guittone 's von Arezzo Dichtung
und sein Verhältniss zu Guinicelli von Bologna,* Leipzig.

[2] *Purgatorio,* xxiv. 54-56.

was Guido Guinicelli (or Guinizelli) of Bologna, whom Dante calls

> "the father
> Of me and of my betters, who had ever
> Practised the sweet and gracious rhymes of love."[1]

For general purposes the schools may be distinguished as the Sicilian and the Tuscan, but between them stands an intermediate, transitional group composed almost entirely of Florentines. Such were Chiaro Davanzati, Maestro Francesco, Maestro Rinuccino, Maestro Migliore, The Complete Damsel, and Pacino Angiolieri. Of these, by far the most important is Chiaro Davanzati, already mentioned as a follower of Guittone.

But Chiaro in his time played many parts. First he essays the Provençal style, developing a theme *Chiaro Davanzati.* of Sordello: *Bel cavalier me plai que per amor.* Then, in emulation of Guittone, he discourses on the mysteries of theology, and renounces ordinary love as of the Devil. Towards the end of his career — he was dead in 1280 — he succumbed to the influence of Guinicelli. Yet, through all these phases and fashions, he manifests a freedom and spontaneity which are full of augury. In his writings, as in those of his countrymen and contemporaries generally, may be remarked a tendency to greater ease and naturalness, especially in those dialogues betwixt lady and lover, of which examples have been left by Chiaro himself and a certain —

---

[1] *Purgatorio*, xxvi. 97-99.

surely this was a nickname—Ciacco dell' Anguillaia.
In compositions like these, archaisms, and Proven-
çalisms, and Guittone's "dear rhymes" and precious
periods, give way to a grace and eloquence founded
on simplicity. Doubtless the reason is that the Florentines had begun to feel at home in these half-foreign
modes, on which they were now to bestow the impress
of their own artistic temperament.

This assertion of the native Florentine element is
symbolised by Rustico di Filippo, a man of plebeian
Rustico di birth, and apprenticed by his father to the
Filippo. silk-trade. Nevertheless, he appears to
have been of some little note, as Brunetto Latini
addressed to him, when rather more than thirty,
his *Favolello*. Rustico is a noticeable mixture of
Democritus and Heraclitus, being equally strong in
humour and pathos. The insipidities of the Troubadour lyric he exchanged for the passionate breath
of deep feeling, and, singing the pangs of love, wept
in good earnest. But Rustico can laugh as well as
weep, though some have detected in his most boister-
ous mirth an undertone of melancholy. He delighted
in drawing portraits of singular people, and drew them
in a way that reminds us of Peter Pindar:—

> " When Messer Messerino God did make,
>   It was believed He wrought a miracle ;
>   Since of each kind the creature doth partake,
>   Bird, beast, and man were satisfied right well.
> For in its throat it counterfeits a drake,
>   And in its shapely loins giraffe I spell,
>   While in its vermeil face—a dainty cake !—
>   A man 'twill be, according as they tell.

> Again, in singing it is like a crow,
>   And, as to knowledge, 'tis a beast outright,
>   And man in vesture doth it imitate.
> God, when He made it, little had to do,
>   But 'twas His wish to demonstrate His might,
>   So strange a thing it pleased Him to create."

I referred above to the *Favolello*, a poetical epistle addressed to Rustico by Brunetto Latini [1] (d. 1294 or 1295), probably from France.   Several cir-

Brunetto Latini.
cumstances have conspired to raise Latini's fame higher than is, perhaps, his due.   First, there is the well-known passage in the *Inferno*, especially the line—

"M' insegnavate come l' uom s' eterna."

And, secondly, there is Villani's testimony regarding his services to the Florentines.   These allusions show that, in his age and country, Latini was an important civilising force ; nor can we well resist the conclusion that Dante felt himself under specific obligations to him.   It is not a forced or unnatural interpretation of the famous line that Dante owed the idea of the *Commedia* to Latini's prior experiment, the *Tesoretto*. Formally, the origin of the *Tesoretto* was as follows : Latini had gone to Spain as envoy of the Republic of Florence.   In returning he met on the plain of Ronces-valles a scholar on a bay mule coming from Bologna.

---

[1] Latini or Latino ?   It is extremely difficult to say.   A man ought to know his own name, and Brunetto calls himself Latino, once in rhyme.   On the other hand, Latino is opposed to Italian usage in the case of surnames.   If Latino, why not Burnetto, for which there is equally good MS. authority ?

Him he questioned about Tuscany, and was informed that the Guelfs had been expelled the country. Latini was heart-broken. Such was his distraction that he lost the highway, and wandered through a wood, where he beheld certain visions. As a fact, he sought refuge in France, which, it may be, the wood symbolises. Anyhow, there is evident kinship between this "selva diversa" and the "selva oscura" of the *Commedia*, while the words "perdei il gran cammino" may well have suggested "che la diritta via era smarrita."

Apart from Dante, the chief significance of the *Tesoretto* lies in its being the earliest specimen of that allegorico-didactic school of poetry which afterwards won such triumphs in Italy. It was, however, in France that allegory first gained an ascendancy. Of that not so much great as famous work, the *Romance of the Rose*, one part had been written relatively not long before by Guillaume de Lorris, while Jehan de Meung was busied at this very time with the continuation. Not only did Latini sojourn in France, but he became, in a literary sense, naturalised [1] there, for he wrote on French soil, and in French prose, an encyclopædia — *Li Livres dou Trésor*. It would seem, therefore, that among the remoter influences which went to shape the Divine Comedy was that of the *Romance of the Rose*, a dry,

The Romance of the Rose.

[1] "Et se aucuns demandoit por quoi cist livres est escriz en romanz selon le langaige des François, puisque nos somes Ytaliens, je diroie que ce est por deux raisons : l'une, car nos somes en France, et parce que la parleure des François est plus délitable et plus commune a toutes gens."—*Li Trésor*, I. i. 1.

pedantic, and tedious allegory,[1] both directly and by the fascination it exercised over the mind of Dante's guide, philosopher, and friend, Brunetto Latini.

And here let me say something as to the metre. The *Romance* was written in ordinary short couplets

Short metre.

of eight syllables; the *Tesoretto*, in heptasyllabic couplets, which Latini appears to have thought the nearest approach in Italian to the French metre. The choice of such a verse for so high and serious a theme was unquestionably bad, and proves Latini deficient in the poetic instinct which, in giving expression to thought and feeling, infallibly seizes the appropriate form. To be honest, it is only by courtesy that Latini can be styled poet at all. He was essentially a schoolman, who posed as a versewriter for the object of conciliating the ignorant, of rendering his studies popular. Indeed, the *Tesoretto* may be deemed, and this is its gravest censure, a second edition, in another language and on a much smaller scale, of *Li Trésor*.

On awaking from his stupor, the disappointed Guelf encounters Nature. Nature is a woman, of whose

Scholasticism in excelsis.

outward lineaments—hair, brow, eyes, lips, teeth—is vouchsafed a needless, and (it must out!) stupid, description. The more needless and stupid, since the lady is a confirmed blue-stocking, and lectures the poor man on the Creation, the Fall of the Evil Angels, Man, the Soul and its Faculties, the Four Elements, the Seven Planets, and other

[1] Lorris is not so bad, but the other's contribution is much larger.

theological, philosophical, and astronomical topics.
Geography next, and the Flora and Fauna of the East.
Then Latini, bidden to continue his journey, passes
into the domain of Virtue, and thence into a flowery
meadow ruled by a naked boy — here designated
Pleasure—with bow and arrows. With Pleasure, as
his constant attendants, are four ladies, Fear, Desire,
Hope, and Love. From this place of peril Latini owes
his escape to the good offices of Ovid, a circumstance
that rather surprises us until we remember that the
most sensual of poets—thief to catch thief—compiled
the *Remedies of Love*. Latini, upon this, repents of his
sins, and finds himself, not on Mount Pisgah, but on
Mount Olympus, where Ptolemy, an old man with
white face and white beard, prepares to induct him
into the mysteries of astronomy. The *Tesoretto*, never
having been finished, ends jerkily.

In relation to the destiny, the future content, of
artistic verse, the most notable portion of the *Tesoretto*
is that concerning love. Not indeed that
What is love? it contains anything new. Latini merely
adopts the views of Provençal and Sicilian predecessors, with whom the question, What is love ? had
long been a favourite topic. Their answer was that
love has its source in pleasure. The vision of beauty
sweeps through the eyes into the soul, and taking up
its abode in the heart, allows the mind no rest from
distracting thoughts. All this may be perfectly true,
but only touches the surface. It was in attempts to
show, not how love is begotten, nor what are its
effects, but what love in its inmost essence is, that

the *dolce stil nuovo* had it birth.   In other words, the
new was a philosophising style.[1]

After the account given of the general tendency
of things down to the second half of the thirteenth
Guido   century, this statement may seem para-
Guinicelli.   doxical. It was natural to expect that a
refined Tuscan lyric would arise out of a fusion of
the more graceful popular poetry with the Troubadour
art—there, in Florence. Everything points to such a
dénouement. But this is precisely what did not
happen. Guido Guinicelli—Dante's " father "—was
a jurist of Bologna. Born about 1230, he appears to
have died, an exile, in 1276.

Although Guinicelli is credited with the invention,
not all his poems were composed in the " sweet new
style." It came to him, seemingly, as a happy inspiration, quite late in his career. Before adopting it he
had proved and tested himself, like Chiaro Davanzati,
in certain existing styles. He wrote, for instance, an
ode (*Lo fin pregio avanzato*) in the obscure manner of
the Provençal equivocal rhymes. Afterwards he professed himself a disciple of Guittone, to whom he sent
a sonnet, addressing him as " caro padre mio," and
inviting his criticism. In speaking of the " sweet
new style," Dante contemplates neither this nor that,
but, pre-eminently, the *canzone* beginning *Al cor gentil
ripara sempre amore.*

In this mystical ode we find reconciled two conceptions of love hitherto regarded as antagonistic. On

---

[1] The standard work on Brunetto Latini is that of Thor Sundby,
Brunetto Latinos Levnet og Skrifter, Copenhagen, 1869. There is an
Italian translation by Renier (Florence, 1884).

the one hand, there was the Troubadour idea which, *The "sweet new style."* though veiling itself in Platonic phrase-ology, conceives of love as something sensual and carnal. When Guittone and Chiaro Davanzati reach the age of reflection, they abjure this passion as sinful, and adopt another sort of love —love to God and the Blessed Virgin. Guinicelli, on the contrary, whilst accepting all that the Troubadours predicate of woman, goes a step further, and finds in love—sexual, but not sensual, love—an emanation of Deity.

Love is the portion and inheritance of the gentle heart, and evil natures have neither part nor lot therein. Just as a star imparts its influence to a precious stone, when purified by the sun, so woman enamours the heart that is pure and true, and free from guile. The symbols of love—Guinicelli can, as it were, only speak in parables—are the sun in high heaven, and God in His higher heaven. Lest the latter figure should seem too bold — nay, blasphemous and profane — to those accustomed to a lower view of love, Guinicelli in his last stanza accuses and defends himself:—

> " ' My lady,' God shall ask, ' what daredst thou ? '
>   (When my soul stands with all her acts reviewed ;)
> ' Thou passedst Heaven into my sight as now,
>   To make Me of vain love similitude.
>   To Me doth praise belong,
>   And to the Queen of all the realm of grace
>   Who endeth fraud and wrong.'
> Then may I plead : ' As though from Thee he came
>   Love wore an angel's face :
> Lord, if I loved her, count it not my shame.' " [1]

---

[1] Rossetti, *Early Italian Poets*, p. 25.

The fourth line has been sometimes interpreted, "You yielded to vain love, deceived by appearances and believing them to be mine." Such an interpretation, whatever may be said for it on other grounds, completely stultifies both the stanza itself and the whole poem. As heat is in the physical world, and as God is in the spiritual world, so love is in the moral world; and God, as a beneficent principle, may rightly and fitly symbolise His creature, when misrepresented and defamed. The recantation in the final stanza is only apparent.

The question may be asked, What is there to distinguish this philosophic poetry from the versified philosophy of Brunetto Latini? The answer is contained in the terms of the question. In Guinicelli's case philosophy may have supplied the material, but the material was transmuted by the workings of a truly poetic nature instinct with high feeling, and aglow with genuine fervour. In such an atmosphere thought loses its severer features and passes into that condition of enthusiasm in which all things are possible. In themselves, however, endeavours to fathom and to analyse love, to dissipate its mystery, are peculiarly infelicitous, and in that sense I would gladly barter all that Guinicelli and his disciples ever wrote for a score of verses from the *Lover's Tale*.

A criticism.

> " Love lieth deep : Love dwells not in lip-depths.
> Love wraps his wings on either side the heart,
> Constraining it with kisses close and warm,
> Absorbing all the incense of sweet thoughts,

So that they pass not to the shrine of sound.
Else had the life of that delighted hour
Drunk in the largeness of the utterance
Of Love ; but how should earthly measures mete
The Heavenly-unmeasured or unlimited Love,
Who scarce can tune his high majestic sense
Unto the thunder-song that wheels the spheres,
Scarce living in the Æolian harmony
And flowing odour of the spacious air,
Scarce housed within the circle of this Earth,
Be cabin'd up in words and syllables,
Which pass with that which breathes them ?   Sooner Earth
Might go round Heaven, and the strait girth of Time
Inswathe the fulness of Eternity,
Than language grasp the infinite of Love."

It is not quite certain how far Guinicelli's poetry was imitated at Bologna. Some writers assume that *At Bologna.* he had no following there, and that the "sweet new style" reappeared only in Tuscany. Three Bolognese writers, however, whom Dante praises conjointly with Guinicelli, were probably more or less influenced by the poet-philosopher —namely, Guido Ghislieri, Fabrizio (or Fabruzzo) dei Lambertazzi, and Onesto di Bologna. As regards the two former, we have little or nothing on which to base an opinion, but in one of Onesto's odes occur the following lines, which, though perhaps textually faulty, express the central and characteristic idea of the new verse :—

" Quand' egli appar, Amor prende suo loco
  Sendo deliberato, non dimora
  In cor che sia di gentilezza fora."

Nevertheless, it was in Tuscany, and especially at

Florence, that the style inaugurated by Guinicelli *The importance* was most fully developed. So much was *of Florence.* this the case that this poet's star underwent a partial eclipse.   Dante's allusion to the two Guidos— Guinicelli and Cavalcanti—and the danger to which both were exposed by his own rising fame, is well known to students of the *Commedia* :—

> " So has one Guido from the other taken
>   The glory of our tongue, and he perchance
>   Is born, who from the nest shall chase them both."

These words indicate that, in Dante's eyes, the most important member of the school hitherto was Guido Cavalcanti.   Before coming to him, however, it is desirable to pay rather more attention than they ordinarily receive to some of his colleagues — if " adversaries " be not the better term.

The phrase "sweet new style" may lead incautious persons to imagine that this Tuscan poetry is particu- *Characteristics* larly easy of comprehension.   There could *of the new verse.* be no greater delusion.   Guinicelli himself, when taxed by Buonagiunta with obscurity, replied, "The man of wisdom doth not lightly run"; while Frescobaldi rivalled Guittone in the art of making himself intentionally difficult and abstruse.[1]   Besides his difficulty, Frescobaldi has another quality which

[1] "It would be very hard to recover the meaning of those verses ; even if one succeeded in recovering it, and after long reflection and patient care could say, ' I seem to have found it,' the fact would still remain that those verses represent a manner which has been sub- stituted for preceding manners" — when a critic of the calibre of Signor Adolfo Bartoli can write like that, the general reader may form his own conclusions as to what is in store for him.

will assuredly not commend him—he cannot, by any stretch of imagination, be deemed cheerful company. His mind is always feeding on its own griefs, and on the thought of death. He sees in death the end of all his torments, and, accosting the Last Enemy, bids him, since he is glad of his coming, come. Naturally, this way of thinking indisposes him for the half-adulterous homage the Troubadours paid to married women, and leads him to fix his regard on the *giovinetta*. When the question is put to him point-blank by a poet named Verzellino, Which is to be preferred as a mistress, a pleasing dame or a maid? Frescobaldi unhesitatingly decides for the latter.

This point of view he shares with Lapo Gianni, who, finding himself at a loss for a metaphor to describe a young lady whom his heart desires, pitches on the now extremely worn comparison of an "angel from Heaven," and the less familiar but equally distinctive phrase "*sister* of Love." The chastity of the Tuscan muse is as the chastity of marble; and noting this, critics have been induced to ask, Is the object of their worship real and human? She floats before us in almost spectral beauty, and the whole being centres in the eyes, a glance from which sets men longing. Greeting from one so exalted is almost too great a condescension, and is in itself a source of blessing. "Beata l' alma che questa saluta!"

All here, in fact, is spiritual, even the terminology. Nothing is more irksome to us moderns than the constant recurrence of the words *spiriti* and *spiritelli*. True it is that we employ a

Spiritualism.

similar locution ourselves when we talk of one's *spirits*, but probably no one using it attaches a specific value to the barometrical phrase. The Tuscans, on the contrary, certainly did attach to it a specific value, though commentators are puzzled to state precisely what. Practically, our choice is limited by the nature of the case to two interpretations. One is that the soul is attended by a multitude of little hobgoblins— so the diminutive *spiritelli* would imply—or, at any rate, by a plurality of spirits whose existence is sometimes confounded with her own. If this explanation be not accepted, then the only alternative is to consider that the term *spiriti* or *spiritelli* denotes the qualities or functions of the soul as a complex organism. This is the more likely as these poets invest the members of the body with a personality rendering them psychologically distinct, both from each other and from the body as a whole. One thing, however, appears certain, that these spirits, whatever they are, have to do with the soul's terrestrial existence, and do not accompany her beyond the grave. In Dante's ode, *E' m' incresce di me sì malamente*, the departing soul embraces the spirits who weep at losing her. The climax is reached in a sonnet of Cavalcanti:—

> " Per gli occhi fere un *spirito* sottile,
>   Che fa in la mente *spirito* destare
>   Da qual si move *spirito* d' amare,
>   E ogni altro *spiritello* fa gentile.
> Sentir non po di lu' *spirito* vile :
>   Di cotanta virtù *spirito* appare ;
>   Questo è lo *spiritel* che fa tremare
>   Lo *spiritel* che fa donna umile.

> Poi da questo *spirito* si move
>   Un altro dolce *spirito* soave,
>   Che siegue un *spiritello* di mercede
> Lo quale *spiritel spiriti* piove
>   Che di ciascuno *spirit'* ha la chiave
>   Per forza d' uno *spirito* che 'l vede."

No wonder Orlandi, though himself addicted to the casuistry of love, observed, " Through too much subtlety the thread is broken." This Guido Orlandi is not an engaging personage. Perhaps none of the group can be accused of undue modesty,—Lapo Gianni, for example, speaks of his own " noble intellect,"—but in self-conceit Orlandi surpasses them all. To Dante he says, with an air of ineffable patronage,

A poetical joust.

" Willingly I spare thee "; while he was indiscreet enough to break a lance with the passionate Guido Cavalcanti, who had ventured on the seemingly harmless expression, " would make Love weep." Orlandi rebukes him for this. " True love," he declares, " neither laughs nor weeps "; and, having referred the sciolist to Ovid, winds up with the comical threat, " Of my cross-bow beware, and stand in dread." The other replied in a strain of characteristic pride and contempt; but as Orlandi was by no means crushed, he continued to act as a foil to his far superior antagonist. It is not too much to say that poets like Guido Orlandi and Gianni Alfani owe whatever importance they possess to their being, as it were, rebellious satellites of Guido Cavalcanti.

It is extremely probable that a sonnet of Orlandi, *Onde si muove, e donde nasce Amore?* gave rise to what was considered then and long afterwards Cavalcanti's masterpiece, although he himself states that it was written at the request of a lady. I refer to his celebrated ode, *Donna mi prega perch' io voglio dire*, in which he discourses, but in the driest and dreariest fashion, on the nature of Love. I have dwelt so long on this topic that I may well be excused from analysing the poem, which to-day has no worth as literature. It is pleasanter to turn to those sides of Cavalcanti's poetry which are more directly human, —to his love for the *forosetta*, for the young lady of Toulouse, for Monna Lagia; to his satire of the Frati Minori, and the pretended miracles of Madonna di San Michele, which no doubt confirmed his inherited reputation as an unbeliever; and, lastly, to his bitter exile, of which Dante was the unwilling instrument, and that pathetic swan-song, *Perch' i' non spero di tornar giammai*. His *ballatette* are singularly pure and fresh, and reproduce, especially in the dialogue, somewhat the manner of the old French *pastourelles*.

In Cino da Pistoia the Tuscan lyric, instead of contemplating love as something external, as matter for scientific investigation, becomes introspective, and analyses its effects on the human heart. Cino thus stands in approximately the same relation to Petrarch as Guinicelli to Dante, only that Petrarch is so resolute a Melchizedek. His verse breathes a profound melancholy, and this melancholy does not arise wholly from the vicissitudes of love. Statesman and exile, some of his best efforts were inspired by yearning for his country.

" Deh quando revedrò 'l dolce paese
        Di Toscana gentile,
     Dove 'l bel fior si veste d' ogni mese,"

sings he, in one place; and in his answer to Dante's plaintive sonnet the regret again asserts itself as the master-feeling. It is superfluous to point out how the sense of banishment must have been a bond of union for the two poets, and the partnership in sorrow is consecrated by Cino's affectionate address—" Beloved brother mine, with pains enwrapt."

Side by side with this thought, this aspiration, this intensity of emotion, there flourished a poetry which *Modish poetry.* may be called, by comparison at least, the poetry of common life. While Cavalcanti's proud spirit, like Milton's, "dwelt apart," the gay society of Tuscany held on its way, and the young spendthrifts of Siena actually formed a club — the *brigata godereccia* or *spendereccia* whereof Dante speaks —for dissipating their fortunes in wanton extravagance. This world of fashion had its laureate in Folgore di San Gemignano, who composed a "garland" of sonnets setting forth what each month had to offer in the shape of fresh amusements. They were parodied by an Aretine poet, Cene di la Chitarra, who appears to have taken umbrage at the swagger of Folgore, and who therefore opposed to the garish glitter of the courtly scene - paintings the plain and humble realities of the country. Folgore wrote a second "garland" on the days of the week.

Still more realistic were the sonnets of Cecco Angiolieri. Cecco was a thorough Bohemian, who

I

detested family life and loved drinking and gambling.

Realism. There were, he says, three things in which he delighted—

> "Cioè la donna, la taverna, e 'l dado."

He had, to be sure, some excuse in a niggardly father, and his ugly wife was always quarrelling with him. For these ills he sought and found consolation in the company of a shoemaker's daughter, Becchina. Cecco unbosoms himself without reserve, even where the obligation to be silent is heaviest. He anticipates with eagerness his father's death. It seems an eternity in coming, and when at last it does come, tells the denizens of hell not to despair because one—himself, to wit—has escaped thence. Whatever may be thought of Cecco's sentiments, it is impossible not to admire the vigour, the pungency, the directness of his style, which are felt as a welcome relief after the mist and moonshine of the *dolce stil nuovo.* His very exaggeration makes you laugh, and that in spite of your desire to be a moral person and a good Christian. Who can fortify himself against the dare-devil humour of a sonnet like this?

> "If I were fire, I would burn up the world;
>> If I were wind, with storms I would it shake;
>> If water, I would make of it a lake;
>> If I were God, Hellwards it should be hurl'd.
> If I were Pope, I should be blithe and pearl'd,
>> For all true Christians I would cause to quake;
>> If Emperor, d'ye know what line I'd take?
>> All heads I'd lop, till round as bandrols furl'd.

> If I were Death, I to my sire would hie ;
>   If I were Life, I would not with him stay ;
>   My mother also should not live but die.
> If I were Cecco, as I am to-day
>   And was yestreen, the pretty wenches I
>   Would keep, old ugly ladies give away."

Such was the incorrigible sinner whom Dante tried, but failed to reclaim.

From what has been said, it is evident that Dante, as a young man, was in close personal relations with other poets of the time. Indeed, during his lyrical period he freely identifies himself with them.

Young Dante.

> " Guido, I would that you, and Lapo, and I
>   Might be bewitcht and to a barque consign'd,
>   That o'er the sea might fare with ev'ry wind,
>   At your sweet will and mine, 'neath the blue sky ;
> So that nor Chance, nor outer weather sly
>   Might interpose an obstacle unkind,
>   But we, still dwelling in one heart and mind,
>   Might more desire each other's company.
> And Monna Vanna, and Monna Bice, then,
>   With her who is the tale of thirty o'er,
>   Might the good wizard set with us aboard ;
> And there be alway talk of love outpour'd,
>   And each of them be happy in this lore,
>   E'en as I ween that we should be, we men."

Even in the *Commedia* there are traces of this brotherhood, and Dante checks his sense of superiority with a *forse*. At present, however, attention must be confined to the *Vita Nuova* and *Canzoniere*.

The *Vita Nuova* paints the devious course of Dante's love for Beatrice. The meaning of *nuova* in this connection is not quite clear. It may refer, physically,

The main problem. to the season of youth, or, spiritually, to the conversion wrought in him by the purifying efficacy of this transcendental attachment. The exact nature of this attachment is the hardest psychological puzzle in literature. The question raised is whether his passion was wholly ideal, regarding no single human being, or whether there was in it something earthly, concrete, personal. The general trend of opinion favours the latter view, but the former position is defended, with considerable force and ingenuity, by a distinguished Italian critic — Signor Adolfo Bartoli. Indeed, some of his arguments are such as no candid mind can resist. It is no longer possible, even for those who espouse the opposite theory, to insist on the literal accuracy of every statement in the *Vita Nuova*, and Signor Pio Rajna, in his interesting essay *La Genesi della Divina Commedia*, though siding in the main with Herr Gaspary, frankly concedes as much. But he holds, as I believe, rightly, that the *Vita Nuova* is not on that account a mere tissue of fiction, a romance, but, on the contrary, an authentic document of actual human experience.

Who or what was Beatrice ? Was this the real name of a real woman ? In what may be termed the "text" of the discussion Dante himself speaks as follows—"Nine times now, since my birth, the heaven of light had returned almost to the same point, with regard to its own gyration, when to my eyes first appeared the glorious lady of my mind, who was called Beatrice by many who did not know *che si chiamare.*"

The style is dignified, but vague. What do the last
words signify ? Bartoli construes apparently, " come
chiamarla." Is this likely ? On a matter of idiom it
is risky for a foreigner to express an opinion, but the
more natural interpretation would seem to be, not
" did not know her right name," but " knew only the
sound of her name and not its hidden meaning." This
appears to be Gaspary's notion, since he renders " did
not know that she was really *beatrice*, the bestower of
blessing."

Pio Rajna regards the name as a kind of *senhal*,
such as the Troubadours used in order to express
The common their feelings more freely ; and, in point of
story. fact, Boccaccio declares that the lady was
called Bice. Daughter of an " ancient " citizen of
Florence, Folco Portinari, she wedded a knight, Messer
Simone de' Bardi, and died in the twenty-fourth year
of her age. All this seems circumstantial enough,
and Boccaccio avers that it came from a trustworthy
person, who knew Bice and was related to her. On
the other hand, Buti, who lectured on Dante at Pisa
soon after Boccaccio's death, observes in his *Comento*
that, while some might believe that Beatrice had been
flesh and blood, yet " it was not so."

This is nothing less than a categorical denial of
Boccaccio's statements, and, as Scartazzini points out,
proves at least that there could have been no widely
spread or firmly established legend on the subject.
But an *ipse dixit* of the kind is not all that is required
to upset Boccaccio's credit. From his mode of imparting the information, it was evidently a family

secret, of which the world in general was likely to know nothing. Recollect: Bice was wife to Messer Simone. But, more than that, Dante, as he confesses, used all his efforts to prevent the truth leaking out, and he rejoices in the success of those efforts. Nevertheless, there are "undesigned coincidences"—*e.g.*, the death of Folco Portinari on the last day of 1289, and the allusion to the death of Beatrice's father in the *Vita Nuova*—which tend to confirm Boccaccio's testimony.   Dr Scartazzini, who is held in such just esteem for his learned and industrious studies, has a theory of his own. He believes that Beatrice lived, though as Beatrice to the poet only; that she was never the wife of Simone or of any other man; that she died whilst still marriageable; that Dante not only loved, but was loved by, her; and that in due course she would have become his bride, had not the match been hindered by "morte villana e di pietà nemica." He does not hold out any hope of discovering who Beatrice was. She was a Florentine lady, and—that is all.

If Beatrice was not flesh and blood, what was she? Well, there is a fairly obvious response to this inquiry. *The "abstraction" theory.* She was an abstraction. That being granted, the next thing is to ask, What sort of abstraction? What may we suppose her to symbolise? Writing in the last century, Biscioni maintained that she symbolised philosophy. But, evidently, this will not do. Dante did indeed, both in the *Convivio* and the *Commedia*, personify this idea, but in neither case was Beatrice the symbol. Rossetti, with his anti-papal mania, saw in her the figure of the

Holy Roman Empire, while Perez asserted that she represents a mediæval figment—Active Intelligence. Bartoli shrewdly perceives that none of these conjectures will stand, so he comes forward with a fourth solution, *i.e.*, that Beatrice is—just *donna*, the ideal of womanhood. What Dante celebrates is precisely what Lapo, what Guido, what Cino, what all the poets of the *dolce stil nuovo* had celebrated; and if he tops them all, it is not that he is helped by any external motive, but he is what he is by virtue of his own innate gifts, keener feeling, a finer touch, a richer imagination, and so on.

This, however, merely begs the question. That there was a good deal of sheer conventionalism in *Origin and nature of love.* the Tuscan, as in the Provençal, school of poetry, may be allowed, but that these poets never were in love, or, being in love, never attempted to describe their feelings, is not only an unlikely proposition, but suggests a hopeless disbelief in the " eternal verities." Signor Bartoli indeed is at no pains to conceal his opinion that love in our sense is a quite modern invention. He maintains that, in the golden or flourishing age of romance, such a thing was unknown, and that if we wish to meet with those ideas hitherto falsely attributed to Dante, we must wait until the time of Byron, and Goethe, and Leopardi. At the close of the thirteenth century the only love of which poets knew anything was that of the Provençal *albata* and part of the *Roman de la Rose*,—in other words, the most naked and unblushing sensualism.

That Byron's conception of love should be considered higher, more spiritual, than that of Dante seems to me a *reductio ad absurdum ;* but, in a matter like this, it would be manifestly improper to appeal to prejudice. I may, however, observe that, if Bartoli is right, then all those explanations so ingeniously framed to account for the phenomenon—such as the softening influence of Christianity, the cult of the Virgin Mary, &c.—may henceforth be laid by as useless. Not, I must confess, that I have ever paid much heed to these explanations, which, in my estimation, are only a little less absurd than the opinion before impugned. The inventor of romantic love has been claimed by one authority—Mr E. F. M. Benecke—to have been Antimachus of Colophon, a friend of Plato. If this be so, we are already a long way from Byron and his contemporaries. But is there not something essentially puerile in these speculations ? Surely the distinction between love and lust is fundamental in human nature.

I need not recall the familiar lines of *Venus and Adonis,* though, from a chronological standpoint, they are absolutely fatal to Bartoli's proposition. Lust is excited through the bodily senses and finds its fruition therein. Love, on the contrary, arises out of a conviction, true or false, of moral excellence—tenderness, fidelity, capacity for self-sacrifice, combined perhaps with graceful manners, tact, and helpful accomplishments as the outward expression of these qualities—in the person beloved. It is just this subjective or imaginative element that, in the eyes of some, has made romantic love ridiculous. But love is love, not lust, and romance, where it exists, is due to collective impressions of the better side of human nature, focussed for the time on a given individual. That Dante, of all men, was incapable of such feelings, I, for one, wholly decline to believe.

It is useless to ignore the fact that here, as generally, the personality of the critic counts for much. If *Poets' love.* he has culled all his ideas of love from the dry study of books, or if his love has passed easily and rapidly from hoping and dreaming into realisation, satiety, perhaps disillusion; or if, like most of us, he is a dull prosaic creature enamoured of success, then he may well be baffled by the delicate, shy, all-spiritual homage of the *Vita Nuova,* content to forego its reward. To poets, however, the sentiment is quite intelligible. The following passage from Goethe's *Tasso,* though it does not refer to Dante, supplies, so far as I can judge, a perfect analysis of his mind and heart as influenced by this early attachment:—

> " Hier ist die Frage nicht von einer Liebe,
> Die sich des Gegenstands bemeistern will,
> Ausschliessend ihn besitzen, eifersüchtig
> Den Aublick jedem andern wehren möchte.
> *Wenn er in seliger Betrachtung sich*
> *Mit deinem Werth beschäftigt, mag er auch*
> *An meinem leichtern Wesen sich erfreun.*
> Uns liebt er nicht—verzeih, dass ich es sage !
> Aus allen Sphären trägt er, was er liebt,
> Auf einen Namen nieder, den wir führen,
> Und sein Gefühl theilt er uns mit : wir scheinen
> Den Mann zu lieben, und wir lieben
> Mit ihm das Höchste, was wir lieben können."

The expression "lady of my mind," of which Bartoli
makes so much, undoubtedly means "my feminine
*A personal
Beatrice.* ideal," but the preceding expressions
clearly point to an incarnation of that
ideal. Reading the *Vita Nuova* in this light, the
thought of a personal Beatrice forces itself upon us
with absolute conviction. Though I can perceive no
valid reason for rejecting the Portinari tradition, belief
in it is optional; that there was a girl in the case,
this, it seems to me, is a downright necessity. Without her, the *Vita Nuova* loses nine-tenths of its meaning, and of its interest more than nine-tenths. But
let us look at the book.

The general character of the work is well described
by Boccaccio. "He in the first place, while the tears
The Vita
Nuova. for the death of his Beatrice were still
fresh, as nearly as possible in his twenty-
sixth year, put together in a little volume, which he
entitled *Vita Nuova*, certain small works, such as
sonnets and *canzoni*, made by him in rhyme at sundry
times before, wondrously beautiful. Over each of
them, separately and in order, he wrote the causes
that had led him to make them, and, after, he placed
the divisions of the foregoing works." The only doubt
that can attach to this account respects the last chapters, which, on chronological grounds, appear to have
been added later. The bulk of the *Vita Nuova* was
certainly in writing in the spring of 1291.

As Boccaccio states, each section has three sub-
sections—the historical introduction, the poem itself,
and the commentary. According to Signor Casini,

who has produced a most valuable edition of the *Vita Nuova*,[1] the whole work is divisible into five parts. The first (chapters i.-xvii.) contains Dante's youthful love, the praise of Beatrice's physical beauty, and the arts he employed to conceal his love from his ill-wishers (1274-1287). The second (chapters xviii.-xxvii.) contains the praise of Beatrice's spiritual beauty, and the presentiment of her early death (1287-90). The third (chapters xxviii.-xxxiv.) includes the whole period of Dante's grief for the death of his mistress (1290-1291). The fourth (chapters xxxv.-xxxviii.) relates the episode of the gentle lady, of whom Dante became enamoured as if to console himself for the loss of Beatrice (1291-1293). And the fifth (chapters xxxix.-xlii.) depicts the struggle between his new love and the memory of the old, and Dante's return to the love and worship of Beatrice.

The incidents of the story are few and extremely simple. When Dante was not quite ten years old, *Falling in love.* there appeared to him a youthful angel, clad in a very noble hue, a lowly and honest red, and girt and adorned as became her tender age, for Beatrice was just nine. The result of this apparition was an immense commotion among the spirits who made their abode in and about Dante's fleshly tabernacle. The Spirit of Life exclaimed with trembling: *Ecce Deus fortior me, qui veniens dominabitur mihi.* The Animal Spirit said to the Spirits of Vision: *Ap-*

---

[1] *La Vita Nuova di Dante Alighieri, con introduzione, commento, e glossario.* Florence, 1890. Sir Theodore Martin's translation will be found useful by English readers.

paruit jam beatitudo vestra. And the Natural Spirit cried: *Heu miser! quia frequenter impeditus ero deinceps.* The reign of Love had begun in Dante's heart.

Nine years later, the same youthful angel again appeared, clad this time in a very white hue, and walking between two gentle ladies, her elders. And, by reason of her ineffable courtesy, she greeted him with such effect as to bring all heaven before his eyes ("mi parve allora vedere tutti i termini della beatitudine"), and cause him to see and describe *Visions* the first of a series of visions. Bartoli has said very happily that the *Vita Nuova* "proceeds by way of visions," of which there are contained in all seven. Neither Bartoli nor Pio Rajna accepts these visions as actual occurrences; but the truth, perhaps, is not so self-evident as these writers pretend. I recollect the shrewd remark of the old gentleman in the *Essays of Elia,* who tested the prospects of a poetical aspirant by asking, "Young man, what sort of dreams have you?" A born poet, and absorbed by thoughts of love, Dante may have dreamed dreams, and seen visions, innumerable. If not, he exercised his just prerogative in feigning them.

In the first sonnet Dante tells how Love appeared to him. In his hand he held Dante's heart, and in his *Dante's first sonnet.* arms, asleep and wrapt in a cloth, Dante's lady. Love awoke her and fed her, all humble and fearful, with that glowing heart, and thereafter Dante saw him go away weeping. This sonnet the young poet sent to all the "vassals of Love," the famous troubadours of the time, that they might pass sentence on it. He received many replies (some of them, we know, not too complimentary), and among them was one from Guido Cavalcanti, who answered,

"Vedesti al mio parer ogni valore."

The allegory does not appeal to modern taste, but its rich symbolism—and this is the important thing—did appeal to the taste of Dante's contemporaries. The last line, as Dante himself points out, was unconscious prophecy.

It is hardly worth while perhaps to go over, one by one, the "incidents" of the *Vita Nuova*. They possess, for the most part, a purely subjective interest. It is these visions that are the kernel of the work, and, above all, that great dream of which all have heard, and which inspired in Dante the divine ode, *Donna pietosa e di novella etate*. The prefatory prose, *His great* however, is the quintessence of poetry. *dream.* "A few days after this, it befel that in a certain part of my person a dolorous infirmity overtook me, whence I suffered continuously most bitter torture. . . . On the ninth day there came to me a thought concerning my lady. And when I had mused of her somewhat, I returned in thought to my own feeble life, and seeing how slight was its duration, whole though it might be, I began to weep within myself at so great misery. And, sighing heavily, I said within myself, 'It must needs be that the most gentle Beatrice do sometime die.'

" And thereat so strong a bewilderment smote me that I shut my eyes, and began to agitate myself like one distract, and to imagine in this wise: that (at the beginning of my fantasy's wandering) there appeared to me divers faces of dishevelled ladies, which said to me, 'Thou wilt surely die.' And after these ladies, divers other faces, dreadful to behold, which said to me, 'Thou art dead.'

" Thus my fantasy beginning to wander, I came to this—that I knew not where I was. And methought I saw ladies going dishevelled along the way, wondrous sad, and methought I saw the sun darken so that the stars showed of a colour that made me judge that they were weeping, and methought that the birds flying through the air dropped dead, and there were very great earthquakes. And wondering at such fantasy, and dreading not a little, I imagined that a friend came to me, and said: 'What knowest thou not? Thy rare lady is departed this world.' Then began I to weep very piteously; and not only did I weep in imagination, but I wept with my eyes, bathing them with real tears.

" I imagined that I gazed towards Heaven, and methought I saw a multitude of angels that were returning upwards, and they had before them a very white cloudlet. And methought these angels sang gloriously, and the words of their song were these: *Osanna in excelsis*, and I heard nought else. Then methought that my heart, where was so great love, said to me: 'True is it that our lady lieth dead.' And thereat I went to see the body wherein had lain that

most noble and blessed soul. And so strong was the
wandering fantasy that it showed me this lady dead.
And methought ladies covered her head with a white
veil, and her countenance had so great a look of
humility that it seemed to say : 'I am beholding the
source of peace.'

"As I thus imagined, there fell upon me so great
humility through beholding her, that I called Death,
and said : 'Most sweet Death, come to me, and be not
churlish, forasmuch as thou must have become gentle,
in such quarter hast thou been. Now come to me, who
much yearn for thee ; and do thou behold it, for already I bear thy colour.'"

Towards the end of the *Vita Nuova* Dante records
how he saw a young and very beautiful lady gazing
compassionately at him from a window.

Infidelity.

She became to him his lady of pity and
consolation, and, as Scartazzini guesses, was none
other than his future wife, Gemma Donati. Dante's
own account of her is as follows : "I say and affirm
that the lady of whom I became enamoured after the
first love was the most beautiful and honest daughter
of the Ruler of the Universe, on whom Pythagoras bestowed the name of Philosophy" (*Convivio*, ii. 16).
This passage, however, must be read in conjunction
with others, and in no way affects the existence of
the "gentle lady" in a literal, as well as allegorical,
sense.

The unfaithfulness to which he confesses was
only for a time. Before the record closes we find
mention in it of a sharp spiritual conflict. Dante's

remorse is terrible. He curses his eyes for their vanity, and tells them that Death alone should cause them to forget "our lady." Finally his heart triumphs over his eyes, and he concludes (save for the benediction) with the memorable words: "I hope to say of her what never was said of any." The application of these words to the *Commedia*, their relation as promise and performance, is obvious and universally admitted. What is considerably less familiar to most persons is an earlier, more obscure, perhaps wholly fortuitous anticipation of the same great achievement in one of the *canzoni*. Dante is under a cloud. Beatrice, displeased with him, withholds her greeting; but this tacit rebuke does but lift her in his esteem, renders him more reverent. He pictures to himself an angel crying aloud in heaven, and claiming Beatrice as the only boon that heaven yet lacks. The saints all support this petition, and Pity alone defends Dante's cause. God charges His beloved to suffer "their hope" to remain during His pleasure in the world. Yonder is one who looks to lose her, and who will say to the vile, "I saw the hope of the blessed."

I have mentioned earlier in the chapter that Dante borrowed the *sestina* directly from Provence. His *sestine*, as well as certain *canzoni*, excite interest other than attaches to the mere form, since they are sensuous, and erotic, and so unlike the lyric, whether of the *Vita Nuova* or *Convivio*. A great pother has been made over the cold and unimpressionable *pietra*. Who was she? Nobody knows, but it is conceded on all hands that she was neither

A difficulty.

Beatrice nor yet the Lady of Consolation. These poems attest sympathy on Dante's part with the frankly carnal and sexual, no less than with the intellectual and spiritual, kinds of love; but, suggestive as some of the phrases are, I do not think it necessary to conclude that there was ever a time in Dante's life when he gave rein to his passions. These, if sins at all, were probably sins of imagination. Whatever view we may be disposed to take of these un-Dantesque compositions, one way of escape which might at first appear open is absolutely barred. We cannot dismiss them as apocryphal, for that which is perhaps the most " objectionable "—*Così nel mio parlar*—is cited in the *De Vulgari Eloquentia*. My own solution is that contained in the lines already quoted :—

> " Wenn er in seliger Betrachtung sich
>   Mit deinem Werth beschäftigt, mag er auch
>   An meinem leichtern Wesen sich erfreun."

If these lines do not — they surely do — apply to Dante, Petrarch, at least, would have adopted them *Petrarch and Laura.* with eagerness. The most important event of Petrarch's life, from a personal and psychological standpoint, occurred on the 6th of April 1327, when he first saw in St Clara's Church at Avignon the lady whom he calls—and very likely it was her actual name—Laura, and immediately fell in love with her. The identity of this lady is not altogether free from doubt, but, in spite of the clumsy frauds (the sonnet, the medal, &c.) with which its earliest champion sought to support the theory, it is not in any way improbable that she was the daughter of Audibert de Noves; that she wedded in 1325 Hugh de Sade, by whom she had eleven children; and that she died in 1348 of the plague. As regards this last point, some have found rather fanciful confirmation of it in Petrarch's ode, *Standomi un giorno*, where he uses the expression "tempesta oriental" of the storm. Plagues, like the wise men, came from the East. The day and the hour when he first saw Laura are scrupulously recorded in his sonnet, *Voglia mi sprona*, but nowhere in his writings does he give any hint that she was the wife of Hugh de Sade, and many have doubted whether she was a married woman at all. The chief evidence in favour of the common belief is the general agreement of the manuscript notes in Petrarch's copy of Virgil with Laura's will produced by the Abbé de Sade in the latter half of the eighteenth century. The genuineness of both documents has, however, been called in question.

So far as outward development is concerned, Petrarch's love for Laura was as barren as that of Dante for Beatrice. Neither poet knew the joy of possession. To Dante, as I have attempted to show, this was not a subject for regret; but Petrarch, it will hardly be gainsaid, felt otherwise. It seems evident that, had the matron's virtue not been inexpugnable, there were phases of his passion when he would have welcomed a frail moment. But a frail moment never came, and though they may have met, as we say, in society, there was no question of reciprocal affection. When the poor lady was gone, and it mattered little what were his speculations concerning her, Petrarch salves his wounded vanity by telling himself that *now* she is not utterly indifferent. While she lives, this is the very thing he complains of—her obduracy, her cruelty.

Petrarch, in his moments of soberness, recognises the folly of this attachment. He sighs over lost *The spirit and* days and nights spent in idle thoughts, *the flesh.* and he prays the Father of Heaven that he may return to another life and fairer enterprises. The sonnet enshrining this petition was written eleven years after his subjection to the "tyrannous yoke," and was doubtless inspired by the solemnities of the fast. But when his prayer is answered, and he obtains some relief from his yoke, even then he is not satisfied—

> " Oimè ! il giogo e le catene e ceppi
> Eran più dolci che l' andare sciolto."

He has loved so long that to cease from love would be a sort of suicide. And yet, when she is dead, he would not, if he could, see her once more alive. Not for her sake—he is too great an egoist for that—but inasmuch as her death was a providential deliverance from trouble and temptation. Now that the danger is past, he is profoundly thankful that she never yielded to his wishes—

> " Oh quant' era peggior farmi contento ! "

And, again—

> " Benedetta colei ch' a miglior vita
> Volse il mio corso, e l' empia voglia
> Lusingando affreno . . ."

Were it not for the "white lies" in which Petrarch
can be shown to have indulged, I should be inclined
to take these hints literally. Avignon was in the
heart of Troubadour-land, and, morally, in bad odour,
while Petrarch himself was very far from being immaculate. But the general character of his allusions
would imply that their acquaintance was rather distant; and, in Petrarch's verse, an ounce of fact leavens
an indefinite amount of imagination. He professes to
know what he is very unlikely to have known—for
instance, the precise manner of Laura's passing. The
description in the *Triumph of Death* is admirable,
but is written so as to suggest that he was present on
the occasion; and who will credit that? Is not the
entire passage a reminiscence, not of Laura's removal
from the world, but of the *Vita Nuova?*

This raises the larger question of this poet's relations with his predecessors. Petrarch would have us
Inconsistencies. believe that he was a kind of poetical
Pallas, that he owed nothing to earlier
rhymers. It seems that his long silence with respect
to Dante had given rise to suspicions of envy and
jealousy. In a letter to Boccaccio he denies this
imputation, remarking that, when a young man, he
had purposely abstained from reading poetry in the
vernacular lest he should be betrayed into imitation.
It is extremely unfortunate, but no less indubitably
true, that no reliance can be placed on this, and
little on any other of Petrarch's assertions, however
deliberate. Thus in his sonnet *S' io avessi pensato* he
declares that he sought

" Pur di sfogare il doloroso core
     In qualche modo, non d' acquistar fama ;
     Pianger cercai, non già del pianto onore,"

whereas in his *Poetical Epistles* he affirms the contrary,
that he had written his Italian verses for the sake of
glory. So also, with regard to his professed ignorance
of Romance poetry, the statement cannot be received
implicitly. It may be that he did not possess a
wide acquaintance with modern productions, but it
is simply incredible that he should have lived at
Avignon yet know nothing of Provençal letters; and
equally so that he should have obtained such a
mastery of Italian verse without a novitiate in
the art.

Of actual verbal imitation the *Canzoniere* certainly
contains but little. Commentators long
Obligations. ago pointed out the resemblance between
Petrarch's

" Benedetto sià 'l giorno e 'l mese e l' anno "

and Peire Vidal's

" Ben aial temps el jorns e l' ans el mes."

The ode *Mai non vo' più cantar* is an essay in the
" obscure manner " of the Troubadours, while *S'il dissi
mai* is an *escondig*, in composing which Petrarch had
probably before his mind Bertran de Born's *Eu
m' escondisc domna que mal non mier*. If we turn to
the Italian poets, it is hard not to think that the
sonnet *Gli angeli eletti e l' anime beate* was suggested by Cino's consolatory ode to Dante on the

death of Beatrice.   Petrarch says that the denizens
of Heaven press round his lady—

> " Piene di *maraviglia* e di pietate."

They say among themselves—

> " Che luce è questa, e qual *nova beltate ?* "

In the earlier and ruder poem we find analogous
expressions—

> " Secondo ch' era qua giù *maraviglia*
> Cosi lassù somiglia."

And again—

> " Per *nova cosa* ogni santo la mira."

Petrarch feigns that Laura, in her celestial progress,
half turns from time to time to see if he follows.   But
neither is Beatrice indifferent.   Dante's spirits, which
" often make that voyage," have brought back tidings
that she was welcomed by the angels with sweet
laugh and song; and Cino goes on to say, " she
speaks of you to those blessed ones," and " prays God,
their true Lord, to comfort you."

The resemblances are not perhaps so close as
absolutely to exclude the theory of coincidence.
The Triumphs.   Suppose the two poets to have lighted by
accident on the same germinal thought,
and they would be certain to develop the idea in
much the same way.   Anyhow, these isolated loans
are very trifling matters.   Weighed against Petrarch's
solid and well-earned reputation, they are as dust in
the balance.   The case of the *Triumphs* is no doubt

somewhat different.   In projecting the series he went, so to speak, out of his way.   He was born to be, not a painter, but a singer.   He did not see—he felt. Then why should he have attempted poetry so directly opposed to his own natural genius?   The reason is plain.   Just as with respect to his *Africa* his emulation was fired by the *Æneid*, so, in later days, the glory of Dante's *Comedy* rendered him ambitious of a like success.   That this was his motive is proved by the identity of the metre.

Petrarch designed his poem on a scale not less magnificent than that of Dante.   Like Dante, too, he dealt with vast questions, affecting humanity as a whole, in relation to his own vicissitudes.   The general idea is that of a vast procession, or series of processions, similar to the triumphs of victorious Roman leaders as pictured in the bas-reliefs of ancient monuments —for example, in the "historical poem" of Trajan's Column, the sculptures whereof

> " wind aloft,
> And lead through various toils up the rough steep
> Its hero to the skies."

In Petrarch's scheme Love triumphs over Man — Charity over Love—Death over Charity—Fame over Death—Time over Fame—and God over Time.   Each of these conquerors is attended by a train of celebrities, most of them taken from ancient history or legend.   The poem is a failure.   The fundamental notion — that of an endless succession of the dead filing before the eyes of the spectator—does not admit of variety of incident or of detailed description. The *Triumphs* are dreary lists of names. Perhaps Boileau was thinking especially of these compositions when he wrote—

"Un sonnet sans défaut vaut un long poëme."

Petrarch has written many sonnets of the sort—quite worth his long poem.

It is entirely in accord with what we have already seen of Petrarch's character that he should affect to despise his Italian rhymes. He calls them *High breeding.* *nugæ* and *nugellæ*, and intimates that, had he known they would be so popular, he would have taken more trouble with them. No wonder Villemain exclaims, "Hypocrisie de poëte, Messieurs!" Petrarch's MSS. are full of corrections, but, correct as he might, he could never bring his verse to that condition of flawlessness for which his artistic instincts perpetually craved. And it is just this which offends us. This sparkling smoothness as of a diamond, this eternal worship of form, this determination to risk nothing—such things are bound to pall. We admire his high breeding, we almost envy his unfailing distinction of manner, and yet—and yet we soon tire of the company of this poetical fine gentleman. Coleridge has said of the Italian poets of the fifteenth and sixteenth centuries, "They placed the essence of poetry in the art. The excellence at which they aimed consisted in the exquisite polish of the diction combined with the avoidance of every word which a gentleman would not use in dignified conversation, and of every word and phrase which none but a learned man could use." Who introduced this ideal, and, in other respects, set the fashion for many generations to come? Well, it was not Dante.

Petrarch was the first of moderns to realise the potentialities of style. The beauty of Dante's phrase *A master of* is inseparable from the beauty of his idea. *style.* It is the soul expressing itself in the face. With Petrarch style is distinct from, independent of, even antagonistic to, natural charm. It is a thing to study, to take pains with, to improve. As your milliner might define it, it is the Muse's *parure* and *coiffure.* Melody and grace—these are the objects of Petrarch's solicitude and toil. His verse is as unsubstantial as gossamer; and that is why the *Triumphs* fail. For an epic, even an allegorical epic, you must have a solid foundation. As regards the lesser and better poems, Petrarch chooses his themes at random. His sentimental temperament can turn to account the most trivial incident, the most fleeting impression. Like the chameleon, he can extract nutriment out of the very air. He does not startle you with much originality. He soliloquises simply, and you are tempted to say that there is nothing new, that somewhere, at some time, you have heard most of it before. But never, believe me, in that magical form. The rhythm, the order of the words, are imperative; and hence it is that Petrarch is practically untranslatable. Take them out of their setting, rob them of the accompaniment of their music, and his thoughts seem commonplace. For Petrarch was not, like Dante, an

observer of outward things. He did not fill a note-
book with prospective metaphors and similes, as
Tennyson is said to have done, and as Scartazzini
suggests was the practice of the great Florentine in
his travels. In fact, Petrarch has nothing of the
botanist. He is the high priest of egoism, of intro-
spection, the prophet of the individual heart.

Let no one suppose, however, that Petrarch was
only a dreamer, that he had no robuster qualities.
Patriot and moralist. He was genuinely attached to his country,
and in one sense a better patriot than even
Dante, whose love for Italy, always less than his love
for Florence, was almost suffocated in his desire for
the accomplishment of an impossible dream. Petrarch, the guest of France, involved in no civil broils
and blinded by no theoretical prejudices, thought
much more of the Italian nationality, of Italy as a
whole, and, in so far as he had any unselfish aim, it
was for the reconciliation of his quarrelsome and misguided countrymen. He prayed, and to all appearance prayed earnestly, for the surcease of strife between the different commonwealths, for the peace of
Italy. At the close of his eloquent and impassioned
ode, *Italia mia, benchè 'l parlar sia indarno*, he observes, addressing his poem—

> " Proverai tua ventura
> Fra magnanimi pochi a chi 'l ben piace.
> Di' lor : Chi m' assicura ?
> I' vo gridando : Pace, pace, pace."

In this same ode he puts his finger on one of the
worst features in contemporary politics—namely, the

growing employment of mercenary troops, who, as he says, "play with death," surrendering instead of fighting whenever it suits their purpose. That this poem possesses both force and feeling was shown very clearly five centuries later, when it was enthusiastically cheered by the Italian revolutionists, and its recitation prohibited by the Austrian Government. As for force, I do not know where in literature to look for a more scathing denunciation of Papal corruption than Petrarch's sonnet on the court at Avignon. Commencing "Flame from the sky upon thy tresses rains," it speaks of chambers where

> "thy girls and old men go
> Wantoning, and with bellows, fire, and glass,
> Beelzebub moves nimbly to and fro."

It concludes by pointing a contrast between all this luxury and the privations of the Early Church; and the last line is also the strongest—

"Now liv'st thou so, that the stink reaches God."

With regard to technique, Petrarch is the reverse of an innovator. He follows the rules laid down by Dante in the *De Vulgari Eloquentia;* and *Technique.* his sonnets are all of the simplest type. Variations occur principally in the tercets, and concern the order of the rhymes. It is worthy of remark, however, that Petrarch was one of the first to employ the madrigal. This was a literary adaptation of pastoral song, and consists of from two to four triplets, with a concluding couplet. The couplets might be increased from one to three; and a form of madrigal

was found having no couplets, and composed of
three triplets. Later, madrigal - writing became a
craze with Italian rhymers, and was parodied in
madrigalesse.[1]

And so we come to the subject of Petrarch's influence on the Italian lyric. I cannot dwell at length
on this topic, but it is expedient to offer
some remarks by way of warning. "Pe-
trarchism" was not immediately fatal to the *dolce stil
nuovo*, echoes of which are audible in certain, pre-
sumably youthful, songs of Fazio degli Uberti. Nor
were these the only jarring notes. Already I have
touched on the moralising tone of one of Petrarch's
disciples — Antonio Beccari. Others of the school
thought less of love and more of politics. All, however — and this it is that stamps them as true
"Petrarchists" — unite in paying close attention to
form. In striving to be correct, they necessarily lost
some of that energy and freedom which in its highest
manifestation we term genius; and tended to sink,
as in the time of the Renaissance they did sink, into
mere formalism and pedantry. Among "Petrarchising"
versifiers of the fourteenth century the Cinquecentists,
better critics than poets, were perhaps right in assigning the palm to Buonaccorso da Montemagno; but
nowadays it is more interesting to recall the effect
of Petrarch's example on writers of the calibre of
Giovanni Boccaccio and Francesco Sacchetti, who,

His disciples.

[1] There is still perhaps no more generally serviceable edition of the
Canzoniere than that of Leopardi, with the additions of Ambrosoli
(Florence, 1870) or Camerini (Milan, 1876).

though remembered rather as novelists, have bequeathed a considerable body of verse.

That Petrarch's influence did not extend to the Welsh mountains may be taken for granted; but, curiously enough, at the very time he was airing his grief about Laura there flourished in the West Davydd ab Gwilym, commonly known as the Welsh Petrarch. Davydd's Laura was a certain Morvudd, with whom he eloped, but whom he had the mortification to see united by parental constraint to the "Little Hunchback." The pair again ran away, but force again parted them, and Davydd was condemned to pay a heavy fine. The men of Glamorgan, admiring his talents, came forward and discharged the fine, but could not release the bard from his unlucky attachment. Although he has been called the Welsh Petrarch, Davydd's poetry rather contrasts with Petrarch's, especially as regards appreciation of Nature. The following lines, from a translation by A. J. Johnes, will afford some idea of his style :—

The Welsh Petrarch.

> " Thou Summer ! father of delight,
>   With thy dense spray and thickets deep ;
>   Gemmed monarch, with thy rapturous light,
>   Rousing thy subject glens from sleep !
>   Proud has thy march of triumph been,
>   Thou prophet, prince of forest green !
>   Artificer of wood and tree,
>   Thou painter of unrivalled skill,
>   Who ever scattered gems like thee,
>   And gorgeous webs on park and hill ?
>   Till vale and hall with radiant dyes
>   Became another Paradise !

> And thou hast sprinkled leaves and flowers,
> And goodly chains of leafy bowers,
> And bid thy youthful warblers sing
> On oak and knoll the song of spring,
> And blackbird's note of ecstasy
> Burst loudly from the woodbine tree,
> Till all the world is thronged with gladness,
> Her multitudes have done with sadness !"

This is more like Chaucer and Walther von der Vogelweide than Petrarch; and at least one English poet agrees with Welsh ideas of beauty. Like the bards, he admires trees of equal growth. In *Iarlle sy Ffynnawn*, Kynon, in relating his adventures, says:—

"And it chanced at length that I came to the fairest valley in the world, wherein were trees of equal growth."

Similarly, in a tale by Gruffydd ab Adda, a bard slain at Dolgellan about 1370, we find:—

"In the furthermost end of this forest he saw a level green valley, and trees of equal growth."

With these passages compare the description in the *Flower and the Leaf* of an arbour:—

> "Wrethen in fere so well and cunningly,
>   That every branch and leafe grew by mesure,
>   Plain as a bord, of oon height by and by."

Joy in sky, and sea, and field is a characteristic shared by Davydd ab Gwilym with the somewhat *Bards and* older Rhys Goch. The bards loved birds *birds.* —the cuckoo, the nightingale, the lark, the thrush, &c.—and Rhys Goch, by these aerial couriers, sends messages to his lady-love:—

" I placed my affection
Upon a slender-waisted maid,
One who is a second Essyllt,
Of the hue of the waves of the raging sea ;
The beauty which adorned her
Became to me an arrow,
For she shot me
With her glances.

.   .   .   .

Go, thou Blackbird,
To the proud and slender maid,
And unto her show
How much for her I grieve ;
And thou, Thrush,
Singing on beautiful branches,
Take all my plaint
To the brilliant fair," [1] &c.

Between Rhys Goch and Davydd ab Gwilym, how-ever, exists an important difference in technique.
Rhetorical artifice. Although there had long been an element of alliteration in Welsh verse, it had been based in the main on the ordinary rules of prosody and rhyme. This may be seen from the original of the above quoted lines :—

" Serch y rhoddais,
Ar ddyn feinais,
Hoen geirw mor gwyllt
Bun ail Essyllt
Ei thegwch hi
Bu'n saeth i mi,
E'm saethes honn
O'i golygon," &c.

It was, however, a common artifice to compose whole

[1] Translated by Thomas Stephens.

stanzas, and even poems, of lines commencing with the same letter and in some cases with the same word—*e.g.*,

> " Oedd breisg freisg ei fyddin
> Oedd brwysg rwysg rhag y godorin,
> Oedd balch gwalch golchiad ei lain," &c.

We find traces of the same thing in Troubadour verse. Arnaut de Marueil, in one of his poems, addresses his mistress thus:—

> " Vos saluda ; e vostra lauzor,
> Vostra beautat, vostra valor,
> Vostre solatz, vostre parlar,
> Vostr' aculhir e vostr' onvar,
> Vostre pretz, vostr' essenhamen,
> Vostre saber, e vostre sen,
> Vostre gen cors, vostre dos riz,
> Vostra terra, vostre pays."

And Dante, in his inscription over Hell-gate, twice repeats the opening words—

> " Per me si va nella citta dolente,
> Per me si va nell' eterno dolore,
> Per me si va tra la perdita gente."

Here it is evident the solemn iteration is peculiarly effective, and answers the purpose for which it was no doubt designed. In Welsh poetry it was Cynghanedd. more a question of sound than sense, and out of this practice grew that poisonous *cynghanedd*, destined until the present century to be the bane of Kymric literature. The beginnings of this pest are already perceptible in the writings of Davydd ab

Gwilym. All that is signified by the word *cynghanedd* cannot be noted here. It had something in common with Icelandic and Anglo-Saxon alliteration, which, as a tax on ingenuity, seems bad enough, but *cynghanedd*, or consonancy, is much worse. The *englyn*, before the introduction of *cynghanedd*, ran thus :—

> " Nid oes ym Davyt dawn orvod—ar bawb
>   Arbennigyawl Nebod
> Cadyr rwyf cadarn glwyf glybod
> Can llonyt byw yn dyt bod." *

The only noticeable features in this stanza are the retention of the same rhyme in the four lines, and the recurrence of the consonants *r*, *b* in the first and second lines. After the introduction of *cynghanedd*, the correspondence of consonants was compulsory in every line—*e.g.*,

> " Ber*v*ain yw'r avr a bar*v*og,—ar*wav l*ais
>   Un hir*v*lew a chorniog ;
> Naid hyd llethr*au* creigi*au* c*r*og
> A'i *n*aw*dd* yw'r graig ddan*n*e*dd*og."

In Walter's *Dissertation on the Welsh Language*, the following lines are given as a specimen of "cross consonancy" in English, but, though clever, they are far from reflecting the complex and exacting nature of full-blown *cynghanedd* :—

> " A *f*ien*d* in Phoebus' fane he *f*oun*d*,
>   That y*onder g*rew yet u*nder g*round,
>   *Sp*rung from the *sp*awn of *Sp*ite ;
>   The Elf his *sp*leen durst not di*spl*ay,
>   Nor act the *d*evil in the *d*ay,
>   But at the *n*oon of *n*ight."

While Italy was rising step by step to the sublimest expression of poetical feeling, in France the best *New French forms.* talents seemed engrossed with the construction of a formulary. The old simple schemes, which had sufficed for Thibaut de Champagne, for Gace Brulé, and for Colin Muset, were discarded in favour of strict, in some cases very strict, laws, at once a challenge to technical ability and a grievous hindrance to a free and natural style. Under the new conditions, to write verse was not too easy; to write poetry, almost impossible. The only compensation was that these pedantic limitations counteracted a tendency to diffuseness, the characteristic besetment of this decadent age.

Let us first dispose of the various forms of the new French lyric. The *chant royal* corresponds in a measure to the Italian *canzone*, being reserved *The chant royal.* for lofty and serious themes. The name is closely connected with the literary competitions of which I have spoken, and in which the poet winning the first prize stood forth as *King*. The *chant royal* was composed of five strophes. Each strophe consisted of eleven lines, and each line of ten syllables. Not only were all the strophes identical in plan, but the same rhymes were retained in the same order, while the last line of the first was repeated at the end of each succeeding strophe, and formed the refrain. At the close of the poem came the *envoi* of five lines addressed to the prince or president, and recapitulating in brief what has preceded.

The ancient name of the popular dance-song was

balete, and it appears to have run thus—*ababcCC.*[1]

The balade. The later *balade,* on the other hand, generally ran *ababbcbC.* This form is an abridgment, as it were, of the *chant royal,* though it might be truer to describe the *chant royal* as a degenerate offshoot, or wilful corruption, of the *balade.* However that may be, the *balade* consisted of three strophes, having the same metre, the same rhymes, and, of course, the same refrain ; and it concluded with a half strophe forming the *envoi.* The number of lines in a strophe, and the number of syllables in a line, were left to the poet's discretion. Generally, there were eight or ten lines, and seven, eight, or ten syllables. Later authorities — *e.g.,* Sibilet in his *Art Poétique* (1548) — prescribe that the number of lines should correspond to the number of syllables ; but this rule does not appear to have been universally followed, at any rate by the older poets.

The simple *rondel,* afterwards known as the *triolet,* had only one strophe of eight or seven lines, and

The rondel. either one or two rhymes. Where there are seven lines, the first line only constitutes the refrain. In the case of *rondel* everything turns on the refrain. The simplest form of the simple *rondel* was $A^1A^2aAaaA^1A^2$. If, however, the refrain rhymed AB, the scheme became $ABaAabAB$. With regard to the number of syllables in a line, they range from one to ten, and the lines may be regular or

[1] The capital letters, here and elsewhere, indicate the one, two, or three lines of the refrain.

irregular. Here is a *rondel* entirely composed of monosyllabic lines:—

je
dy
que
je
le
vy
je
dy.

But a *rondel* was not necessarily simple, and the longer the refrain, the longer the *rondel* became. Thus the refrain *ABBA* resulted in the scheme *ABBAabABabbaABBA*. By means of a five-lined refrain with a three-lined resumption, or a six-lined refrain with a two-lined resumption, *rondeaux* were formed twenty-one or twenty-two lines in length. The tendency, however, was to diminish both the length and the importance of the refrain. The earlier *rondeau double*, afterwards known as the *rondeau quatrain*, consisted of twelve lines, and the later *rondeau double* of fifteen lines, each with a single refrain-line. The schemes of the *rondeau quatrain* and the *rondeau double* were respectively *AbbaabAabbaA* and *AabbaaabAaabbaA*. Here is an example of the *rondeau quatrain*, by Charles of Orléans:—

> " Gardez le trait de la fenestre,
> Amans, qui par rues passez :
> Car plus tost en seres blessez
> Que de trait d'arc ou arbalestre.
> N'allez a destre n'à senestre
> Regardant ; mais les yeulx baissez :
> *Gardez le trait de la fenestre.*
> Si n'avez medecin bon maistre,

> Si tost que vous serez navrez
> A Dieu soyez recommandez.
> Mors vous tiens ; demandez le prestre.
> *Gardez le trait de la fenestre.*"

Often only the first word of the refrain was given, followed by "etc."; but this was a slipshod device, and ruinous to the metrical effect.

The school of Charles of Orléans invented what may be termed an imperfect rondeau—the *bergerette,* of which the distinctive feature was the re-ception in a separate compartment of two new rhymes—for example, *ABBAcdcdabbaABBA.* The *virelai* (earlier, *vireli*) is simply a *bergerette* expanded into several strophes, with the refrain repeated only at the conclusion of the last strophe.

The bergerette *and* virelai.

There are many sorts of rhyme. The *rime léonine* or *riche* is supposed to be formed of two masculine rhymes, but in practice is often synony-mous with the feminine rhyme. *Rimes equivoques* or *equivoquées* are those in which simple are rhymed with compound words or combinations of words : *metent ; entremetent,* or *volagement ; vol a je ment.* The rhyme is said to be *annexée* when the last syllable of one line is the first of the next, and *fratrisée* when the last word of one line is the first of the next. The following strophe of a *ballade* by Eustache Deschamps will illustrate most of these peculiarities :—

Varieties of rhyme.

> " Lasse, lasse ! malheureuse et dolente
> Lente me voy, fors de souspirs et plains,
> Plains sont mes jours d'ennuy et de tourmente.
> Mente qui veult, car mes cuers est certains ;

> Tains jusqu'à mort, et pour celli qui j'ains,
> Ains, mais ne fut dame si fort atainte,
> Tainte me voy, quant il m'ayme le mains.
> Mains, entendez ma piteuse complainte."

The *rime batelée* is that in which the last syllable of
one line is the middle syllable of the next.   When all
the lines of a strophe, or all the words of a line, begin
with the same letter, the rhyme is *senée*.   It is *cour-
onnée* when the last two words of the line have the
same ending:—

> " La blanche columbelle belle,"

and *emperière* when the rhyme is thrice repeated:—

> "En grant remord Mort mord."

It would be possible, availing myself of treatises like
Henri Croy's *Art et Science de Rhétorique*, to fill many
pages with such details, but I prefer to
devote the remainder of my space to the
poets composing in this style.   The earliest was Guillaume de Machault (*c.* 1284-1377), who attached himself to the person of successive monarchs (Philippe le
Bel, Jean II., Charles V.), and sang their achievements.   Machault was rather a minstrel than a poet;
and, as a musician, he displayed some originality by
inventing new airs (" des tailles nouvelles ").   These
airs gave considerable vogue to his verse, but, on his
death, partly from the flimsy nature of its support, his
fame suddenly collapsed.   Like other poets of the
school, he lived to be extremely old; it was an age
of rapid transition, and Machault clung to Old French
forms, though he failed to renew their pristine fresh-

ness and gaiety. He left a vast legacy of *ballades, rondeaux, chants royaux*, besides historical poems and *dits*. In commencing the *Dit de la Harpe*, he harps on the harp thus :—

> " Je puis trop bien ma dame comparer
> A la harpe et son gent cors parer
> De xxv. cordes que la harpe ha,
> Dont roys David par maintes fois harpa ;
> Et vraiement qui aimme de la harpe
> Le tresdous son et sagement en harpe
> Et le grant bien des cordes en harpent
> Trop miex le pris que d'or fin un arpent
> Et pour itant weil aprendre a harper," &c.

Whatever we may choose to term this, it is certainly not common-sense. The quality of common-sense is *Eustache Deschamps.* the note of Machault's admirer Eustache Deschamps (1328-1415), who, not quite for-tunately, has been saved thereby—saved from absurd-ity, but saved also from being a poet. A distinguished critic is of opinion that it would be well if arrange-ments could be made for a complete edition of Deschamps' writings.[1] Why ? Because he was so shrewd an observer of current events, and one finds in his verse so many valuable hints on the moral and political history of the fourteenth century ! Deschamps was a plebeian, and during his lifetime went by the name of Eustache Morel. This was not a patronymic, but a surname, due to his dark complexion :—

> " Chacuns me dit : tu es lais garnemens,
> Gros visage as, tu es *noirs et hallez*."

---

[1] The Société des Anciens Textes has agreed to meet this, perhaps not very wide, demand.

The other name was derived from a house near Vertus, of which he tells us—

> " Dehors Vertus ay maison gracieuse,
> Où j'avoye par long temps demeuré,
> Où pluseurs ont mené vie joyeuse.
> Maison *des champs* l'ont pluseurs appelé."

Although Deschamps was not a poet endowed with fine sensibilities or creative imagination, he could write manly verse, and it is by no means fanciful to surmise that his frank, blunt style was just the style to please Bertrand du Guesclin, whose death indeed he deplores in a *ballade* full of mournful energy :—

> " Estoc d'oneur, et arbres de vaillance
> Cuer de lyon espris de hardiment,
> La flour des preux et la gloire de France,
> Victorïeux et hardi combatant ;
> Saige en voz fais et bien entreprenant
> Souverain homme de guerre,
> Vainqueur des gens et conquereur de terre
> Le plus vaillant qui onques fust en vie :
> Chascun pour vous doit noir vestir et querre.
> Plourez, plourez flour de chevalerie ! "

If I am driven by conscience to refuse to the long-lived "faiseurs" the coveted name of poet, the objections no longer hold in the case of Jean Froissart (1337-1410). Great in prose, he is not equally great in verse, but a delicate fancy, a lively, graceful, and melodious style, assuredly do not count for nothing. These French writers have a strong claim on the attention of English students from their influence on Gower and Chaucer. Gower may be

Froissart.

reckoned one of them, and Chaucer was flattered by
Deschamps as a "great translator"! It is curious
that one generally so well-informed as the late Professor Ten Brink should have attributed to Chaucer
the invention of the daisy-cult. I will not expose
myself to similar risk of error by nominating Froissart
as the inventor, but he unquestionably wrote a *Dittié
de la Flour de la Margherite*, whence, in all likelihood,
Chaucer borrowed the idea:—

> " Elle est petite
> Blanche et vermeille et par usage habite
> En tous vers lieus, aillours ne se delite.
> Ossi chier a le preel d'une hermite,
> Mes ch'elle y puist croistre sans opposite,
> Comme elle fait les beaus gardins d'Egypte
> Son doulç vëoir grandement me proufite
> Et pour ce est dedens mon coer escripte
> Si plainement
> Que nuit et jour en pensant je recite
> Les grans vertus de quoi elle est confite,
> Et di ensi ; li heure soit benite
> Quant pour moi ai tele flourette eslite,
> Qui de bonté et de beauté est dite
> La souveraine et s'en attenc merite,
> Se ne m'i nuist fortune la trahite," &c.

There is no common-sense in that, but daintiness,
and charm, and ease, and serenity.

Christine de Pisan (1363-1420) is avowedly a follower of Deschamps, dutifully subscribing herself "ta
Christine de disciple et ta bienveillante." Although she
Pisan. essayed many kinds of composition, including the most frivolous, she, like her master, is most at
home in serious political and patriotic subjects, and

she treats them with masculine vigour.   Among her *ballades* is one that reminds us of the *Combat des Trente*, since it hails the victory of seven Frenchmen over seven Englishmen, in 1403, at Montendre near Bordeaux; and her last poem was a *dittié* in honour of the triumphs of Jeanne d'Arc.   It is a noble pæan, wherein is expressed all the joy of a woman, all the eloquence of a statesman, and all the gratitude of a saint.   Besides an allegorising *Roman d'Othéa et d'Hector*, otherwise known as the *Cent Histoires de Troye*, Christine wrote a number of *dits moraux* addressed to her son Jean Castel, and designed, like Lord Chesterfield's Letters to his Son, as a preparation for life,—*e.g.*,

> "Se tu as estat ou office,
>   Dont tu te mesles de justice,
>   Gardes comment tu jugeras,
>   Car devant le grant juge yras."

Lastly, in the controversy regarding the *Romance of the Rose*, Christine championed the honour of her sex, with excellent effect, in an *Épître au Dieu d'Amour*.

The *Livre des Cent Ballades* is precious as throwing light on the literary dissipations of French gentlemen *The* Livre des at the close of the fourteenth century. Cent Ballades. The work consists of a great "debate" on love, opened by an old knight who counsels a young bachelor to be loyal, while a lady defends inconstancy and caprice.   Unable to decide the point, the young man submits the question to thirteen lords, three of whom return a witty, evasive answer, seven side with the old knight, and only two are found to support the

lady. The principal scene of this "debate" is a water-
meadow by the Loire, where a gay company of ladies
and gentlemen is assembled, but the meeting with the
knight takes place on the road between Angers and
Pont-de-Cé. The *Livre* was supposed to have been
written by Marshal de Bouciqualt, then between
twenty and thirty years old, and certain of his friends,
during an expedition "oultre-mer"; but the latest
authorities are opposed to this belief.[1]

[1] These writings are not specially easy of access. Interesting specimens may be found in Leroux de Lincy's *Recueil de Chants Histor-
iques;* and Scheler has published an edition of Froissart's poems
(Brussels, 1871). Mr Paget Toynbee's *Specimens of Old French*
(Clarendon Press) will be valued.

CHAPTER IV.

DANTE.

" HIS biography is, as it were, irrecoverably lost for us."
This was Carlyle's dictum several decades ago, and
Lost biography. nothing has happened since to necessitate
a revision of the sentence. Rather, the
effect of much toilsome research and anxious sifting of
evidence, instead of adding to our knowledge, has
been, at least in some directions, to take away that
little which we flattered ourselves we possessed. As
in other departments of history, so here beliefs which
have entered, so to speak, into the very marrow of our
consciousness—have become almost articles of faith
with us—must be yielded up before the powerful
search-light which is being turned on so many dark
coigns of the Middle Ages. The final result may be
happy. The process may end in an authentic biography of Dante not devoid, let us hope, of that

warmth, that colour, that particularity which lend so
great, however spurious, a charm to the "romances"
that served our predecessors in lieu of genuine fact.
But for this the time is not ripe ; and, with regard
to many statements, the most that can be claimed for
them is that they are provisionally correct.

Things being in this predicament, it is natural to
ask—What are our sources of information ?   At first
these might seem ample.   A multiplicity
The Trattatello.
of "Lives" is found to exist, some of them
quite early, and one going back to the generation following that of Dante.   Assured of this fact, we might
well suppose it a simple and satisfactory expedient to
procure the biographies, read them, and digest them at
our leisure.   Nobody could be blamed for this illusion;
however, it *is* an illusion.   These "Lives," most of
them, are not independent works.   They are to be
traced with hardly an exception to one original —
Boccaccio's famous Little Treatise in Praise of Dante.
Its very title is enough to render this composition
suspected.   If it was wished to learn the truth about
such-and-such, the last place in which to seek it would
be a speech delivered at his funeral, when the force of
the adage "Nothing but good of the dead" is most
felt and appreciated.   The *Trattatello* is not actually
a funeral oration, but it is conceived in the spirit, and
executed in the style, of a funeral oration ; and therefore its authority cannot be received as final.

Boccaccio's general character and achievements will
be dealt with later.   Meanwhile, it is requisite to
assume an acquaintance with this writer as the author

of the *Decameron.* That Boccaccio was a novelist is not an irrelevancy—a circumstance that can be rightly ignored. While it would be unjust to affirm that a novelist is incapable as such of treating historical subjects seriously, it must be evident to the least reflecting that he is exposed to peculiar temptations, and trammelled by predilections from which other, less fanciful, beings are exempt. If we find him devoting disproportionate space to the romantic elements of the story—that is no more than we should expect; nor ought it to be much of a surprise, if the habitual and irresponsible exercise of the inventive faculty should disgust him at times with a mutilated and imperfect presentation, and cause him to substitute for the rude, the simple, and sadly stupid truth the rainbow hues of a glowing imagination.

Considerations like these addressed themselves in the fifteenth century to the sober inquiring mind of Leonardo Bruni, who wrote in sarcastic terms of the "love, and sighs, and scalding tears," which formed the staple of Boccaccio's contribution. Instead of the showy rhetoric and trivial subject-matter of the Little Treatise, Bruni proposes to himself an historical relation of "the weighty and substantial parts" of Dante's life, nor, all things considered, does this Aretine secretary of the Republic of Florence disappoint. It was obvious at the first that, coming when he did, he would have to forgo many of the advantages open to his predecessor. Nobody who could remember Dante, or who could furnish accounts drawn from personal knowledge or the disclosures of

A critical "Life."

trustworthy informants, was any longer in existence.
On the other hand, Bruni, from his official position,
had full access to documentary evidence still obtain-
able ; and this he professes to have used.

If we could be sure, as he more than once asserts,
that he had inspected Dante's letters, the testimony of
At loggerheads.   Bruni would be of priceless value. It
would assume the character of a reprint,
a literary testament, a posthumous autobiography,
at least in part. But what security is there that
Bruni was not, like so many others before and since,
the victim of imposture ? Another consideration
which impairs the worth of this witness is the spirit
of contradiction he displays to Boccaccio, who, daring
as he may have been, cannot have invented always
and everywhere. This antagonism declares itself in
things which it was idiotic to affirm, and only less
idiotic to deny—for example, Boccaccio's solemn intimation that Dante, austere even in infancy, despised
the caresses of his mamma. This fortunate conjecture
might well have been left to refute itself ; but when
Bruni proceeds to emphasise the matter by announcing
that the youthful Dante, for all the warmth of his
studies, bated not a jot of social intercourse and enjoyment, instinctively we pause. Truly, "love, and sighs,
and scalding tears " are much more in accord with the
tenor of Dante's juvenilia than the festal scenes in
which Bruni would depict him as moving.

Besides these "Lives," what have we ? First there
is the all too brief notice—the *rubrica dantesca*—of
Giovanni Villani. Villani's sincerity is above sus-

picion; but since it is human to err, good intentions
are not everything, and on the score of
Villani.
accuracy even Villani may be impeached.
For all that his few words are extremely precious, for
—let us not forget—they are the words of a contemporary.[1]   Something also may be gleaned from the
old commentators, who, however, commit all the bad
actions proper to the tribe, such as purloining from
the text, eschewing real problems, and furnishing
needless explanations.   Again, there are the public
archives, whence, at the present time, the chief additions to our knowledge may be looked for; and,
lastly, there remain, as a test and touchstone of
imagined discoveries, the works of Dante himself.

With materials so sparse, so heterogeneous, so diver-
gent, prediction becomes easy; around this carcass of
contention the eagles of debate will gather
Descent.
together.   There is indeed hardly a circumstance of Dante's life, including the incident of his
birth, which has not at some time formed the battle-
field of controversy.   He was born, it is now generally
admitted, in the year 1265; and probably in the
month of May.   It is conceded also that he was of
Florentine parentage; but inasmuch as his father's
party—the Guelf—was then in exile, it is not absolutely certain that he was born at Florence.   He came
of a family which was at least respectable; to assess
its exact importance is a task of some difficulty.   Villani says, "This Dante was an honourable and ancient

---

[1] The "Life" by Filippo Villani, which is only mentioned to avoid
possible confusion, is a worthless abridgment of Boccaccio's.

citizen of Florence, of Porta San Piero, and our neighbour," but this need not imply that he belonged to the class of nobles, a supposition which other passages of the chronicle seem expressly to exclude. One ancestor of Dante appears to have attained distinction—namely, a certain Cacciaguida whom he lauds in the *Paradiso*. This old Florentine, it seems, had been a valiant soldier of the Cross, and the Emperor Conrad had knighted him, but the honours thus acquired had not been handed down. "Verily," says the poet, apostrophising Nobility, "thou art a coat that quickly shortens"; and, as Cacciaguida warns his descendant against inquiring too closely into their antecedents, we are perhaps justified in assuming that the family had never, except in the case of this glorified quartermaster, exceeded the rank of the better sort of citizens. There are other arguments tending to the same conclusion, but on these it is not necessary that I should enter.

Dante's father is stated to have been a lawyer, and, singularly enough, a person of little mark and likelihood. Indeed his insignificance was a byword. When Dante was young, he appears to have bandied "unparliamentary" sonnets with his friend and destined brother-in-law, Forese Donati, whom he describes as a son of "I know not whom," while Donati retorts, "As for you, your vileness and cowardice shows only too plainly that you are the son of Alighiero." As these expressions are rather strong, we must suppose them to have been used during some period of misunderstanding; but the taunt, brutal at

Parentage.

M

the best, would have been entirely pointless if the conduct of Dante's father had not provided some occasion for it. Whatever his fault may have been, and it is difficult to think that lukewarmness as a Guelf was not part thereof, it did not operate as a bar to matrimonial alliances. Alighiero married, first a lady of whom all that is known is her name, Donna Bella, and secondly, Lapa di Chiarissimo Cialuffi. By the former he had a son, Dante, while Lapa was mother of Francesco Alighieri and a daughter. All this is now clearly ascertained, but until quite recently the names were given in the reverse order, and it was Lapa, not Donna Bella, who was believed to have died, perhaps in childbirth. Alighiero died at some date between 1270 and 1279, whence it is possible, and indeed probable, that Dante tasted something of the tender mercies of an autocratic step-mother. Anyhow, it is a notable fact that nowhere in his writings does he make mention of his father, his mother, his brother, his sister, or any relation whatsoever.

It makes this strange circumstance yet stranger that Dante does allude to the "dear and good paternal image" of Brunetto Latini. To be sure, his warm regard does not preclude his assigning him to one of the circles of Hell and blackening his memory with an atrocious charge, but this he does not willingly. Dante is supreme Gonfalonier of Justice! As we know, in a general way this Latini, "the worldly man," is very far from obscure; his precise relations with Dante are somewhat of a mystery. Was he his tutor in the common acceptation of the term?

Education.

Or was he merely a friend of the family, whose shining talents variously displayed aroused the wonder and admiration of the growing boy ? The latter alternative is more probable, but, frankly, we cannot say.

That he had other instructors is certain. It would be easy to make too much of the interview with

> " His Casella whom he woo'd to sing,
> Met in the milder shades of Purgatory."

Such evidence points to taste rather than to positive acquirements, though the inference that Dante's songs were set to music at Florence is no doubt sufficiently interesting. With regard to drawing, we have it on the best authority—his own—that he had some practice therein. The story of his absorption on his lady's death-day, when he was found by persons of distinction designing angels, was certainly not recorded with any intention of vaunting his accomplishments.[1] Whether he could paint also, I shall not attempt to decide. His profound delight in portrait and miniature is manifest in his writings, and it might be just to credit him with at least the rudiments of the art. These studies, perhaps, as well as the help derived from Ser Brunetto, belong to that secret process by which men of genius form themselves; but it is scarcely a question that Dante, in addition to this, received the best education the age could afford.

With parentage and education it is natural to associate another sort of influence—that of early companionships. Each step hitherto has been for us a

---

[1] *Vita Nuova*, § xxxv.

surprise. The laws of heredity and environment have
both in turn been defied, and the poet's
Friendships. development has proceeded in accordance
with a principle that eludes us, unless we figure it as
the law of repulsion and rebound. Alighiero as father,
Latini as godfather (in the realm of fame), and now,
to cap all, Cavalcanti as friend—it is certainly per-
plexing. Not indeed that there was anything strange
in the youthful and ambitious Dante paying court to
a poet of Guido's genius and renown. That was the
most probable thing in the world. Cavalcanti was full
ten years older than Dante, and so by comparison a
mature man; but he may have been flattered by the
lad's attentions, and, without much thought or concern,
extended to him his patronage. Here, however, is the
amazing thing—Cavalcanti was by all accounts an
atheist, an odd acquaintance, truly, for one who was
to chant the splendours of the Glory Infinite, the
Light Eterne.

Returning for a moment to those quarrelsome sonnets, the genuineness of which, amidst so much that
has become apocryphal, is comparatively secure,
Forese was a huge gormandiser, so that Dante must
needs reckon among his friends a "cook's oracle," a
mediæval Heliogabalus. Yet, withal, the greeting
between these erstwhile revilers in Purgatory, where
Forese, lean and gaunt, is expiating his folly, is one
of the most touching episodes in the whole of the
cantica—

> "That face of thine, which dead I once bewept,
> Gives me for weeping now no lesser grief."

Besides Guido Cavalcanti and Forese Donati, Dante, as we know, was acquainted with Cino Sinibuldi and Lapo Gianni. Three out of the four he associates in terms of generous approval — possibly all; if the "unum alium," whom for some reason he declines to name, can be his friend and enemy, Donati.

I am seeking to trace the exterior life of Dante, otherwise from the topic of his friendships it would be inevitable that I should pass to that of his first love. But apart from the fact that *In the field.* this first love pertains to the inmost core of his being, and was perhaps solely an ideal phase of his existence, the theme has, for good and sufficient reasons, been already disposed of elsewhere. Suffice it to say that the departure of Beatrice — that is Dante's style; "partita da questo secolo"—occurred on the 19th of June 1290, when she was twenty-three, and he just a year older. This love-affair, or what is symbolised by it, occupied a considerable time, during which the poet was called upon, more than once, to prove his valour in action. From his mode of speaking it might be inferred that opportunities of the sort were rather frequent. Certainly, at this epoch, the condition of Florence was far from peaceful, and there were street-brawls innumerable. On two occasions the city arrayed her forces against external foes, and Dante in the flush of youthful vigour could not be spared from the ranks. At Campaldino (or Certomondo), on the 11th of June 1289, a battle was fought between the Florentine Guelfs and the Ghibellines of Arezzo, which in its changes and chances antedated Naseby. The squad-

rons of Florence, borne down by the Aretine horse, fell
back on the support of the infantry; and the steadi-
ness of the foot-soldiers, combined with the dispersion
of the enemy, finally gave the victory to the Guelfs.
Dante, who was in one of the cavalry troops, describes
the trepidation, and at last the great joy, with which
he marked the varying fortunes of the day. The
following August he was present at the siege of
Caprona, when the garrison, after an honourable re-
sistance, surrendered on terms.

We come now to his marriage. At some date before
1298—it is impossible to settle exactly when—Dante
took to wife Gemma Donati, a woman of
A Xanthippe? family, who bore him several children.
Rumour has not been kind to this poor lady, vilified
through successive ages as a termagant or shrew. The
author and propagator of the scandal was Boccaccio,
who based it on the supposed complete separation of
the couple after Dante's exile. But this is less than
just. I yield to none in reverent admiration for Coleridge, for whose frailties, remembering his lofty and
generous aspirations, I am eager to admit any excuse;
but it would be folly to pretend that the fact of his
quitting Sara and her family casts any valid reflection
on the wife of his youth. If Gemma can be identified
with the "gentle lady" of the *Vita Nuova*, and there
have been more unwarrantable conjectures, then the
marriage was one of affection, not a conventional
arrangement patched up, like that of Montaigne, to
satisfy relations. The subsequent parting is explained
only too easily by the grim logic of the situation.

Allowing, however, that there were jars, it is absurd —I was going to say Quixotic, but Quixote would have disdained such a thing—to throw all the blame on Gemma Donati. To say nothing of the irritability of poets, of which it is evident that Dante abundantly partook, it must have been a severe trial to a wife of average sensibility for her husband to be always and openly celebrating the transcendent virtues of another. Nor is it any answer to say that Beatrice, at any rate in death, was a phantasm, a mere abstraction. It is altogether too much to expect from a simple Florentine lady the power of nicely discriminating between the real and the ideal, when this very problem has baffled the ripest intellects and is likely long to remain an apple of discord between rival schools of criticism.

The irritability of poets! Was it ever better exemplified than in the case of Boniface VIII., the *Shepherding* "shepherd turned wolf"? Dante would *the sheep.* seem never to have satisfied himself that justice had been done on this malefactor of the Lateran. Much of this may have been righteous indignation; but, on the other hand, it must not be forgotten that Boniface was Dante's evil genius, a sort of haunting vampire whose lust of power had blotted out the prospect, the fair prospect, of his life. The antagonism between them goes back to the very earliest years in which Dante can be believed to have taken part in public affairs. In 1293 was accomplished the memorable reform of Giano Della Bella, by virtue of which none of those citizens denominated "great" or "noble" could succeed to any office of state. These Ordinances of Justice, as they were called, naturally gave great umbrage to the disfranchised, and in 1295 the nobles and great men essayed a counter-revolution. Among other expedients they despatched from Campania a "free and bold cavalier" whose special mission it was —on the principle "Smite the shepherd and the sheep will be scattered"—to slay Giano Della Bella. I cannot here follow the story to its conclusion; but it is important to note that the cavalier in question came, as Dino Compagni alleges, with the approval of Pope Boniface VIII., "then newly created."

In 1300 the same pope again interfered in the domestic affairs of Florence. The general condition of things was as follows. The Ghibellines had been cast out; the nobles and great men had been reduced to impotence, and all persons ambitious of office were required to enter themselves as members of some "art"—that is, some trade or profession. If it be true, as proverbial wisdom assures us, that indolence is always mischievous, the converse ought also to hold, and the statesmanship of Giano should have issued in profound tranquillity, in universal contentment. Excellent in theory, but in practice how different! Faction had indeed been expelled, but not the spirit of faction, which was always engendering new causes of strife. When they had nothing else to fight over, the citizens adopted as a pretext the rival claims of two great houses, the Cerchi and the Donati; and though they were all nominally Guelf, they could not rest until they had formed themselves into two new

Civic broils.

parties in certain features reproducing the old. These were the Neri and the Bianchi. In a republic one cannot serve the state and ignore divisions of party. Dante was a Bianco. He further qualified himself by joining the sixth of the seven Greater Arts, which was that of the physicians, but included also artists.

The magistracy of Florence at this time consisted of a Gonfalonier and six Priors. Dante, having already graduated as Counsellor, was, on the 15th of June 1300, advanced to the Priorship, and held office until the 15th of August following. Far too much stress has been laid on this honour, which circulated with such rapidity as to justify almost any citizen in hoping for its attainment. On the other hand, the cares that beset the post rendered it a thankless distinction for any but a sincere patriot. Coincidently with the date of Dante's accession to office Pope Boniface sent to Florence a high dignitary, Cardinal Fra Matteo d' Acquasparta, with the title of "peace-maker." Had the pontiff's motives been pure, no conduct would have better become the Vicar of Christ; but there is reason to think that Boniface, reviving the pretensions of Gregory VII. to universal jurisdiction, sought to profit by their unhappy dissensions, so as to draw the Florentines into acknowledged dependence on himself. The Bianchi, being then masters and suspecting some such design, refused to obey, and the cardinal-legate departed, leaving the city under an interdict and sentence of excommunication. Thus foiled, Boniface, still deeply persuaded of the need of reconciling the Florentines, appealed to the arm of flesh, and on the 1st of November 1301 Charles of Valois marched his forces into the city. The Bianchi fled in confusion, while the Neri, faithful servants of the Church, received their due reward.

Væ victis ! The houses of the Bianchi were rased, their goods confiscated; and Dante especially was

Exile.

sentenced on the 27th of January 1302 to a fine of two thousand florins. This was to be paid within three days, and, in default, all his belongings were to be declared public property. In any case he was to suffer banishment for two years, as well as perpetual exclusion from office and emolument, as a cheat! On the 14th of March 1302 a second decree was fulminated against him, setting forth that he had neither answered the citation nor paid the fine, and condemning him to be burnt alive, if ever he should fall into the power of the Republic. In fact, to adopt the style of our own Civil Wars, he was henceforward to be treated as a malignant. Even after his death Dante was still for the Florentine official the exile, the foe of the Guelf party, the Prior who had been guilty of dishonesty.

Bruni asserts that, at the time this storm burst, Dante was at Rome on an embassy to the Pope. It

Patrons.

is, however, not improbable that he was at Florence or in the immediate neighbourhood, whence he succeeded in making his escape. The bulk of the exiles settled at Arezzo, and, in alliance with the Ghibellines of this and other towns, made a vigorous attempt to recapture Florence, finally without avail. Dante then betook himself to Verona, where he was hospitably entertained by the Scaligeri;

and, in 1306, the Marquis Francesco Malaspina availed himself of his services in the conclusion of a peace with the Bishop of Luni, Antonio di Canulla. These are the only intimations respecting the early years of his wanderings which can be properly regarded as certain. For the rest, the claims of various towns to have sheltered him are on a par with his many— mostly apocryphal — missions, with which in some cases the hospitalities may have been confused. Anyhow, for us, the period is densely obscure.

The account most generally received is that of Villani — namely, that Dante proceeded first to *In journeyings* Bologna, and then to Paris and other *often.* parts of the world, for purposes of study. An old tradition has it that on his first disappointment—the death of his lady—the poet enrolled himself among the Frati Minori of the Order of St Francis. It is known, however, from his own description, that the source to which he then applied for consolation was neither Holy Scripture nor the pious exhortations of departed saints, but the writings of pagan moralists. Felled by this second disappointment, Dante may well have thought it a fit occasion for the resumption of his cherished studies. But here arises a question which touches in a greater or less degree the whole period of his exile—Whence did he obtain the means to perform these long journeys and provide for his bodily needs ? That he was for a time dependent on the generosity of strangers is proved by a famous passage, which shows also how bitterly he regretted the necessity. It has been suggested that he sought to minimise his obligations by teaching—that he repaired to the different universities as much in the character of a professor as in that of a student. But if this was so, why did he not avow it? Can it be that he was conscious of exposing himself to some vulgar taunt, like that levelled at Milton by Dr Johnson? It is possible.

Whether or not there occurred that notable incident narrated by Boccaccio, and recalling the prowess of the Admirable Crichton, it is beyond a doubt that Dante sojourned at Paris. He himself alludes to this stay in the *Paradiso*, where he speaks of Sigier and the Rue du Fouarre.[1] At Paris, it is believed, Dante heard of an event that filled him with the wildest joy, and caused him to decide on an immediate return to Italy. This was the descent into the peninsula of the Emperor Henry VIII. Dante, with the sanguine spirit of an exile long without a solitary ray of hope, beheld in a vision his own restoration to Florence in the wake of the Imperial arms; and in due course the forces of Henry actually beleaguered the city walls. Meanwhile the poet, with untimely confidence, threatened his enemies with the direst penalties. He thus sealed his own fate, for

A mirage.

---

[1] Though the coincidence is probably accidental, there is a curious analogy between some verses of Rustebeuf and Dante, both imitated from Scripture :—

> "Vous qui etes parmi la voie,
> Arestés vous ; et chascuns voie
> S'il est dolor tel com la moie,
> Dist sainte Eglise."

> "O voi che per la via d' Amor passate,
> Attendete e guardate,
> S' egli è dolore alcun quanto 'l mio grave."

presently the besieging army drew off, the Emperor sickened and died, and Dante was once more abandoned to his own apparently feeble resources.

There now began over again that tedious round of involuntary travel rendered, we may believe, all the

Perpetual motion. harder by the memory of this third great disappointment. At first, indeed, he is said to have withdrawn to the monastery of Santa Croce di Fonte Avellana; but his vehement nature could not long support the monotony of the cloister. In 1313, on the death of Clement V., he wrote a burning epistle to the cardinals, firmly reproving their shortcomings, and exhorting them to a better choice; and, in 1316, he had the poor satisfaction of learning that his compatriots had been overthrown in a fearful battle at Montecatini by a noted captain of the age, Uguccione della Faggiuola. What lends immense dramatic interest to the circumstance is the probability that Dante was residing at Lucca at the time, under the protection of this very man! At Lucca also he formed a platonic acquaintance with a lady happily named, for rhyming purposes, Gentucca. Platonic, for it is absurd to suppose that Dante would have referred to the matter had the censure to which he alludes been just. The old commentators, construing too literally the self-reproaches of an exalted nature, readily admitted the grossest imputations on the poet, and, among other crudities, accused him of falling in love with a woman who had a *goître*. That afflicted but too fascinating lady is now perhaps finally abolished; and the last blot of which it remains to clear his memory is that serious charge of embezzlement. On this subject all that can be said now is that his own protestations of innocence, and the trend and tenor of his writings, may well be set in the judicial scale against the weakness of human nature and the temptations and traditions of the office.

The words which Dante puts into the mouth of his ancestor Cacciaguida, "I came from martyrdom unto *Nunc dimittis.* this peace," are applicable perhaps to the close of his own earthly life, passed at Ravenna. There, honoured by the sincere friendship of Guido Novello da Polenta, and holding possibly some high position in the college, he gave himself to the completion of his great work. The last act of his career was eminently worthy of him, being a mission to Venice on behalf of his patron, and in the cause of peace. His efforts were repulsed, and on his way home he was seized with an illness. He died at Ravenna, the 13th of September 1321, and was buried in the chapel of the Madonna, hard by the Church of St Francis. His funeral lacked no element of distinction that could reasonably have been present—"the habit of a poet and a great philosopher," a sorrowful train of doctors, and a valedictory oration pronounced by Guido da Polenta himself.

From the gloom of Dante's life in the world we pass to the refulgency of that inner life of which he has *Dante's Trilogy.* traced for us the outlines in imperishable art. The *Vita Nuova,* of which I have already spoken, is the first part of what has been excellently termed a literary and psychological trilogy.

Dante's spiritual life exhibits three phases, and each
phase is represented in his writings—more particularly, in the *Vita Nuova*, the *Convivio*, and the *Commedia*, severally.   The credit of this discovery belongs
primarily to Dionisi, but the analysis will always be
associated with the name of an illustrious critic, Karl
Witte, who not only adopted it, but, recognising its
importance, developed and systematised it in his essays,
Über Dante; Über das Missverständiss Dante's; and
Dante's Trilogie.[1] Those who espouse this doctrine
consider that Dante, in relation to his inner experience,
lived through three epochs which may be defined as
the age of peace, the age of conflict, and the age of
reconciliation.   Already in the *Vita Nuova* we hear
the ominous, but still distant, thunder of a "molta
battaglia," but, as we have seen, the story ends with
the benediction as of a calm and radiant sunset.   Possibly this touch may have been added after the *Convivio* had been abandoned unfinished, and at the
moment when the *Commedia*, typifying a complete
change of view, was assuming definite shape in his
mind.   The *Convivio* or *Convito* is the memorial of the
second or philosophising period to which Dante afterwards looked back with regret and disapproval.   His
recantation occurs in Canto xxx. of the *Purgatorio*,
where Beatrice addresses the "pious substances":—

> "Some time did I sustain him with my look ;
>   Revealing unto him my youthful eyes,
>   I led him with me turned in the right way.

---

[1] *Dante Forschungen*, vol. i. pp. 1-65, 141-182.

> As soon as ever of my second age
>   I was upon the threshold and changed life,
>   Himself from me he took and gave to others.
>
> .   .   .   .
>
> And into ways untrue he turned his steps,
>   Pursuing the false images of good,
>   That never any promises fulfil," &c.[1]

Neither here, however, nor in the *Convivio*[2] do we find evidence of an utter apostasy from the faith such as Witte does not scruple to attribute to him. Undue absorption by philosophy is probably what is meant. Boccaccio tells us that in his riper years Dante felt shame at having written the *Vita Nuova;* and it is perhaps to this shame that we owe the *Convivio.* Disgusted with the simplicity of his early work, Dante girded himself for an allegorical exposition of his poetry as more in harmony with his mature age. In other words, he quitted the lover to become the man of science, the philosopher. His method is to select certain of his lyrics and to make them serve as texts for learned dissertations on the manifold aspects of human knowledge or speculation. Originally he proposed to treat fourteen *canzoni*, but only three are actually introduced. Whether Dante projected a work on the scale that this would imply, may be doubted. It is more likely that, with the progress of the composition and the incessant flow of ideas, the need of fresh lyrical inspiration ceased to be felt.

The objective value of the *Convivio* is not large, and consists chiefly in the aid which it affords towards

The Convivio.

---

[1] Longfellow's tr.

[2] To the English reader may be commended Mr Hillard's translation (London : Kegan Paul, Trench, Trübner, & Co.)

deciphering the more difficult passages of the *Commedia*, and especially the *Paradiso*. This, however, is only another way of saying that the *Convivio* is prized as a key to the mind of Dante—that Dante is the real subject. These abstract studies interest us, if they do interest us, as forming the cartilage of the mighty intellect which puts on flesh and blood in the *Vita Nuova* and the *Commedia*, whereas the *Convivio* is the articulated skeleton, or, if you will, the nervous system laid bare to view. Dante is a schoolman, an Aristotelian. The position of Aristotle in his eyes is sufficiently indicated by such phrases as "glorious philosopher to whom Nature revealed her secrets," "master and guide of the human reason," and, in the *Commedia*, "master of those that know." His authority is rejected only when it conflicts with the doctrines of Christianity, as, for instance, in the theory of the Heavenly Intelligences.

In the introductory lyric Dante discusses the nature of nobility or gentleness, and corrects "the false judg-*What is nobility?* ment of those who hold that the source of gentleness is riches." This was a vital principle of the entire school, beginning with its founder. Guinicelli's great "epoch-making" poem, to which Dante refers, illustrates the point of view in a pregnant antithesis:—

> "The sun strikes full upon the mud all day;
>   It remains vile, nor the sun's worth is less.
> 'By race I am gentle,' the proud man doth say;
>   He is the mud, the sun is gentleness." [1]

---

[1] Rossetti's tr.

N

To concede that an "uomo da niente," be he of the Uberti of Florence or the Visconti of Milan, may be gentle by right of birth, would make nonsense of philosophy. As Dante states it with epigrammatic felicity, "it is not the race that ennobles the individuals, but the individuals the race." He accounts for the difference between souls in conformity with the opinions of Aristotle and the Peripatetics. A generative virtue, proceeding from Heaven or residing in the combined elements, passes with the human seed into the womb. There the formative virtue, supplied by the soul of the begetter, prepares the organs for the celestial virtue, and the soul becomes quick. It then receives from the Mover of the Heavens the potential intellect, which renders it capable of appropriating all the universal forms as they exist in its Producer, in a measure depending on its nearness or otherwise to the First Intelligence. The potential intellect is a gift from God, a divine ray, and identical with nobility. It is bestowed only on certain elect souls of happy constitution, which are naturally adapted for its reception.

> "For God doth grant it only to the soul
>   That in her person whole
>   He seeth stand ; so that to sundry men
>   Draws nigh the seed of bliss immaculate,
>   God-planted in the soul well situate."

Dante betrays a special pride in this definition of nobility as the "seed of bliss," since it embraces the four causes of the Aristotelian philosophy — the material cause in the words "nell' anima ben posta";

the formal in the words "ch' è seme"; the efficient in the words "messo da Dio nell' anima"; and the final in the words "di felicità."

If this be nobility, what is love? It is "the union of the soul and the thing beloved," a union sooner or *The philosophy* later inevitable. The soul, as it proceeds *of love.* from God, is simple. Its diversities arise from secondary causes, or from the matter into which it descends; but as the human soul is the noblest of begotten forms, it receives more of the divine nature than any other. And since its being depends on God and it is preserved by Him, it naturally desires to be united to God, in order to strengthen its own existence. As in the good qualities of Nature reason shows itself divine, it follows that the human soul unites itself with them the sooner and more thoroughly the more perfect they appear; and this appearing takes place according as the soul's cognition is clear or impeded. The union of his soul with the gentle lady Philosophy is the love to which Dante alludes in his ode "O Love that in the mind," &c. Some passages of this poem are so warm as to suggest that it was originally indited with a quite different intention, —that it was only by an afterthought that the gentle lady to whom he gave himself after the death of Beatrice was identified with Philosophy. And this becomes more probable when we consider that Dante had a fourfold system of interpretation—the literal, the allegorical, the moral, and the anagogic,—the last, which is "above sense," having reference to those spiritual things which are spiritually discerned. It is, however, only right to point out that such a view somewhat contradicts Dante's explicit and repeated declarations that virtue, not passion, was the "moving cause," the inspiration of his poetry.

Among the distinctions with which this work abounds is one that relates to his verse as such. In the *tornata* of the first poem—Dante uses the term for convenience, though, as he says, he seldom conformed to the practice out of which it arose—occurs the following apostrophe:—

Distinctions.

> " O Song, I think they will be few and rare,
>   Those whom thy argument will not appal,
>   So hard and difficult thou speakest it ;
>   Therefore if peradventure it befall
>   That thou before some persons needs must fare,
>   Who unto thee may seem not shrewd of wit ;
>   Then pray I thee, do not all comfort quit,
>   Saying unto them, O mine own story dear,
>   ' Mark ye at least how beauteous I appear.' "

By way of comment on this portion of the ode, and especially the concluding line, Dante affirms that a poem has, or should have, two qualities—*bontà* and *bellezza*. *Bontà* has to do with the sentiment; *bellezza* with the embellishment of the words. In this case the *bontà* will be hard to reach ; only a few will succeed in grasping it, but there will still remain an element of pleasure more or less attainable by all, consisting in the grammatical construction, the rhetorical order, the music of the rhythm, which things constitute the *bellezza* of the verse. Thus Dante, though he deems the *bontà* the most delightsome, is unwilling to send any class of readers empty away.

The *Convivio*, or *Convito*,[1] is an intellectual feast of which the poems are the meat, and the comments *Dante's audience.* the bread—the *barley-bread*. Dante wishes to be liberal of his good things; so he addresses himself, not to the literati, whom he charges with covetousness, but to princes, barons, knights, and other noble folk, both men and women, unskilled in Latin. From certain allusions, the book seems to have been written in 1308 or 1309, and the initial section contains a pathetic and very eloquent passage alluding to his own exile.

Dante was the first of Italians to discourse philosophy in the vernacular; and, while admitting its *The question of language.* imperfections face to face with Latin, he stoutly champions his mother tongue against the pretensions of Provençal or any other *volgare*. Besides a spirited defence of the language in the *Convivio*, Dante devoted to the topic a separate treatise in Latin. The title of the work — sometimes, but wrongly, given as *De Vulgari Eloquio*—was *De Vulgari Eloquentia*. That *Eloquentia*, not *Eloquio*, is right is proved by the occurrence of the former in the treatise itself, as well as in the *Convivio*, where it is promised. The importance of the point depends on the meaning we

---

[1] The question of the title is of little importance. Most modern writers prefer *Convito*. The name occurs eight times in the work itself, and in all these cases twenty-four MSS., including the oldest and most authoritative, read *Convivio*.

attach to these expressions. Are they synonymous?
At first, we should probably answer, No! We should
understand by *eloquentia* a distinguished sort of
speech, what Dante calls in this very discourse
"illustrious vulgar," while *eloquium* might be employed to describe speech in general. But it is not
at all certain that Dante did not use *eloquentia* also in
this latter sense. It is evident that Pietro Alighieri,
in his *Commentarium*, did. In any case, the scope of
the work seems to require such a construction, since
the treatise deals, not only with the "illustrious
vulgar," but with vernacular speech under all its
aspects.

The *De Vulgari Eloquentia* [1] consists of two parts,
of which the first is concerned with philology, the
second with various forms of verse. It is
Preliminaries. noteworthy as the earliest attempt in
modern times to treat these subjects scientifically,
and, further, as having been composed by the greatest
poet of the age. But, with all its merits, it is a
fine instance of the inefficiency of the scholastic or
a priori method of conducting inquiry. The treatise opens with a distinction between vernacular and
grammatical speech, and, in contradiction to the *Convivio* which regards Latin as the nobler, assigns the
preference to the vernacular. A good deal of space is
then taken up with such puerilities (as we should
deem them) as the question what language was spoken
by Adam, and whether he acquired the faculty of

[1] This treatise has been Englished by A. E. F. Howell (Kegan Paul,
Trench, Trübner, & Co.   London : 1890).

speech within or without the Garden of Eden. Next it deals with the building of the tower in Sennaar, the confusion of tongues, and the dispersion of the human race. Thus by slow degrees it arrives at the topic of the Romance languages, which are distinguished by their symbols of affirmation into three groups, those of *oc*, *oil*, and *si*. With this, however, is adopted the more obvious geographical division, Spain, France, and Italy, including in Spain Provence, and excluding apparently Castille. For all three languages a common origin is recognised, and priority is claimed for none of them, except inasmuch as the "founders of grammatical speech," whoever they may have been, selected *sic* for the purpose of affirmation. Here may be noted a change in the terminology. In the *Convivio* "Latin" is opposed to "vernacular," and Dante is careful to point out that the sovereign language takes no account of particular vernaculars, such as German, French, &c. They are all, and simply, *volgare*. In the *De Vulgari Eloquentia*, on the other hand, the terms "Latium" and "Latinus" are appropriated to Italy, though in one place, to avoid mistake, Dante inserts the qualifying epithet. Grammatical speech is "quædam inalterabilis locutionis identitas diversis temporibus atque locis" — a kind of superior Volapük, in fact.

Coming to the Italian language, Dante passes in review fourteen of the principal dialects, though he *The Italian* intimates that, were all the local varieties *dialects.* and sub-varieties to be included, they would amount to more than a thousand. The worst dialect,

he says, is that of the Romans, which is not a vernacular so much as a wretched *patois* of all the Italian
vernaculars. Dante says nothing of the characteristic
Roman drawl; but, tested by any good standard, Rom-
anesco is no doubt a speech of solecisms. This fact
will be appreciated in the light of a specimen taken
from a burlesque poem entitled *Meo Patacca*. This
was the name of a bravo who was going to the relief
of Vienna at the time of the siege by the Turks, but
vented his fury on the poor Jews of Rome instead.

> " Era quell' ora ch' i Pizzicaroli
>   Con le partiche aggiustano le tenne
>   Innanzi alle lor mostre, e i Fruttaroli,
>   E ognun che robba magnaticcia venne ;
>   Perche pè fa servizio a i Nevaroli,
>   El caldo insupportabile se renne,
>   E allora il Sol, se non ci son ripari,
>   Scalla le robbe, e scotta i bottegari."

However, the other dialects were not too good. Hitherto Sicilian had stood on a different footing from the
rest, owing to the literary prowess of those "illustrious.
heroes," the Emperor Frederick and his son Manfred;
but the Sicilian thus praised was not the Sicilian of
the ordinary inhabitants, of which Dante gives us a
sample in the line—

> "Traggemi d' este focora se t' este a bolontate."

Similarly, the people of Parma say *monto* for *molto*.
But, besides these local dialects, there is a Latin, a
common Italian language, which is "vulgar" in relation to grammatical Latin, but, compared with the

dialects, "illustrious, cardinal, aulic, and courtly."
These adjectives might lead us to suppose that there
was spoken in the peninsular courts a purer form of
Italian than elsewhere. It is clear, however, from the
context that the words are used largely in a figurative
sense, just as we speak of the Queen's English. Those
who actually determined the fashion of classical Italian
were not everyday courtiers, courtiers by profession,
but poets and scholars like Dante himself and those his
contemporaries cited in the following section. It is
rather extraordinary that, in treating of the dialects,
Dante shows no favour to the Florentine, although it is
certain that it approached much nearer to the "illustrious vulgar" than any of the rest.

As regards the second, or metrical, portion, I have
already made some allusion to it in the preceding
chapter. The treatise is certainly hard reading, though
I do not know that I am prepared to accept Gaspary's
criticism, that it was practically useless for purposes of
illumination. As an "art poetical" it is, even within
its existing limits, neither accurate nor complete, and
at the point where it breaks off the sonnet and the
ballata still remain to be treated. But some of the
later chapters are invaluable, and, regarded as a whole,
it is the most precious treatise on the formal side of
poetry since Aristotle.

The circumstance that the *De Vulgari Eloquentia*
is in Latin proves that it was designed for learned
The De   readers. The same remark applies to an-
Monarchia.   other treatise, the *De Monarchia*. The date
and intention of the latter work has been much de-

bated. Gaspary is of opinion that it was produced in the last years of Dante's life, and the words "sicut in Paradiso Comediæ jam dixi," which appear in the majority of the MSS., support this view. On the other hand, Boccaccio affirms that the book was written at the time of the Emperor Henry's visitation, when the subject was engaging all minds, and the interest felt in it was wrought up by practical events to fever-pitch. The question, however, is extremely complicated, and the *pros* and *cons* as stated by Dr Scartazzini [1] are so evenly balanced that it is next to impossible to arrive at a definite conclusion. On the face of it probability inclines to Boccaccio's conjecture. I say "conjecture," but it may of course be that Boccaccio possessed positive information. The value of Boccaccio's testimony is always an unknown quantity.

Leaving this point undecided, the *De Monarchia* is a contribution to the burning controversy of the *High policy.* age regarding the limits and the mutual relations of civil and spiritual authority. St Thomas Aquinas had dealt with the theme in his day, and had found, as was natural in a churchman, for the Pope. Moreover, two contemporaries of Dante—John of Paris in his *De Potestate Regia et Papali*, and Engelbert of Admont in his *De Ortu et Fine Romani Imperii*—had embarked on the same topic; but, apart from any consideration of authorship, neither of these writings has a tithe of the interest attaching to the *De Monarchia.* Nor

[1] *Dantologia*, p. 289 *et seqq.*

is this due wholly and solely to the greater profundity of the latter, its wider scope, its more vigorous handling. The antagonism between pope and prince was general, but in Italy the friction attained to white heat. In the small autonomous republics of the peninsula the question of papal or imperial supremacy had a vital effect on the fortunes of individuals and families, forming as it did the dividing line between the two great parties, the Guelfs and the Ghibellines. So far as the protagonists—those mighty spirits who in bygone days had sought to bring the question to an issue—were concerned, the quarrel had already spent itself. Henry and Hildebrand, Adrian and Alexander, Frederick Redbeard and Frederick of Sicily, the two Innocents and Gregory IX., had been succeeded by the weak Henry and the unworthy Boniface. But the hatred and bitterness remained, and the condition of Italy at this time might be fairly set forth as one of " wounds, and bruises, and putrefying sores."

The vehemence of the Italians is easily understood. Italy was not a nation—it was only a geographical *The shade of* expression; and yet common descent, com-*Cæsar.* mon speech, common traditions, impelled the people to seek some rallying-point, some palladium, which, while gratifying their pride, might be useful also in preserving their liberties, and procuring for them protection. The idea of the Roman Empire, in however shadowy a form, had never ceased to operate, and from the time of Charlemagne had been linked with the Emperors of Germany, who claimed to inherit the sceptre of the Cæsars. On the other hand, the Pope, with his seat at Rome, and exercising by virtue of his office universal jurisdiction, might be regarded as standing for the present against the dead past.   The Italian nobility naturally bent to the central figure of feudalism, while the free burghers were staunch adherents of the Papacy.   In the hour of need the latter could count also on the effective support of France.

In the *De Monarchia*[1] Dante probes the whole question to its bottom.   By "monarchy" he under-
Compromise. stands single and supreme dominion, and by "temporal monarchy" imperial as distinct from ecclesiastical rule.   He then proceeds to state the principal divisions of the inquiry, which are as follows: First, whether monarchy is needful for the wellbeing of the world.   Secondly, whether the Roman people has rightfully taken upon itself the office of monarchy.   And, thirdly, whether the authority of monarchy depends immediately on God, or on some minister or vicar of God.   These points are discussed in as many books, in which scholastic deductions are buttressed by quotations from Scripture and the Church Fathers.   Dante's general conclusions may be inferred from the following sentences: "Wherefore man had need of twofold guidance answering to the twofold end—namely, the Supreme Pontiff, who, according to Revelation, should conduct the human race to the life eternal; and the Emperor, who, according to the teachings of philosophy, should guide the human race to temporal happiness. . . . Which

[1] Translated by F. J. Church (London: Macmillan).

truth, indeed, as regards the last question, is not to be received so strictly, but that the Roman Prince is subject in some degree to the Roman Pontiff, since mortal happiness is ordained in a certain sense to happiness immortal. Therefore let Cæsar observe towards Peter that reverence which the first-born son ought to observe towards a father, so that, illumined by the light of paternal favour, he may irradiate with the greater efficacy the world over which he has been set by Him alone who is governor of all things both spiritual and temporal."

Closely connected with the *De Monarchia* are certain Latin epistles. According to Boccaccio there existed in his time a quantity of such epistles, and *The Letters.* it is much to be deplored that he was not at the pains of transcribing them instead of filling his sheets with vaguely eloquent periods that rather tantalise than satisfy. It is somewhat singular that during the present century the tale of letters has fluctuated considerably. Witte in 1827 knew of six, and previously there were only four. In 1842 the number had risen to fourteen, but at least eight of this total were afterwards demonstrated to be forgeries. To-day Signor Casini is ready to admit the authenticity of the following epistles: (i) that to the princes and peoples of Italy on the descent of Henry VII., between September 1310 and January 1311; (ii) that to the Emperor Henry, April 16, 1311; (iii) that to the Florentines, May 31, 1311; (iv) that to the Italian cardinals, 1314; (v) that to a friend at Florence, 1316; and perhaps (vi), that to Can Grande della Scala (very

important, if genuine), describing the aim and fundamental ideas of the *Commedia*.

Dr Scartazzini, however, is sceptical. Villani mentions by name "three noble epistles"—one to the
Government of Florence, another to the Emperor
Henry, and a third to the Italian cardinals—as having been written by Dante; and, while treating with
scant consideration some of the fourteen pretenders,
Scartazzini would fain allow the genuineness of the
epistles purporting to be those mentioned by Villani,
but cannot reconcile it with his conscience to say, with
Poletto, that they are beyond all controversy "fattura
di Dante." As Renier had before pointed out, Villani's
words might have inspired in some humanist the whim
of composing scholastic exercises befitting the circumstances. For my own part, I have failed to discover
any trustworthy criterion, though the character of the
MSS. is by no means reassuring.

The authenticity of the Latin eclogues has also been
called in question, but with immeasurably less reason,
Dante's eclogues. and except by critics like Prompt, ready to
doubt anything and everything, the verses
are usually received as genuine. In the spring of
1319, when Dante was at Ravenna, he was invited by
a learned professor, Giovanni di Virgilio, to visit
Bologna, and reproached in a Latin "carmen" for
casting pearls before swine, *i.e.*, writing poetry in the
vernacular. Dante replied in an eclogue—curiously
enough, the first since the days of Virgil—in which
he styled himself Tityrus, Giovanni Mopsus, and a
certain Dino Pierini, with whom he was staying,

Meliboeus. The invitation was declined on political grounds, Bologna being anti-imperial. The professor, however, very insistent, repeated the invitation in an eclogue promising Dante, among other delights, an opportunity of meeting the poet and historian, Albertino Mussato. Even this prospect failed to move Dante, and, in a second eclogue, he again courteously refused the offer. Apparently there was a lion in the path. " Quis Polyphemon, ait, non horreat ? " Romeo dei Pepoli, or King Robert of Naples, or one of the Caccianimici (*Inferno*, xviii. 48) may have been Polyphemus.

It is hardly worth while to dally with the *Seven Psalms*, the *Profession of Faith*, and the rest of the apocrypha; but it is well to state that the *Quæstio de duobus Elementis*, received by Gaspary as authentic, is almost demonstrably the fabrication of a later age. On this point the arguments of Dr Scartazzini are practically conclusive; but recently the matter has been taken up afresh by Mr Paget Toynbee in the columns of *Literature*, and with the same result.

We come at last to Dante's greatest work—the *Commedia*. The topic is so vast that it is impossible to do justice to it in any number of pages that might be set aside for the purpose in the present volume; but I will attempt to deal with, at least, the essentials. And first let me try to correlate the *Commedia* with other works of Dante already described. In the sixteenth canto of the *Purgatorio* are plainly audible echoes both of the *Convivio* and the *De Monarchia*, and of those

The Comedy.

passages in the treatises to which I have directed
particular attention :—

> " Forth from the hand of Him who fondles it
>   Before it is, like to a little girl
>   Weeping and laughing in her childish sport,
> Issues the simple soul, that nothing knows,
>   Save that, proceeding from a joyous Maker,
>   Gladly it turns to that which gave it pleasure.
> Of trivial good at first it tastes the savour ;
>   Is cheated by it, and runs after it,
>   If guide or rein turns not aside its love.
>
> . . . .
>
> Rome that reformed the world accustomed was
>   Two suns to have, which one road and the other,
>   Of God and of the world, made manifest.
> One has the other quenched, and to the crosier
>   The sword is joined, and ill beseemeth it
>   That by main force one with the other go." [1]

Lines like these are more than chance reminiscences
of past studies. The ideas therein expressed are the
informing principles, the invisible structure which lies
behind the outer adornment. The *Commedia* is, in
truth, " fearfully and wonderfully made," and it is not
surprising that partial and, so far, inaccurate views
have obtained as to its scope and meaning. But it
has always been recognised, even by those who have
themselves failed to penetrate beyond the "literal
sense," that it is inspired by a profound purpose, and
is something more than a sequence of boldly drawn or
softly shaded pictures,—that it has *bontà* as well as
bellezza. It is an illustration on a gigantic scale of
fourfold senses, literal, allegorical, moral, and anagogic.

[1] Longfellow's tr.

The force of the last adjective, "that which leads up to God," is easily seen in the light of the *Commedia*.

Quadruplicity. Ere it concludes, the great poem conducts us to the very throne of the Eternal; and it typifies, in its several stages, the steps by which the soul, on departing from sin, becomes holy and free. The *Commedia* is distinctly, and before all, an edifying work. It has also a moral aim. It aspires to render men, not only saints, but good neighbours and worthy citizens. Thus it may be regarded as a didactic treatise, a long *ammaestramento*, a Whole Duty of Man. Thirdly, it is a study of the human soul, its virtues and its vices, its powers and its defects, and, in obedience to the fashion of the day, Dante translates his ideas into object-lessons, concrete examples, embodied truths, overt signs, and pregnant hints, woven harmoniously into a simple vast plan. This is the allegory, the symbolism of the Divine Comedy, the nice decipherment of which has proved a fountain of strife to generations of subtle and ingenious, bellicose and opinionated commentators.[1] Lastly, there is the literal sense, which any one can see is the destiny of man hereafter.

Looked at from another point of view, the subject of the poem is Dante himself—Dante the exile, of *The personal whom Florence was unworthy, and who, element.* amidst his woes and wanderings, continually asks himself, What am I? Whence?

[1] Biagioli is perhaps the worst. He calls Venturi "sozzo can vituperato," while Zani de' Ferranti calls *him* "quel grammatico inurbano."

Whither? Bereft first of his mistress, then of his city, to which he was attached almost or quite as passionately, he had lost as it were his significance. He was alone. In such circumstances the realm of imagination, to which he had always more than half belonged, became paramount, absorbing. But henceforth imagination was for Dante a consecrated thing; it was *vision*. The busy scenes around, Florence, Italy, the world, all took their colour, and derived their meaning, from the contemplation of the eternal truths of which the *Commedia* was to be the storehouse. To adopt a phrase of Spinoza, Dante beheld things "sub specie æternitatis."

But Dante believed in an eternal world topically as well as tropically. Once by the bier of Beatrice he had entered within the veil; and now when all earthly occupations, all secular interests, had in a sense dropped away from him, the future, the great future wherein the loose threads of time and space—the sundered ties, the temporal losses, the inexplicable failures, the injustice, the ingratitude, the pain — would be ravelled up into luminous consistency, stared him perpetually in the face. Boccaccio tells us that when some women of Verona saw Dante pass, one of them observed, "See you the man that goes to Hell, and returns when he lists, and brings up news of those below?" "Forsooth," replied a gossip, "you must speak truth. Don't you see what a crisp beard and what brown hair he has, through the heat and smoke down there?" The story is not all a parable.

Dante's motives, then, were certainly personal, and

they were mainly two—love of Beatrice and all that
Nebulæ. Beatrice connoted, and that sense of justice
which in his passage through life had
suffered so many rude shocks and contradictions.
This, however, does not preclude the possibility that
others may have been possessed by these or similar
feelings in an inferior degree. The seclusion of the
cloister provided just that aloofness from the world,
just those opportunities for reflection, that Dante was
afforded in his bitter exile. Certain it is that the
state of men's souls after death had occupied the
attention of numerous writers before Dante, and not
only of speculative theologians but of poets. Some
critics, attaching too much importance to the fable,
have looked for the germ of the *Commedia* in one or
other of the productions of the mediæval eschatologists.
The true germ was beyond question those impalpable
reveries, those liquid visions of the *Vita Nuova.* But
it cannot be denied that the *Commedia* differs from
these in its solidity, in its abundance of " hard fact."
In other words, the poem has a history independent of
the poet.

During the Middle Age, certain Irish compositions
—Irish by virtue of their birthplace, but written in
Antecedents. Latin—had achieved considerable vogue.
Such were the *Purgatory of St Patrick,* the
Voyage of St Brandan, and the *Vision of Tundale.*
Both Herr Gaspary and Signor Pio Rajna have been
much impressed with the resemblance of the *Vision* to
the *Commedia*, and the Italian critic is convinced that
Dante had read the work either in Latin or the ver-

nacular. Of course, if we do as Rajna does, if we set
down an analysis of the *Vision* and forget for the
moment all possible alternatives — the *Æneid,* the
Tesoretto, &c.— the similarity is very striking, and
almost drives us to think that Dante was at least on
bowing terms with the dream of Tundale. But we
must not lose sight of the fact that the Middle Age
was simply saturated with the thought of a future
state—that in describing Hell, Purgatory, and Paradise, Dante was dealing with a theme the most
widely popular he could possibly have lighted on.

Writing on the Divine ·Comedy before Dante,[1]
Labitte reminds us that Dante visited France, and he
points out that the churches and cathedrals
A caution. of that country teem with sculptures and
paintings, some of them old enough to have caught
the eye of the great poet himself. The remains of a
wall-painting in the crypt of the Auxerre cathedral
show the triumph of Christ exactly as Dante has
depicted it in the *Purgatorio.* The Mystic Rose might
have come from the church of Chartres, while the
gates of manifold churches, including that of Our Lady
of Paris, were brimful of suggestions for a writer pro-
posing to treat the penalties of Hell. It is needless
to discuss whether Dante actually availed himself
of such hints, but the fact that they *were* available
should put us on our guard against too ready an
acceptance of any particular theory concerning special
obligations.

I shall not pursue the subject further more than to

[1] *Revue des Deux Mondes*, iv. Série, 1842.

point out that these borrowings, real or imaginary, do
Originality. not affect in any true sense the question
of Dante's originality. The charge of
plagiarism is one with which mediocrity or absolute
total insignificance revenges itself on genius. As your
groundling conceives the matter, almost all literature
is plagiarism. *Julius Cæsar* is stolen, and no acknowledgment neither, from Plutarch. Chaucer and
Boccaccio are worse " rievers " than any Hielandman;
and Tennyson, in a modified way, is hardly better. It
is the same with music. Mendelssohn and Gounod
have seized on other men's themes, therefore let their
names be clean put out. Meanwhile the great reputations, like so many impregnable Gibraltars, remain
unimpaired; and the stickler for literary morality is
left to ruminate Molière's delicious retort, " Je prends
mon bien où je le trouve."

Signor Alessandro D'Ancona has some excellent
remarks on this topic,[1] the burden of them being that
Dante brought order out of chaos and thus established
an indefeasible right to what before had belonged to
anybody or nobody. Yes; that is it. The old monks
possessed the same materials, and they had tried to
create out of the formless mass an intellectual world.
But they lacked something—something essential; the
power that could mould and shape, that could
dominate and inspire, that could make dry bones
live. In a word, they lacked *originality.*

The great characteristic of Dante's genius is its
plasticity. It converted what was rough and unhewn

[1] See *I Precursori di Dante* (Florence, 1874).

into perfect symmetry, and rendered it clear, definite,

A new creation. intelligible. It sounds an odd assertion, but this result was due, in no small measure, to his partiality, or—we may say—his superstitious regard, for the number three and its multiples, of which there are already traces in the *Vita Nuova*. The schoolmen had divided the world to come into two main partitions—Heaven and Hell. The whole of Hell was situate underground, and comprised Hell proper, the abode of lost angels and spirits of the damned; Purgatory, the sojourn of penitent sinners; the Limbo of unbaptised infants; and the Limbo of the Fathers, known also as "Abraham's Bosom," and inhabited by just men dead before Christ's coming. Heaven consisted of the visible sky or firmament; the Spiritual Heaven, the home of saints and blessed angels; and the Intellectual Heaven, scene of the Beatific Vision. Dante changes all that. Hell, to be sure, he places underground, where it stretches from the surface of the earth to the centre. But Purgatory is a mountain at the antipodes, a distinct place altogether. Signors Vaccheri and Bertacchi deny this, identifying the Hill of Difficulty at the outset of the poem with the Mount of Purgatory, and making the avenues of the two spheres of punishment contiguous.[1] The suggestion, however, does not appear very plausible. If Dante really began his itinerary at a point in the opposite hemisphere, it is strangely unlike him not to record the circumstance fully and plainly. He

[1] *La Visione di Dante Allighieri considerata nello spazio e nel tempo.* Turin, 1881.

would certainly, I think, have written some prefatory lines explaining and defending his presence at the ends of the earth. But this he has not done. Finally, Dante's Heaven is an adaptation to spiritual purposes of the Ptolemaic system. The earth is the centre of nine heavens, those of the Moon, Mercury, Venus, the Sun, Mars, Jupiter, the Fixed Stars, the "Primum Mobile," and, enveloping all, the motionless Empyrean, which seems to have been without sun or star save God Himself.

The three topographical divisions naturally suggested the three divisions of the poem. The two *Symbolism.* opening cantos, reckoned for convenience part of the *Inferno,* are in a way common to all three *cantiche.* I leave out of account the idea that the Mount Delectable is the Mount of Purgatory as too improbable, but the conjunction of Virgil and Beatrice is significant. They are to be Dante's guides, Virgil through Hell and Purgatory, and Beatrice through Paradise. This early mention of Beatrice is of importance as showing that Dante had returned to the spirit and temper of the *Vita Nuova.* But the Beatrice of the *Vita Nuova* is not absolutely the Beatrice of the *Commedia.* She figures in the later and greater work as a gracious personality, and, literally, as an angel; but the influence of the *Convivio,* of that middle period of reflection, continues to be felt, and Dante is no longer satisfied with Beatrice as a fair and virtuous lady. Without forfeiting any of her natural charms she has become to him an emblem, but the emblem of what he now deems the most precious thing in the world—Theology.   And so we come to that thorniest of topics, Dante's symbolism.

Allegory is everywhere in the *Commedia*.   It is, if I may return to an old metaphor, the nervous system *Dante and Tennyson.* of the poem.   But just as the nervous system has certain ganglia, certain centres, so also in the *Commedia* are certain passages, the comprehension of which is vital to the understanding of the whole.   The opening cantos of the *Inferno* and the concluding cantos of the *Purgatorio* are of this order.   In the latter case the symbolism is so elaborate that I cannot attempt to deal with it here.   In the general exordium, on the other hand, the mechanism is comparatively simple, and may therefore well serve as a pattern.   The poet feigns that midway in the journey of life he found himself in a dark forest, and this wild forest lay in a valley.   The place was very horrible, insomuch that Dante can scarce bear the remembrance of it.   As little can he state how he entered it, for he was oppressed with sleep at the time. This is Dante's way of describing human birth.   Let us not forget those key-lines :—

> " Forth from the hand of Him who fondles it
>   Before it is, like to a little girl
>   Weeping and laughing in her childish sport,
> Issues the simple soul, that nothing knows," &c.

Or, as Tennyson puts it, vocatively:—

> " O dear Spirit half lost
> In thine own shadow and this fleshly sign
> That thou art thou—who wailest being born
> And banished into mystery, and the pain
> Of this divisible-indivisible world," &c.

This "divisible-indivisible world" is the forest of the *Commedia,* which expresses in concrete terms what *"Read Ezekiel!"* the great English poet in his later years essayed to define in philosophic language — the bewildering incoherence of this perpetually changing congeries of atoms, the coexistence in the same object of identity and difference, baffling the human intellect. But where Tennyson speaks of a shore, Dante uses the figure of a valley. This image is quite in keeping with the terminology of the *Convivio,* where a "substantial form" is said to *descend* into matter. There can be little doubt, however, that the valley of this first canto is Ezekiel's Valley of Dry Bones. If any one will examine the thirty-seventh chapter of the sacred book, he will speedily recognise the point of the comparison. The orthodox anagogic interpretation of the prophecy is that the Valley of Dry Bones represents the world of unredeemed and unregenerate humanity. Without impugning this view, which indeed is essential to the completeness of the analogy, it is clear that the prophecy had a simpler, more immediate application—an application that concerned the political condition of the Jewish nation divided into the rival kingdoms of Judah and Israel, and doomed to captivity among the heathen. A brighter prospect, however, is in store for the hapless race. "And I will make them one nation in the land upon the mountains of Israel; and one king shall be king to them all: and they shall be no more two nations, neither shall they be divided into two kingdoms any more at all. . . . And David my servant shall be king over them; and they all shall have one shepherd." It is hardly needful to insist how well all this suits with the state of contemporary Italy, the land of Guelfs and Ghibellines, specially as viewed by one with Dante's imperialist longings. There are numerous passages in the *Commedia* proving how ill-founded he deemed the papal claim to temporal dominion, and how injurious in its effects. And we have already seen that, according to Dante's philosophy, the welfare of humanity depended on unity of rule, Peter being supreme in his sphere, and Cæsar in his.

> " Midway upon the journey of our life
> I *found* myself within a forest dark."

The word " found " is important. It indicates Dante's awakening to the consciousness of his real predicament. Though he knew it not, he had been in the dark forest all his life until the year 1300, which is approximately the date of the commencement of the poem, and ostensibly of its entire action. The great work, however, occupied him many years. Very likely, as Scartazzini suggests, it was composed at a variety of times and places. When at length it was approaching completion, the whole of the events connected with Henry of Luxemburg's ill-fated expedition belonged to the past. But Dante still adhered to the pretended date of his mysterious travel, and, indeed, takes advantage of it to assume the language of prophecy. His David is the unlucky German prince, whom he rewards with a heavenly throne, but with regard to whom, in his purely earthly *rôle*, he is compelled by dire necessity to forgo the sanguine and confident tone of the prophet of old.

In seeking to escape from the dismal valley, Dante comes to a hill up which he endeavours to climb. But *The three beasts.* the hill is steep, and each time his efforts are frustrated by the appearance of a wild beast—first, a leopard; then, a lion; and, finally, a wolf. The hill, what does it typify? Not true happiness, probably. For that we must wait till the end of the next *cantica* and the glorious vision of the Earthly Paradise. The Mount Delectable of the proem symbolises, I believe, rather than happiness itself, the mirage of happiness, the delusive pleasures of mere worldly prosperity to which moral goodness contributes not a jot. Observe, the moral and anagogic senses are here inextricably entwined. Dante is not only a representative man; he is also a representative Italian, and these symbols possess a political as well as a spiritual meaning. Indeed, the political application is, of the two, the more obvious and distinct. The leopard is the Florentine democracy; the lion, the royal house of France; and the wolf, the Papacy. But the emblems have a wider significance. They were borrowed in the first instance—so, at least, it would appear—from Jeremiah v. 6: "Wherefore a lion out of the forest shall slay them, and a wolf of the evenings shall spoil them, a leopard shall watch over their cities, every one that goeth out thence shall be torn in pieces." In these words we seem to have clearly expressed the right interpretation of the signs. The lion is Violence; the wolf, Avarice; and the

leopard, Treachery. The two interpretations are perfectly consistent, one being involved in the other.
Scartazzini's notion that the beasts symbolise the lust
of the flesh, the lust of the eye, and the pride of life
appears to rest on what I believe to be a total misconception of the passage. That the Mount Delectable
typifies worldly prosperity, not true happiness, seems
proved by the key-lines already quoted :—

> " Of trivial good at first it [the soul] tastes the savour ;
>   Is cheated by it, and runs after it,
>   If guide or rein turns not aside its love."

And now, at the moment when Dante, recoiling before
those terrible beasts, sinks back into the no less terrible
forest, a guide shows himself. The hapless poet descries a shadowy form, and though unresolved whether
he beholds a man or a shade, accosts it. It is Virgil.
By an extremely poetical touch the laureate of the
Cæsars is depicted as hoarse through long silence.
This, of one dead a thousand years, is a very felicitous
thought ; but, of course, Dante means more than
that. He alludes to the neglect of those lofty studies
of which Virgil was once and now Dante himself
is a chosen vessel. The "accomplishment of verse"
is not, for his Florentine admirer, Virgil's supreme
claim to reverence. Outwardly a poet, he is inwardly
a moral philosopher, a prophet, and—mark it well !—
the grandest representative hitherto of the imperial
idea. Virgil, however, is not in those savage glades
by accident. Unknown to Dante, a little drama has
been enacting in Heaven, and all on his account.

Blessed women, transformed into ministering angels, have discovered his woeful plight and borne the news to Beatrice, who hastened to Virgil, where he abode "lord of the song pre-eminent" among those in suspense (*i.e.*, in Limbo), and tearfully besought his aid. The story has so much real pathos that it seems like sacrilege to rob it of its simplicity, its tender human interest. Yet it is certain that the poet designed it for a parable, and Gaspary has admirably observed that just as the Vision of God was the guerdon and goal of Dante's weird pilgrimage, so a ray of light divine, typified by Beatrice, was necessary to kindle his zeal and prompt his fainting courage. Reason, philosophy, would not suffice for this, though, once the task was attempted, it would guide him a certain distance along the way. That way lay through the endless horrors of Hell and the stern but salutary discipline of Purgatory, which Dante, in the vesture of the flesh, was to behold unscathed, for his edification and enlightenment.

In defining the precise shape of the prison-house of the lost, authorities employ different terms. Fenini

The great jail. likens it to an inverted cone, Gaspary to a funnel, while Leigh Hunt describes it as a "funnel graduated in circles." "Funnel" is a good word, but we must take care that we do not misunderstand what is intended. It is, perhaps, natural to think of the funnel of an English steam-engine, but that is not the idea at all. The funnel proper is a hollow conical vessel with a slender pipe issuing from its vertex, and used for conveying liquids into receptacles with a small aperture. The origin of Hell, in Dante's cosmogony, is the fall of Lucifer, whose huge person, piercing the crust of our planet, hurtled to its centre, where it remained rigid—the pipe of the subterranean funnel. The various circles, degrees, or compartments of Hell, thus conceived, are assigned to different categories of sinners.

The head of the "fell worm" is directly under Jerusalem, while his legs point in the direction of *The Mount of Purgatory.* the Mount of Purgatory, which last is an island in the South Pacific. Communication between the vertex of the abyss and the base of Purgatory proceeds, at least on this occasion, by means of a natural tunnel—a rough, uneven path, and scant of light—and then, a thousand times welcome after the murkiness of Hell, bursts on the weary travellers the cloudless sapphire of the sky, the rippling laughter of old Ocean. But the scenes of misery are not yet at an end. The Mount of Purgatory is, in many respects, a milder analogue of Hell, and, indeed, owes its existtence to the convulsion, the seismic disturbance caused by the descent of Lucifer. The soil displaced by this impact was pushed out on the opposite side of the world and formed an excrescence on the earth's surface. Just as Dante's Hell is a model of engineering, so his Purgatory will exact some praise from your architect. Rising tier above tier, in a series of circular ledges or cornices, it resembles a Roman amphitheatre turned inside out and upside down. On these ledges or cliffs successive orders of penitents realise in drastic fashion the heinousness of their besetting sins, and so work out their salvation. At the summit is the Earthly Paradise, on the portrayal of which Dante lavishes all his poetical resources ; and the advent of Beatrice, which here takes place and is ushered in by mysterious tokens, resolves itself into an apocalyptic vision, entirely precluding familiarity, or even courtesy, on the part of her earthly lover.

As a political pamphlet the *Commedia* is dead. For us moderns the notion of a universal Empire directed by a German is utterly vapid, and has been succeeded in the minds of some by the dream of a Parliament of Man, a Federation of the World. Again, the Union of Christendom must needs be postponed, partly through the fissiparous tendencies of Protestantism, partly through the invincible prejudice which exists in all liberal and democratic countries against the secular and autocratic pretensions of the Papacy, of which Dante himself, sound Catholic as he was in matters of faith, was a resolute opponent. The interest of the *Commedia*, however, lies, not in the dim, speculative background, but in the foreground, in the action. What we care for is the drama, and among the competing accounts of the title—the happy ending, the homeliness of the style, &c.—I do not think sufficient stress has been laid on the thoroughly dramatic nature of the work. For myself, I am by no means certain that the choice of such a title as *Commedia* was not intended to suggest the grim irony, the downright absurdity, of human life. In this connection it is worthy of note that Dante employs this description only in the *Inferno*. In the *Paradiso* the

A comedy indeed.

alternative title *Poema Sacro* is used. Anyhow, the Florentine poet seems to have fairly anticipated the sentiment—"All the world's a stage, and all the men and women merely players."

Dante's Hell is not, what his predecessors had sought to render theirs, a horrible negation of this world of time and sense. Terribly as he makes them suffer, the miserable denizens are still human, nor have all ideas, inclinations, interests been roasted or frozen out of them in the infernal holocaust or lake of thick-ribbed ice. Signor Francesco de Sanctis has remarked, and it is true, that "in the kingdom of the dead is felt for the first time the life of the modern world." Dante may not do what Mr George Macdonald has dared to do — put shops in Heaven ; but he comes very near to this when he associates the happy spirit of Sigier with his old-time lectures in Straw Street. Dante's ordinary method is to stereotype the lot, whatever that may be, of the departed, while fixing in them a vivid sense of the manifold occupations of earth. It is vain for Lamartine, in his studiously depreciative criticism, to pretend that this side of the poem is dead also,—that nobody cares, at this time of day, about the Florentine nonentities that crowd the stage of the *Commedia*. These people are typical, and, being typical, can never become obsolete. To be sure, the force of the allusions cannot be felt now as it was felt by Dante's contemporaries or their immediate successors, when the memory of the persons of the drama was still fresh ; but the emotions awakened in

Human nature.

the poet of necessity extend to his readers, at any rate
to the more sympathetic of them. For Dante does
not behold these strange things with apathy, with
stoical composure. He communes with lost friends,
quarrels with vanished foes. He weeps with those
that weep, and fails not to record his own sensations
—fear, joy, or surprise—at startling turns of events.

When Dante called his poem a "comedy," he may
have known that it did not conform to the technical
A conscious requirements—the unities of time, space,
king. and action—which the ancients postulated
in dramatic compositions. Nevertheless, the *Commedia* is not without an element of unity, supplied in
Dante himself. It is his own personality, throughout
human and impressionable, that renders the poem one.
And here it should be observed that Dante is deterred
neither by false modesty nor by worldly prudence from
openly avowing his sense of his own importance.
Though he may accord to Virgil a primacy among
poets not really deserved, Dante regards himself as
belonging, not only to the same class, but to the same
coterie; and, on arriving at the Noble Castle, he takes
his place, as of right, with the first half-dozen of the
world's bards.[1] Somehow this lofty egotism gives no
offence. We are used to look for egotism in poets
—especially in minor poets—but that is not the explanation. The explanation is that Dante does himself considerably less than justice.

After all the admiration lavished on the *Commedia*

[1] The others are Homer, Horace, Ovid, Lucan, and, of course,
Virgil.

by those who have loved and studied it, it is still a
Dante's
character. question whether, outside a small circle of
Dantists, the cynical remarks of Voltaire[1]
do not continue to apply. The great world gazes, with
more or less of satisfaction, at Doré's illustrations,
and dips hesitatingly into Cary's translation, but the
Commedia, the most glorious creation of human genius,
gains no hold upon its heart. If any part of the poem is
read, it is the *Inferno*, probably as the most sensational.
But an impression prevails that, in limning his terrible
nocturnes, Dante in a way exhausted himself. This
assumption is very stupid and gratuitous, and can only
have arisen from sheer idleness or indifference. It is
the reader, not the poet, who is exhausted; and, in
giving out at this point, he carries away a somewhat
false impression of Dante's character, which he finds
grim, austere, vindictive, and sadly lacking in the
more human qualities of sweetness, tenderness, and
generosity. Even the perusal of the *Inferno*, however,
if we take into consideration the conditions imposed by
the theme, should lead us to think of Dante as something better than a mad misanthrope. The poet had
his hates—and what wonder?—but the most dispassionate survey of life could only have conducted
him to the position of Bishop Burnet. " I find," says

---

[1] "Vous voulez connaître le Dante. Des Italiens l'appellent divin:
mais c'est une divinité cachée; peu de gens entendent ses oracles; il
a des commentateurs: c'est peut-être encore une raison de plus pour
n'être pas compris. Sa réputation s'affirmira toujours parce qu'on
ne le lit guère. Il y a de lui une vingtaine de traits qu'on sait par
cœur; cela suffit pour s'épargner la peine d'examiner le reste."—
Dictionnaire philosophique.

the historian, "that the long experience of the base-
ness, the malice, and the falsehood of mankind has
inclined me to be apt to think generally the worst of
men and of parties." But Dante, while accepting the
necessity of punishment, of retributive justice, exhibits anything but a pharisaical spirit towards the
victims. Indeed, as mirrored by himself, he is at all
times much more a man than a moralist. The incomparable episode of Francesca da Rimini shows how
deeply he can be touched by human love and sorrow;
but it is not his prerogative to pardon what God and
the universal conscience agree in condemning. And
here, it should be observed, Dante's penalties are not
arbitrary. They are suggested by, evolved from, the
faults themselves. The infernal hurricane, which
drives incessantly before it the souls of Paolo and
Francesca, locked in an eternal embrace, symbolises
very well the restless agitation of their culpable love.
So, too, in the Circle of the Violent:—

> " Justice divine, upon this side is goading
>   That Attila, who was a scourge on earth,
>   And Pyrrhus and Sextus; and for ever milks
> The tears which with the boiling it unseals
>   In Rinier da Corneto and Rinier Pazzo,
>   Who made upon the highways so much war."

All these wrong-doers merely reap as they have sown.
They experience the effects of an inexorable law of
nature, and so there is no inconsistency, much less
hypocrisy, in the poet manifesting the liveliest concern
and sympathy as each time he beholds the fatal consequences of sin. For a peccable and erring creature

no course could be so proper. Dante is learning his lesson.

In entering upon the *Purgatorio* we emerge into a softer, serener atmosphere. Dante's biographer Balbo describes it as "perhaps on the whole the most beautiful" of the three great divisions of the poem. I will endeavour to indicate some of its many charms, but first let me insist that the *Purgatorio*, though the mind is no longer awed by the tears and the tragedies of a fixed and irreversible destiny, is by no means deficient in striking situations.[1]   Like its predecessor, it has what a German might call its *Hauptmomente*.   The incidents of Francesca da Rimini, Farinata, Pier delle Vigne, Brunetto Latini, Guido di Montefeltro, Ugolino, &c., are succeeded by others quite as notable, those of King Manfred, Buonconte, La Pia, Sordello, Sapia, and Arnold Daniel.

The Purgatorio.

When Balbo speaks of the beauty of the *Purgatorio*, he is thinking perhaps, most of all, of the magnificent description, continued through several cantos, of the Earthly Paradise, though there are detached passages equally graceful and imaginative.   Mr Ruskin has dilated on the radiancy of Dante's angels, and the topic is worthy of his pen. Has it ever been noticed how thoroughly Franciscan is the poet's regard for birds, and how frequently and happily he draws upon their habits for metaphors and

Dante's aviary.

[1] Miss Norley Chester has treated some of these incidents with much delicacy in a little volume entitled *Dante Vignettes* (London, Elliot Stock).

similes? Already in the *Inferno*, in that matchless
fifth canto, there occur within a few lines of each other
apt comparisons borrowed from the tumultuous motions
of starlings in winter, and, for the nearer sinners, from
the flight of cranes. Later, in the twenty-second canto,
we meet with the more banal image of the duck and
the falcon. The *Purgatorio*, at its very commencement, contains an allusion to the story of the Pierides,
who were changed into magpies; and in the ninth
canto is an exquisite time-note:—

> "Just at the hour when her sad lay begins
>   The little swallow, near unto the morning,
>   Perchance in memory of her former woes." [1]

In the thirteenth canto the eyelids of the envious are
sewn up, like a spar-hawk's; and, in the same canto,
Sapia quotes the old legend of the blackbird which, in
Lombardy, gave to the early spring-time the name "i
giorni della merla." Just as the wings of birds may
have suggested angels, so the song of birds inevitably
reminds Dante of poesy:—

> "Whereat the branches lightly tremulous,
>   Did all of them bow downward to that side
>   Where its first shadow casts the Holy Mountain;

---

[1] As a chronological hint nothing can equal the half-dirge—imitated
by Byron and Coleridge—in the preceding canto:—

> "'Twas now the hour that turneth back desire
>   In those who sail the sea, and melts the heart,
>   The day they've said to their sweet friends farewell,
> And the new pilgrim penetrates with love,
>   If he doth hear from far away a bell
>   That seemeth to deplore the dying day."

> Yet not from their upright direction swayed,
>   So that the little birds upon their tops
>   Should leave the practice of each art of theirs;
> But with full ravishment the hours of prime,
>   Singing, received they in the midst of leaves,
>   That ever bore a burden to their rhymes."
>   —*Purg.*, xxviii. 10-18.

It is needless to multiply instances, but I cannot forbear mentioning the "eagle with the plumes of gold," and that great mystical eagle of the *Paradiso*, composed of multitudinous souls, yet endowed with one mind and with one voice—symbol of the empire of the Cæsars.

It would be agreeable, were it possible, to illustrate in the same way Dante's sense of colour. The *Com-* *media* has several allusions to painting as *The poet as painter.* included in the poet's art (see, especially, *Purg.*, xxxi. 139; and xxxii. 64); and it is part of Dante's poetic gift to view things, even things that are not, with an artist's eye. Thus, in writing of Matelda, he says there appeared to him—

> "A lady all alone, who went along
>   Singing and culling floweret after floweret,
>   With which her pathway was *all painted over*."

In the *Paradiso* Dante takes leave of earth and begins his ascent towards the Divine. The conditions being altogether changed, the critics have *The Paradiso.* of course asked themselves, Is the *Paradiso* a *sbaglio*, a mistake? Gaspary, though a most reverent and sympathetic writer, would seem to answer, in a qualified sense, Yes! He speaks of this last division as "a continual struggle with the ineffable." This is at least a fine phrase, nor can it be denied that it enshrines a large element of truth, only that it appears to assume as a poetical necessity that all verse should include a variety of sensible images, and that, where this is impossible, the subject is incapable of poetical treatment. But may not poetry suggest, as well as project, ideas? Does not Gaspary's canon exclude the very highest sort of poetry, that which we call sublime? To me it seems that, in conning the *Paradiso*, and especially the final canto, I learn for the first time the meaning of that epithet. It may be, as Balbo asserts, that to "the general" the *Paradiso* will always be less pleasant reading than the other *cantiche*. But suppose it were! The last thought that entered Dante's head was to accommodate himself to those who would fain run and read. His great, his only aim was to adapt his verse, as far as might be, to the tremendous exigencies of the theme, and it is from this standpoint and by this standard that he ought to be judged, always remembering the constraint laid upon him not to leave this part of his task unattempted.

Now, how could Dante treat the glories of the celestial world? A merely sensual paradise, the haunt of houris, paved with flowers, perfumed with odoriferous shrubs, freshened with the spray of fountains, and vocal with the notes of amorous nightingales: it would have been easy to depict a place like that, but it would have been a Mohammedan, not a Christian paradise. The heaven of Christendom could only be represented

as something exquisitely pure — a scene of glancing
light, an abode of everlasting song. And that is how
Dante does represent it. He is perpetually alternating
between, or rather associating, these two conceptions,
Here are two examples, culled at random :—

> " Voices divine make up sweet melodies ;
> So in this life of ours the seats diverse
> Render sweet harmonies among the spheres ;
> And in the compass of the present pearl
> Shineth the sheen of Romeo, of whom
> The grand and beauteous work was ill-rewarded."
>
> —*Par.*, vi. 124-129.

> " ' Glory be to the Father, to the Son,
> And Holy Ghost ! ' all Paradise began,
> So that the melody inebriate made.
> What I beheld seemed unto me the smile
> Of the universe ; for my inebriation
> Found entrance *through the hearing and the sight.*
> O joy ! O gladness inexpressible !
> O perfect life of love and peacefulness !
> O riches without hankering secure ! "
>
> —*Par.*, xxvii. 1-9.

Such lines suggest what is indeed the sovereign distinction of the *Paradiso*, its rhapsody. The *Purgatorio*
holds at least one splendid lyrical passage ; but the
Paradiso is always, so to speak, on the verge of breaking away into the limitless expanse of song. If in
some material sense the *cantica* does not show us
Heaven, it shows us what Heaven might be ; and, in
musical phrase, renders its blissful crescendo in organ-
tones of mingled sweetness and power.

With these general observations, it would be natural
that the present section should close, but there are

certain prosaic details, dropped as it were by the way,

Technicalities. which it is necessary to turn back and pick up. As to the verse, there appears to be a technical name for it—*serventese ternario incatenato* —and in all probability Dante was its inventor. It consists of even *endecasillabi* rhyming alternately, and each rhyme, except at the beginning and end of the cantos, is repeated thrice (*ababcbcdc*). It is a great regret that Longfellow's translation, the best for ordinary use, does not reproduce the original rhyming, but Dante himself has declared that the *bontà* is more than the *bellezza*. The rhythmical charm of the *terzina* is at once realised, but it may not be equally evident how well this metre combines the advantages of the couplet and the stanza. The couplet, as has been already remarked, lends itself to the gradual unfolding of the narrative, while the stanza is indulgent to the personal feeling of the narrator, who in this instance is actor also. Thus, even in particulars like these, the intuitive, or instinctive, certainty of Dante's genius triumphantly asserts itself. Indeed, generally, his artistic and spiritual triumph was as complete as his private and political failure.

A remark of Villemain's deserves to rank among the curiosities of literature. " Il [the Divine Comedy]

"Servum pecus." est resté comme un monument original qui n'a point servi de modèle." The context indicates that what the great critic intended by this unguarded deliverance was that Dante has never been imitated successfully, whereas Shakespeare has—*e.g.*, by Schiller. Waiving the latter question, it is allow-

able to believe that Villemain was entirely unaware
to what an extent Dante's poem has served as a
pattern, even if Petrarch and Boccaccio be utterly
ignored. In 1860 Señor Vidal y Valenciano Caytano
contributed to the *Revista de España* an informing
article on Spanish imitators, translators, and commentators of the Divine Comedy. In Italy, during
the fourteenth century, friends and foes alike made
him their model. Fazio degli Uberti, with his *Ditta-
mondo*, an uninspired geographical study, may represent the former; Cecco d' Ascoli, with his insufferably
dry "scientific" *Acerba*, the latter. This Cecco, who
must on no account be confounded with that delightful rogue, Cecco Angiolieri, was transformed in popular
fancy into a wizard—a high compliment, since Virgil
was metamorphosed in precisely the same way. Cecco's
conception of poetry was to exclude from it everything
in the nature of fable, and he piques himself on the
fact that his poem contains none of those passages of
the *Commedia* which Voltaire and other hostile critics
consider redeeming oases. Some lines of the conclusion are worth citing, in order to show the comfortable
self-esteem of this pigmy, and his amusing depreciation of his mighty contemporary. Cecco's metre, it
will be noticed, is a variation of the *terzina* :—

> " Qui non se canta al modo delle rane,
>   Qui non se canta al modo del poeta
>   Che finge immaginando cose vane ;
>   Ma qui risplende e luce ogni natura
>   Che a chi intende fa la mente lieta.
>   Qui non se regna per la selva oscura.
> Qui non vedo ne Paolo ne Francesca," &c.

[The list of works that might be recommended for the study of Dante is practically endless. The catalogue of Part I. of the Fiske collection in the library of the Cornell University—perhaps the best collection in the world—has been just issued, and numbers ninety-one quarto pages, closely printed in double columns. In England there has been a remarkable oscillation between prose translations and translations in *terza rima*. Mr A. J. Butler's labours deserve recognition. He has translated the whole of the *Commedia* into English prose, as well as Dr Scartazzini's *Handbook* (London : Macmillan), and has written an excellent little work on *Dante and his Times* (A. D. Innes). Mr Eugene Lee-Hamilton is the latest aspirant in the field of verse translations, most of which have been dismal failures. On the formal side, Longfellow's is a sham, while Cary's Miltonic effort, if it never sinks very low, is Dante adapted, rather than translated. The writer first studied Dante in Paolo Costa's annotated edition, and an excellent edition it is. In the present work the text of the *Oxford Dante*, revised and indexed by a group of devoted scholars, has been uniformly followed.]

CHAPTER V.

DAWN OF THE RENAISSANCE.

'ECCERINIS'—LATIN HISTORIES—RICHARD AUNGERVILLE—PETRARCH—HIS POPULARITY AND AIMS—RIENZI—PETRARCH'S EPISTLES AND ECLOGUES —HIS EPIC—HISTORICAL WRITINGS—PHILOSOPHY—PETRARCH AND BOCCACCIO—BOCCACCIO'S VERSE—THE 'DECAMERON'—SOURCES— STYLE—FRANCESCO SACCHETTI.

IN early times High Italy was famous as the seat of Provençal verse and North French poetry, imported literatures. It would be inaccurate to de-
Eccerinis. scribe mediæval or transitional Latin as imported; nevertheless, in relation to the blossoming *volgare*, it occupied the same antagonistic position as did they. This antagonism is first recognised as formidable in Petrarch's deliberate conspiracy to undo the work of his predecessor; but the Baptist of the Early Renaissance was Albertino Mussato (born, 1262; died, 1329). Mussato differs from Petrarch in that he is, in all but his choice of language, a thoroughly popular character. Outside literature, the aim of his life was to defeat the ambition of Dante's patron, Can Grande, and the production for which he is best

known—the tragedy *Eccerinis*—was dedicated to the same end. Mussato was a native of Padua, in which city, some sixty years before, Ezzelino da Romano and his brother Alberico had provided a spectacle of tyranny in its worst and vilest shape. To freshen the memory of these events, to fire anew the indignation of the citizens, and thus prevent a recurrence of the episode, was the purpose of Mussato's learned play, in which the chief personage was that son of Satan— literally, in the drama—Ezzelino. In spirit the work is rather lyrical than dramatic. There is no action worth mentioning, and no fine characterisation. With regard to form, it was modelled on Seneca's tragedies, and was never intended to be played. It consists, in a large measure, of long declamatory passages ; and, indeed, the whole of the fifth act is taken up with the report of the horrible death of Alberico and his family. Although faultily constructed and " speaking with tongues," the composition, by reason of its ardent patriotism, profoundly impressed the people of Padua, and the author was publicly rewarded with a wreath of laurel, ivy, and myrtle.

Mussato described himself in official documents as " poeta et historiographus Paduanus." The latter title

Latin histories.

he appropriated on the score of two immense historical works : the *Historia Augusta* or *De Gestis Henrici VII. Cæsaris*, and *De Gestis Italicorum post Henricum VII. Cæsarem.* Mussato here takes Livy as his model, imitating him not only in the use of the period and the " oblique oration," but in terminology. Coeval Italian institutions are

Romanised out of knowledge. We read of tribunes of the people, decrees of the Senate, and cohorts of the army. Occasionally an explanatory note is added as, for instance, that in which the expression "tribuni plebis" is supplemented by the words "quos gastaldiones appellant"; but, more usually, we are left to grope our way unaided, and with a growing sense of misapplied ingenuity. These histories, however, possess considerable value as chronicles. Not only was Mussato truthful and painstaking, but, regarding much that he has set down, an eyewitness. In this respect he contrasts with another Latin historian, Ferreto da Vicenza, who, not perhaps quite voluntarily, acts the part of special pleader for Can Grande. Ferreto, though he expresses admiration for Mussato, is actually, in style and method, superior to the Paduan ; but he of Vicenza does not regard the historian's calling in the same serious light, nor, again, are his statements based on personal knowledge. Mussato and Ferreto were the leaders of a whole school of Latinists, including two older writers, Lovato of Padua and Benvenuto dei Campesani of Vicenza. These scholars, it should be noticed, limit themselves to the linguistic aspect of classical study. Mussato's Latin, though not equal to Petrarch's, is better than Dante's and better than Boccaccio's, but, unlike Boccaccio, Mussato has not cut himself loose from mediæval tradition. His interests and his point of view are those of the mass of his contemporaries.

The *quasi*-ness of Mussato and Ferreto in relation to humanism, of which they have, so to speak, an

ahnung, but not the full revelation, is in England rep-
Richard resented by Gower and Richard Aungerville
Aungerville. de Bury, Bishop of Durham. Aungerville,
as we learn from the Italian scholar, met Petrarch,
and in a learned conversation promised to help in
elucidating the position of the ancient Thule, which
promise he broke. The bishop was a great collector
of books, and author of a Latin *Philobiblon* on his
favourite "hobby." His MSS., it is said, were "more
than all the bishops of England had then in their
keeping "; but he died deep in debt, and his books were
sold to the Abbot of St Albans. The assertion that
they went to enrich the library of Durham College.
Oxford, appears to rest on a clause in his will defining his intention. The *Philobiblon* testifies to an
almost puerile joy in books. Aungerville calls Paris,
on account of its libraries and academic treasures,
the "paradise of the world," and he looks down from
a superior height on the sea of ignorance around. He
might be compared to Reuchlin, only Reuchlin is more
mature, more philosophic. The bishop's love for
antiquity is shown in frequent allusions to the classics,
and his literary ardour in a defence of poetry. Aungerville is therefore in some sort an intellectual ancestor
of Sir Philip Sidney.

It is in Petrarch, however, that the Renaissance first
stirs with life. In his own eyes, and in the eyes of his
Petrarch. contemporaries, Petrarch was great, not on
account of his sonnets, but by virtue of his
attainments as a scholar ; and though none but con-
noisseurs may care to peruse his Latin writings (with

the possible exception of the Letter to Posterity), it is nevertheless difficult to overestimate their historical importance. Petrarch, the Renaissance, the modern world—in this light their significance becomes at once apparent.

Francesco Petrarca was the son of a Florentine notary, Petracco di Parenzo. "Petracco," of course, is *Early years.* a derivative of "Peter"; and the great scholar, finding the name too homely for him, Latinised it. Petracco belonged to the White faction, of which Dante also was an adherent, and it would seem that, as a boy, Petrarch had a passing glimpse of his austere predecessor, possibly in his father's house. Petracco having, with other members of his party, been driven into exile, his son was born at Arezzo. The event occurred on the 20th January 1304. Petrarch's mother, it seems quite determined now, was Eletta Canigiana, and under her tutelage he spent his early years at Incisa, where his ancestors had dwelt, near the upper reaches of the Arno. Thence, in 1310, the family removed to Pisa; and when, through the failure of Henry VII., the Ghibelline cause was finally lost, Petrarch accompanied his father to Avignon, in the south of France, then the seat of the Papal Court. Both at Pisa and at Avignon, the boy was instructed by a certain Convenevole da Prato; and he was afterwards sent to Montpellier and Bologna, that he might study jurisprudence. Petrarch, however, had no taste for the legal profession, having succumbed to the seductive influence of literature. When Petracco died, the youthful student found himself compelled to embrace

the priesthood, an office for which he was essentially
unfitted, though, in a secular sense, it proved extremely
profitable, since it enabled him to enjoy the fruits
of rich prebends conferred upon him by appreciative
patrons.

So far as outward circumstances are concerned,
Petrarch's career offers a notable contrast to that of
Courtier and Dante—a contrast arising no doubt, in part,
courted. from difference of temperament and mental
constitution. Despite his fervid imperialism, Dante
was no courtier. He was a kind of Elijah. Petrarch,
on the contrary, was a finished man of the world. So
much was this the case that he could dispense with
the vulgar arts of flattery. As a young man he succeeded in gaining the attachment of the powerful
family of the Colonnas; and, in later years, he was
everywhere courted by the great and noble, who
appear to have regarded his society as a distinction.
Jacopo da Carrara, the lord of Padua, sent him repeated invitations, and when at length Petrarch
arrived, obtained a canonry for him as an inducement to stay. Again, in 1353, when Petrarch passed
through Milan, Giovanni Visconti, at once archbishop
and lord of the city, almost forced him to remain at
his court. Instead of being, like Dante, a personal
enemy of the popes, Petrarch enjoyed such a measure
of their favour as to receive from Benedict XII. and
Clement VI. a canonry, a priory, and an archdeaconry.

This was obviously a very different lot from Dante's
wretched plight, which, to judge from his own description, resembled that of a tramp, while Petrarch, amply

supplied with means, journeyed in state from one brilliant scene to another, only, however, to confirm the Wise Man's verdict on all things earthly—Vanity of Vanities! If the life of both poets was largely consumed in travel, with Dante this course of action was involuntary. He was always longing for the "dolcissimo seno" of Florence. For Petrarch, on the other hand, continual change was almost a condition of existence. In 1353, Giovanni Visconti sent him on a mission to Venice, in order, if possible, to negotiate a peace between that republic and Genoa. The famous old doge, Dandolo, was then presiding over the destinies of Venice, and after courteously discussing the ambassador's proposals, addressed to Petrarch a personal question, What was the reason of his restless life? There was no doubt one definite and admitted reason; but, apart from Laura, these frequent mutations were probably only the outward symptom of a profound constitutional restlessness, which extended, in a greater or less degree, to every thought, purpose, and action.

The circumstance that Petrarch was chosen on more than one occasion ambassador, is sufficiently striking, *The influence of letters.* nor, perhaps, entirely to be explained by his talent and reputation considered in themselves. Villemain remarks that about this time men of letters began to form a class independent of the clergy, wielding a force like that of the profession named in our day the Fourth Estate, the force of educated opinion. Their influence, though doubtless ill-defined, was real, and accounts for the fact that, at the courts of the new lords, the place once held by minstrels and jongleurs was now taken by scholars and poets. When we find men like Petrarch preferred to high official positions—he might have been Apostolic Secretary had he wished—and intrusted with important diplomatic charges, we are naturally reminded of similar honours paid to literature by successive Governments of the United States—and of Addison.

To return to the Visconti. In 1368 Petrarch was present at the wedding of Violante, daughter of the *The moral* younger Galeazzo, with Lionel Duke of *atmosphere.* Clarence, when, according to the story, he met Chaucer. The brothers Galeazzo and Bernabò Visconti were men of infamous character, and Giangaleazzo, the son and successor of Galeazzo, was, if anything, worse. The annals of the dynasty teem with betrayals and assassinations, yet it could count Petrarch as a friend. Similarly, in one of his letters[1] Petrarch speaks of Jacopo da Carrara, who had procured his lordship by the murder of a cousin, as " a man distinguished for every laudable quality, but especially for an extraordinary and angelic sweetness of character, . . . the lord of Padua, nay, rather, the father of his country." Is there not some inconsistency here ? It is impossible to deny it, but we need not conclude therefore that the writer was a sycophant or a coward. The truth is, that Petrarch at each moment writes as he feels. He is the slave, not of circumstances, but of his own passing mood.

[1] *Fam.*, xi. 2.

It is probable that Petrarch's courage was never subjected to any severe test. As a man of affairs politicians did not take him seriously.[1]
Indulgence.
When he was sent on a mission, he went as an ornamental figurehead, and the prosaic practical work was placed in the hands of a subordinate. The widespread feeling that he was a most estimable man, a man of social charm, a man of learning and genius, but immaculate as a schoolgirl of every dangerous art, conferred upon him an immunity of which he was not slow to avail himself. He did not break with the Colonnas, the Visconti, and the rest, for the simple reason that "they lived with him, not he with them";[2] but he did not permit such friendship to silence him, when, as he conceived, public duty or personal conviction called upon him to speak.

The capacity of the scholar-poet to speak and act for himself is seen more than anywhere else in his association with Rienzi and the *révolution*
Rienzi.
de théâtre. It is indeed not unlikely that Petrarch's inspiration, his constant preaching of a united Italy, was the cause of Rienzi setting about his task. Cola di Rienzi was of obscure origin, his father being an inn-keeper and his mother a laundress, but he studied the classics and perused the inscriptions on the monuments until he not only became penetrated with the thought of Rome's ancient glory, but infected also

---

[1] Petrarch himself was under no delusion. "Ut enim re intelligo, nihilo melior œconomicus quam politicus sum ; omnia hæc unus solitudinis ac litterarum amor abstulit" (*Fam.*, xxii. 12).

[2] *Sen.*, xxvii. 2.

his fellow-citizens. Rienzi's personality appears to have been magnetic. Even Petrarch, writing to him, observes, "When I think of the grave and holy discourse you held with me the other day, at the gate of the old church, I seem to have heard a sacred oracle, a god, not a man." Rienzi, however, was about as well fitted to execute an actual *coup d'état* as Petrarch himself. He was a dreamer and egoist, whose sentimental vagaries, ramifying into filial impiety and absurd and arrogant blasphemy, stamp him as an impostor. If for a time he seemed likely to succeed, it was because the political condition of Rome, and the general misery of the peninsula, afforded a congenial soil for the hardy plotter. The transference to Avignon of the Papal see left the Eternal City a prey to faction. First the Orsini and the Colonnas, rival aristocratic families, contended for the senatorial dignity; then, on the crest of a popular upheaval, the iconoclast Jacopo Arlotta "had the cry." But Arlotta failed, just as Rienzi was destined to fail, because he possessed neither the practical genius nor the force of character requisite for a situation of tremendous urgency.

Rienzi's ideal was the establishment of a Roman republic on the model of the old, but tinctured by Christianity. This was his inflated style: "Nicolò, by the authority of our most merciful Lord Jesus Christ, severe and merciful, tribune of liberty, of peace, and of justice, and deliverer of the Holy Roman Republic." Notwithstanding his ancient friendship with the Colonnas, Petrarch warmly supported the adventurer.

He called him a "new Brutus," and, addressing the citizens, exclaimed, "Honour this man, honour him as a messenger of heaven, a rare gift of God, and hazard your life for his safety." And when Rienzi failed and lay in the prison at Avignon, Petrarch interposed his good offices, and obtained his release on the ground that he was a poet.

In spite of this fiasco, the resuscitation of Italy continued to engage Petrarch's thoughts. He abandoned *A change of front.* —indeed, he could not choose but abandon —the hope of a real Italian awakening, the erection of a strong and stable Italian Government from the Alps to the Strait of Messina. But he fell back on the next best expedient, and espoused what was, in fact, Dante's great panacea, the Ghibelline cult. Directing three letters to Charles IV., he styled him, with Petrarchian pomp, a "new Augustus," and reminded him, with Petrarchian finesse, of such old-world heroes as Camillus, Curius, and Cincinnatus. In 1354, the emperor appeared in Italy. Whilst he was at Mantua, he sent Petrarch a cordial invitation, and the poet in a letter to his friend "Lælius" describes the momentous interview. Petrarch, it seems, presented some coins to the monarch, and, on condition that he played his part manfully, consented to dedicate to him his unfinished work *De Viris Illustribus.* The emperor, on his side, was favourably impressed with Petrarch, who records with evident pleasure that he had "joked and disputed with Cæsar." Characteristically as regards the poet, the matter ended as it began—in a joke, if not in a dispute. Charles was the soul of prudence. He compounded with several states for sums of money, received the imperial crown at Rome, and then he went home. As Matteo Villani observes with pardonable irony, he departed "with the crown for which he had struck never a blow, and with a purse full of money that he had brought empty." It was all very astute, but it was not what Petrarch had hoped, and even expected. Something of his vexation is shown in a letter that he sent after the emperor on his retreat. "Valour," he says, "is not an hereditary boon. While I should not be inclined to believe that you lack the science of ruling or that of making war, you do lack the spring of all actions—the will." [1] In 1368 Charles paid another flying visit to Italy, but by this time Petrarch had come to the conclusion that a Holy Roman Empire, such as he desired to see, must be given up; and the book *De Viris Illustribus*, Charles having proved unworthy of the honour, was dedicated to an Italian.

These fantastic politics, which contemporary statesmen appear to have treated with good-natured levity, *Petrarch's idealism.* would not deserve so much notice were it not that they were part and parcel of Petrarch's *Weltanschauung*. He saw things, not in the dry light of reason, but through the prism of his own fancy and the subdued reflection of a bygone age. It was Petrarch's lament that he was born out of due time. Had he been able to choose, he would have lived in the days of Roman greatness; but inasmuch

[1] *Fam.*, xix. 11.

as there was no "time machine" to transport him out
of the ignoble period to which an unkindly fate had
assigned him, he did his best by incessant study of the
classics to create for himself an ideal atmosphere, to
be in spirit a citizen of the Republic, to hold communion with the mighty dead. Thus he writes letters
to Cicero, Seneca, Varro, Livy, Virgil, Horace, Asinius
Pollio, and Quintilian, and gives his correspondents
Greek and Roman names. A certain German, Lud-
wig von Kempen, to whom he had been introduced at
the palace of Bishop Jacopo Colonna, he calls—though
the compliment is rather overstrained — Socrates;
while Lello di Pietro Stefano is transfigured by an
easy process into Lælius. When the consort of
Charles IV. honours him with a letter apprising him
of the birth of a daughter, Petrarch overwhelms her
with allusions to Isis, Sappho, Carmenta the Sibyl,
Penthesilea, Tomiris, Cleopatra, Zenobia, Lucrece,
Clelia, Cornelia, and Martia. What the good lady
thought of the epistle has not transpired, though she
was probably pleased with the address, as well as confirmed in her opinion of Petrarch as a scholar and a
gentleman.

We, on the contrary, with our ingrained utili-
tarianism, are apt to smile. Certainly, at first it is
by no means easy to sympathise with a state of
mind to which such things are natural. And yet,
if we will only reflect, the matter is perfectly simple.
The Puritans, the Methodists, and others, who have
succeeded in *realising* the Bible, have acted in precisely the same way, drawing upon themselves abund-

ance of ridicule, but that of itself proves nothing. So, again, the romantic cottager's wife names her children after favourite characters in pseudo-society novels; and hostile leader-writers complacently illustrate the blunders of struggling statesmen by metaphors from the last sensational play. The Middle Age did not understand antiquity. The modern world is busy, and reserves its enthusiasm mainly for applied science. But the Renaissance, whatever its faults, was a necessary link in the chain of evolution; and Petrarch, at the cost of his own peace of mind, stood forth as the apostle of the pagan gospel of worldliness, the doctrine of "Carpe diem." Beauty in woman, beauty in nature, beauty in art — these were the objects of his worship, and he knew that the ancients worshipped them too. The Middle Age had not forgotten the old world of Greece and Rome, but, in looking backwards, could not break loose from its own tangle of associations. It picked out for admiration the fabulous heroes, and arrayed them comically in a mediæval costume. Even real personages, like Virgil and Alexander, become fabulous under the transforming hand of the romancer, and dutifully hear mass. What Petrarch effected may be indicated by a comparison between his way and Dante's. The *Divine Comedy* mentions Achilles, Hector, Ulysses, Jason, Theseus, &c., and, in addition, some historical characters like Cato, and Brutus, and Cassius. But all are on a common footing and owe their inclusion to poetical and legendary reasons rather than to solid fact. Petrarch, on the other hand, is attracted by this solid fact, though to him it reveals itself in a liquid guise as poetry.　In his fifth canzone he alludes to

> " Maratona e le mortali strette
> Che difese il Leon con poca gente."

And in the *Triumph of Fame* he introduces Demosthenes, Epaminondas, Alcibiades, Miltiades, and Themistocles.

Petrarch loved Latin, and attempted to make it, for all purposes, his own.　Dante also was at one

Latinity.

time an equally zealous partisan of the stately tongue, but, with more shrewdness than Petrarch, recognised betimes that the future lay with the " dialects."　The result was that the younger writer committed to a dead language much that he had better kept for the living speech of the *Canzoniere*.　Apart from the obvious objection that Latin was known, and could be known, only to a few, it is impossible for the most versatile of men to express himself in a language like Latin with the facility or felicity that he might have attained in his mother tongue.　Petrarch no doubt wrote different Latin from Dante's.　Adoring Cicero as a consummate master of style, he endeavoured to reach the same level of perfection.　Certainly, it would not be difficult to convict him of manifold errors.　This was accomplished by a Florentine critic, who, having pointed out that Petrarch had made a short syllable long, was reviled for his pains *as an ass and a drunkard!*　Such accidents, however, might be looked for in an experimental stage of the study; and the marvel is, not that Petrarch should now and then have committed short for long, but that he should have written—in an academic sense—so well.

Nor can it be alleged that he underestimated his achievements. He seems to have kept fair copies of *Epistles in prose.* all his Latin letters, out of which he afterwards formed four collections. The first and fullest, dedicated to his friend "Socrates," was entitled *Rerum Familiarum Liber*, and comprised twenty-four books and three hundred and forty-seven letters, the latest of which is dated 1366. In 1361, however, Petrarch began a new series—*Rerum Senilium Liber*—to include all letters deemed worthy of preservation to the time of his death. This collection consists of seventeen books and one hundred and twenty-two epistles. The *Variæ* number sixty-nine letters ranging from 1335 to 1373, and omitted for some unknown reason from the previous collections. Lastly, there are twenty-one epistles *Sine titulo*, which bear no addresses, probably because of the perilous nature of their contents. These epistles, indeed, lash the vices of "Modern Babylon," if not with the stinging force, with all the vehement earnestness of Petrarch's vernacular writings dealing with the same theme.

Of the letters generally must be said, what it would have pained and almost killed Petrarch to hear, that their value lies in the matter. He himself took so much trouble to render them elegant and attractive as ever bride or belle in decking her own person, and all this trouble was simply thrown away. The charm of published correspondence is — the exact opposite of Petrarch's labour and aim — that it was never designed for publication; and the ideal letter is one in which these literary forms, these ulterior motives, this cramping sense of the public and posterity, is for the moment laid aside, and the candidate for fame —poet, historian, or essayist—forgets to be dignified, shows himself of the great human brotherhood. Such letters are delightful by reason of their sincerity, their simplicity, their spontaneity; but fashion-plate epistles, unless we have some very particular concern in reading them, repel. "Ars longa, vita brevis." The Renaissance, however, much affected epistolary composition, and of the same stilted, self-conscious kind.

Besides his prose letters, which sometimes degenerate into tracts, Petrarch wrote three books of *Poetical epistles.* poetical epistles. These again are of great importance for the study of his life, and possess many elements both literary and historical in common with the more voluminous collections in prose. They contain also vivid, though too sparse, descriptions of scenery, of such favourite haunts as the deep forest of Selvapiana and the meadows around Vaucluse. The most beautiful of all (the seventh epistle of the first book) discusses the master-topic of the *Rime.* Between these epistles, which appear to have been composed at different periods, and the *Rime* have been noted interesting verbal coincidences, which assist in fixing the chronology of the poems. Take for example the ode *I' vo pensando,* written in the

plague-year 1348, and with it compare the fourteenth
epistle of the first book :—

> " Mille fiate ho chiesto a Dio quell' ale
>   Con le quai dal mortal
>   Carcer nostr' intelletto al ciel si leva."

> " Quis dabit ut pennas, posita gravitate, columbæ
>   Induar alta petens ? . . ."

> " E sento ad ora ad or venirmi al core
>   Un leggiadro disdegno. . . ."

> " Sæpius ambiguam gravis indignatio mentis
>   Digna subit. . . ."

> " Dall' altro non m' assolve
>   Un piacer per usanza in me si forte."

> " Sed retinet mundus, trahit imperiosa voluptas
>   Funestisque ligat nodis violentior usus."

Not wholly unlike Petrarch's versified epistles are
his eclogues. Misled perhaps by Dante's example,
Eclogues. Petrarch adopted an utterly false method
in his treatment of country themes, imparting to them, in fact, an allegorical turn. Now it
will be evident to most that pastoral poetry ought to
find its appeal in the reaction from the strife and stir
of cities. When the Pope or the King of France is
encountered where a simple shepherd was expected,
at once the charm is dissolved. Virgil may in sundry
verses have been guilty of political allusion, but that
is totally different from making such reference a habit.
This the Italians did, with the inevitable result that
the idyll, which ought to connote naturalness and

innocence, became in their hands an ingenious exercise, a rather irritating pastime.

Until a disillusionment occurred rather late in life, Petrarch imagined that his fame would depend on a Latin epic. If Cicero was his idol as a prose-writer, Virgil was his prince of poets.

Coronation.

Just as Virgil had sung the infancy of the Roman power, so Petrarch was eager to renown its lusty youth, when, under the valiant Scipio, it contended with the rival might of Carthage. This must be termed an unfortunate ambition. The highest success he might have achieved would only have given him a name like that of Buchanan or Politian—respectable enough perhaps; but Petrarch wished to be named with Homer, with Virgil, with the intellectual giants. And he chose the wrong road. It is probable that he never could have written a good epic even in Italian. His mind was preoccupied with himself; and, to write a good epic, a man must be merged in the mass, and be capable of a stronger, larger, more lasting enthusiasm than Petrarch's refined nature, temperate emotion, and questioning intellect would admit. Petrarch himself was full of confidence, and the *Africa*, while still inchoate, was made the pretext for a great histrionic triumph, in which, if the paradox may be allowed, he forestalled the applause which was never to come. This was his coronation in the Campidoglio at Rome. Ere he received the wreath he submitted himself to the examination of King Robert of Naples, who, satisfied of his fitness, divested himself of his royal robe and made it over to Petrarch. For splendour and circumstance, the actual ceremony is doubtless, as a recognition of literary merit, unique. Twelve children of the noblest Roman houses, clad in red, recited verses made by Petrarch in honour of the people. Then came six of the principal citizens in green raiment, and bearing wreaths of flowers. Last of all appeared the senator, with a crown of laurel, and occupied the seat of honour. Thereupon Petrarch was called to the sound of the trumpet, and presented himself in a long robe. Thrice he cried " Long live the Roman People ! " Then he knelt down before the senator, who doffed his garland and placed it on Petrarch's head, after which the poet repeated a sonnet in praise of the ancient Romans.

These extraordinary proceedings will serve to convey some notion of the kind of reputation Petrarch had ac-

The Africa.
quired. It may be that they were not so entirely spontaneous as he would have us infer, but the striking fact is that they were in any way possible. Petrarch was lucky. He was taken at his own valuation, and what that valuation was is abundantly manifest in his poem, where, in certain dreams, his birth is foreshadowed as that of a greater Ennius, and Scipio's triumph is associated with his own. All this advertising of self, however, was accompanied by a remarkable slowness and diffidence in giving the poem to the world. During Petrarch's lifetime only thirty-four lines became known, and those by accident ; but, few as they were, they did not content the critics. The verses comprise the last speech of Mago, admiral of the Carthaginian fleet and

brother of Hannibal, uttered as he lay a-dying on the
shores of Sardinia. The Florentines objected to this
speech, which expatiates on the nothingness of human
affairs, that it was incongruous in the mouth of a
dying person, especially of one young in years and
a pagan. The poet was deeply offended at these
strictures. There can, however, be no doubt as to
their substantial justice and propriety, the more so
when we consider — an opportunity denied to the
Florentines—the inconsequent manner in which the
episode is introduced. Perhaps it was this intimation
that the poem, if published, would not be greeted with
indiscriminate adulation, that led Petrarch to lock up
his *Africa* in the privacy of his own closet, and to
expend on it with unceasing diligence the labours
of his file.

The epic, though a failure, was a failure not wholly
unredeemed. Numerous passages might be cited in
which the grandeur of the theme, without much dressing from Petrarch, produces its due effect on the reader.
But, by universal admission, he is at his happiest in
dealing with the story of Sophonisba, where he could
draw on his own experience. Elsewhere the *Africa*,
in violation of Petrarch's own canon, copies too literally the historical account in Livy, and this misplaced
fidelity opposes a fatal check to freshness and originality of treatment. The poem consists of nine books,
but between the fourth and fifth book " multa de-
sunt," whether " valde deflenda " must be a matter of
opinion. The cause and extent of the hiatus are alike
unknown.

The book *De Viris Illustribus*, and the three books *Rerum Memorandarum*, may be dismissed more briefly. *Historical writings.* Like Rollin's *Ancient History*, they were educational. The biographical work may be compared to Plutarch's gallery, save that the personages, with two exceptions, are all Romans; and it is needless to add that these later portraits have little of the undefinable charm which has meant for Plutarch an immortality of fame. The other work, composed of anecdotes so arranged as to illustrate consecutively the four cardinal virtues, may be looked upon as completing the Lives, and, for us, derives its chief interest from contemporary examples relating to Dante, King Robert of Sicily, Castraccio Castracani, Uguccione della Faggiuola, &c. Neither of these compilations, to which Petrarch kept adding during ten or twenty years, was ever completed by him.

Petrarch's writings nearly all exhibit a tendency to moralise. With the progress of years this tendency *Praise of solitude.* becomes more marked. Petrarch, though his guidance affected others that way, himself never fully accepted the pagan conception of life as a feast. His nature was pensive and prone to melancholy, but sadness and disappointment, far from conducting him, like Leopardi, to fierce, implacable revolt, turned his thoughts into another channel. In 1347 Petrarch, always very impressionable, visited the Carthusian monastery of Montrieu, of which his brother Gerard was an inmate, and, captivated with the placid sweets of such an existence, wrote a panegyric entitled *De Ocio Religiosorum*. But Petrarch did not need

R

spiritual motives in order to appreciate solitude. He loved pomp, it is true, but he did not love perpetual pomp. The claims of society were hard to reconcile with study and meditation, and after admitting them for a time, he would shake them off as an intolerable load. In his treatise *De Vita Solitaria* he justifies his preference, alleging, among other things, that a man cannot be an active citizen and preserve his integrity ; and, strange to say, he is very severe on women as the fount and source of every ill. The work is a monument of erudition; but it seems a pity that Petrarch, who, though a scholar and city-bred, could write so well of " green fields and babbling brooks," did not dwell rather, after the manner of Marmontel, on the simple pleasures of country life.

The ascetic tone of these writings characterises also the *De Remediis Utriusque Fortunæ*. The composi-

Petrarch as Stoic. tion was germane to the period, when captains of the people turned despots and were again hurled from their giddy height by the expiring efforts of communal freedom; but, as to practical utility, the work might just as well not have been written. It contradicts itself, and it contradicts human nature. A parent's joy over the birth of a son must be tempered by the reflection that sons are a burden; if, on the other hand, too many sons are born, a man is to remember that sons are a parent's greatest wealth. The balm, however, most generally applicable is that nothing is important. Even to mourn for lost friends is an act of folly. If Stoicism be so good, why, it may be asked, did not Petrarch himself practise it in respect of Madonna Laura? In G. K. Pfeffele's little poem, *Der neue Stoiker*, Herr Thoms, an easy-going skipper, the idol of the sailors, has a trick of saying, " Es hat nichts zu bedeuten." A parrot learns, and exultingly repeats, the phrase. By-and-by the ship is becalmed, and provisions run short. Then Herr Thoms decides that he must strangle poor Poll, but with its last breath the bird gurgles out, " Es hat nichts zu bedeuten." Petrarch's *Remedies* are only a refined kind of parrot-talk.

More attractive is the *De Contemptu Mundi*, written about 1342. Petrarch calls this his *Secretum*, and *Spiritual conflict.* affects that it was composed, not so much with a view to publicity, as to satisfy certain inner needs. There may be a modicum of truth in this statement; but, in point of style, Petrarch was prepared for either event. Probably the declaration was a mere ruse, and he intended from the first to admit the public to his confidence. A favourite author of Petrarch was St Augustine, whose *Confessions* he had always within reach. In the *Secretum* he presents himself in a white sheet, whispers his sins in the ear of the great saint, and echoes St Augustine's sentiments regarding spiritual matters. But even in the book he manifests considerable reluctance to accept the practical conclusion and at once renounce his errors. Before he can forsake the world, he must at least finish the *Africa* and the *De Viris Illustribus*. It would seem also, from the pitiless arithmetic of Signor Bartoli, that there were other pursuits which he was not yet inclined to abandon. About a year

after this very imperfect conversion a natural daughter was born to him.   But Petrarch was not merely
fooling.   The cry that rises in the *Secretum* did not
issue from "feigned lips."   Any one who thinks otherwise omits to consider the fund of religious feeling,
amounting to downright superstition, which at one
time all but consigned his beloved *Rime* to the flames.
Only his capacity for religious emotion is allied with
moral infirmity, and that is one of the reasons why his
character is apparently so complex.   This, however, is
a familiar experience.   St Paul himself confesses, "That
which I do, I allow not"; and Ovid observes in a similar strain—

> "   .   .   .   Video meliora proboque,
> Deteriora sequor." [1]

Petrarch shares their inconsistency.   Pitying himself,
he would gladly flee from his earthly prison-house to
the arms of the Crucified, but doubts and fears hold
him back.   The desire for fame which has clung to
him from boyhood, he cannot give it up.   However,
it is not only ambition that enslaves him.   We cannot
fully comprehend this mental conflict without recollecting that poison of love which, if it continually
tormented him, gained for him, far more than his
erudite Latin writings and untiring research for manuscripts, the coveted renown.   Petrarch spent his last
years at Arquà, on the Euganean Hills, in the com-

---

[1] *Met.*, vii. 20.   It is noticeable that in his ode *I' vo pensando*, in
which Petrarch gives poetical expression to the war in his members,
it is the pagan writer whose words occur to his mind :—

> " E veggio 'l meglio, ed al peggio m' appiglio."

pany of his daughter Francesca and her husband. He was found dead, with his hand resting on a book, the 18th July 1374.

In 1350, when Petrarch passed through Florence on his way to Rome, he met for the first time Boc-
Petrarch and Boccaccio. caccio. In the following year Boccaccio was the bearer of a letter, of which he was not improbably the author, addressed to Petrarch by the Prior of the Arts, the People, and the Commonwealth, announcing the restoration of his paternal property and beseeching him to make Florence his home. Although his mission was not publicly successful, the visit proved very delightful to Boccaccio, since it enabled him to spend several evenings with the poet in his garden.   Boccaccio's attitude towards the older writer—older, however, by less than ten years—is that of a reverent and admiring disciple.   Petrarch is his master, a kind of god on whom he lavishes all those ingenious phrases and periphrases of which worshippers always have plenty.   In one letter he tells him that the name Boccaccio will be honoured by the latest posterity, because it were inconceivable that such an one as Petrarch should correspond with a slight, unmeritable man.   When, however, he learns that Petrarch has stayed with the tyrant Visconti, Boccaccio is shocked.   He regards such conduct as apostasy, and with the freedom of fast and intimate friendship, reproves the wrong-doer.   Still more notable is the way he tries to school Petrarch into due appreciation of Dante.   Himself an enthusiastic votary, he was well aware of Petrarch's indifference and even

scorn. Nevertheless, he sends him a copy of the *Divine Comedy*, which he bids him welcome and admire.

To appraise the relative merits of these pioneers would be an arduous and delicate task. As a Latinist, Boccaccio was doubtless the inferior; but, by way of compensation, he acquired a knowledge of Greek, and by procuring the establishment at Florence of a chair in that language, assisted in promoting the study of classical literature. In all this he was the educator of his time. In disposition, however, Boccaccio was the antipodes of a schoolmaster. He did not exist to teach, to inculcate prudence and morality. He existed to enjoy, and because he found pleasure the ideal of Antiquity, therefore Antiquity interested him. From the charnel-house of the unlovely Middle Age the voluptuous Florentine hasted with nimble foot into the parterre of the old world, radiant with nature and with art. Filled with the spirit of revolt, he did without paltering what Petrarch did with hesitancy and fear. He renounced and ridiculed the asceticism and "other-worldliness" of the Ages of Faith. He sought to kill monkery with a laugh. This bold originality of character was bound to express, as well as impress, itself. If I may so divide the matter, the impression is seen in the Renaissance, the expression in a series of works embodying his own feelings, or, in the case of the *Decameron*, his experience of men and books.

Boccaccio was the son of a Florentine merchant and a Parisian gentlewoman called Jeanne. Giovanni, therefore, bore the names of both parents. Like Dante and Petrarch, he was by force of circumstances a citizen of the world. Born at Paris about 1310, we find him

Parentage and youth. seventeen years later at Naples, where his father proposed to initiate him into the mysteries of commerce. The luxury, the soft climate, and the brilliant natural tints of the southern city, encountered in Boccaccio a responsive and sympathetic disposition, and he easily succumbed to the vision of a beautiful kneeling girl. Maria d' Aquino was, like himself, a "love-child," being the offspring of King Robert and a frail Provençal beauty; and Boccaccio first saw her on Good Friday, 1334, in the Church of San Lorenzo. Giovanni's passion was reciprocated, and for some time the pair seem to have invented or embraced opportunities of meeting. These were no innocent trysts. It was a regular and genuine amour, such as might be predicted from the circumstances and the example of their respective parents. But at length a coolness set in, and Boccaccio vented his disappointment in a sonnet anticipating Time's revenges :—

> " S' egli avvien mai che tanto gli anni miei
>   Lunghi si faccian, che le chiome d' oro
>   Vegga d' argento onde io m' innamoro,
>   E crespo farsi il viso di costei,
> E crespi gli occhi bei, che tanto rei
>   Son per me, lasso ! ed il caro tesoro
>   Del sen ritrarsi, ed il suo canto sonoro
>   Divenir roco sì com' io vorrei,
> Ogni mio spirto, ogni dolore e pianto
>   Si farà riso, e pur sarò sì pronto,
>   Ch' io dirò ; Donna, Amor non l' ha più cara," &c.[1]

---

[1] It may be worth while to contrast with this spiteful effusion a

Boccaccio's sonnets will not compare with those of Petrarch in respect of finish; but his verse is graphic, *The* Filocopo, and that dealing with episodes of Neapolitan *&c.* life has somewhat the effect of instantaneous photography. A prose effort, the *Filocopo*, partakes of the same quality. The meaning of this word is supposed to be "love's labour," but Boccaccio's compounds are truly wonderful.[1] The *Filocopo* is one of many versions of the old French romance *Floire et Blanceflor*, which was probably brought from Greece at the time of the Crusades. On the side of art, the story has often been more worthily presented, but, as autobiography, the work is certainly arresting. A lover goes in search of his mistress. Having put to sea, he is driven by stress of weather to Naples, where he finds her in the midst of a gay company. Fiammetta is, of course, Maria, and the pictures Boccaccio draws of Neapolitan society are no doubt faithful reflections of the scenes

sonnet of Petrarch's on the same theme. The translation is a rash attempt dating from college-days.

> If but my life can so much foil present
>   To my harsh torment, and to all my woes,
>   That I may see, by virtue of life's close,
>   Lady, the light of your bright eyes quite spent—
> The fine gold of your hair with silver blent,
>   And coronals despised, and worldly shows,
>   And that face colourless, which in my throes
>   Makes me afraid and backward to lament.
> Then Love will grant me valiance so keen,
>   That I will show you of mine agonies
>   The years, and days, and hours, what they have been;
> And if my wishes fair the time denies,
>   It cannot fortune but that to my teen
>   At least there come some succour of late sighs.

[1] *Filostrato*, for example, is a horrid mule, its parentage being φιλία and *stratus*, and its meaning "laid low by love."

with which protracted residence in the city had made
him familiar.   The reigning queen, Giovanna, was, as
Villemain observes, a kind of earlier *parousia* of Mary
Queen of Scots, and her court appears to have been
modelled on the Courts of Love.   At any rate, the
questions propounded have a remarkable affinity to the
questions that formed the staple of the *tensos*. With the
Filocopo it is natural to associate two other romances,
the *Ameto* (or *Commedia delle Donne Fiorentine*) and the
Fiammetta.   The former is an unsuccessful attempt
to reconcile idyll and allegory, pagan fable and Christian moral, which things are past reconciling.   The
latter, addressed to ladies, is a psychological romance,
a romance of the heart.   This work is, in some ways,
the counterpart of the *Vita Nuova* and *Secretum ;* but
with this important distinction, that the lady speaks,
or rather is made to speak, whatever may suit her
admirer.   It is certain that the desertion was the act,
not of Panfilo, but of Fiammetta.

Boccaccio was engaged on these works between
1338 and 1343, but his pains were not monopolised
by prose.   Even the *Ameto* is interlarded with terzines ; and, besides these,
he composed a long poem wholly in that metre.
The *Amorosa Visione* extends to fifty cantos, and
the general notion is that of a dream wherein the
poet, in company with a lady, visits the realms of
Fame, Love, Happiness, and the Garden of Wellbeing.   Here also we meet with hopeless contradictions—the form of the Dantesque vision, the
symbolism of allegorical French poetry, and, mingled

The Amorosa
Visione.

with myth and legend, reminiscences of the gentle-women of the Neapolitan court. More notable than anything is the discordancy between the spirit of the poem and that which the consecrated metre would lead us to anticipate. Damnation and purgatorial pains are out of date, and for saints and sinners are substituted heroes, and poets, and lovers. The chief end, the wished-for consummation, is the satisfaction of the sexual passion. It is worth remarking that the identity of Fiammetta and Maria is established by the dedication of the *Amorosa Visione.*

Boccaccio did not confine himself to *terza rima* as a metre. It is impossible to be quite certain about the matter, but there is some reason to suppose that he was really the inventor of that *ottava rima* which was to become, as it were, specialised as the metre of Italian epic. Both *terza* and *ottava*[1] being *rime incatenate*, it is conceivable that the one was evolved from the other. Boccaccio wrote three poems in the octave stanza, the *Filostrato*, the *Teseide*, and the *Ninfale Fiesolano*. These compositions are linked, not only by community of form, but by similarity of subject, as they are all stories of love. The *Filostrato*, which is in eight cantos, or, as the poet calls them " parts," tells of the love of Troilus and " Griseida," young people of Troy. Chalcas, Griseida's father, fore-seeing the ruin of his country, has taken refuge in the Greek camp, and desires to have his daughter with him. Diomed negotiates an exchange, and though the girl parts from her lover with many tokens of sorrow and

A new epic.

---

[1] The rhyme-scheme of the *ottava* is : *abababcc.*

affection, she afterwards yields to the solicitation of
the doughty Greek captain. Troilus, on obtaining
proof of her inconstancy, rushes, in a paroxysm of
grief, to challenge his victorious rival, but, instead,
falls under the spear of Achilles.

The story of Troilus and Cressida has been repeated
in Chaucer's poem of that name, in the *Pastime of
Pleasure*, and in the well-known play. The topic of
Chaucer's relations with the three great Italians must
be reserved for a later chapter; but it may be well to
point out that, with regard to the material, Boccaccio
himself stood in the same position. He cannot even
claim to have been the first in modern times to turn
the narrative to poetical account. The central source
of many works relating to the Tale of Troy was the
Latin history of Guido of the Columns, which was itself
based on the *Roman de Troie* of Benoît de Sainte-More
(*circiter* 1160).[1] Behind this again were the writings of the mythical Dictys and Dares. If therefore

---

[1] In France, where Benoît had first made it popular, interest in the
story was revived through a prose translation of Boccaccio's *ottave* by
Pierre de Beauveau, Lord of La Roche-sur-Yon, Governor of Maine,
and Seneschal of Provence and Anjou. This valiant soldier, whose
name frequently occurs in the chronicles of his time, was a lover and
a poet. He made "de plaisants diz, de gracieuses chançonnetes et
balades"; and, having wooed a lady, fared even as Troilus. For
solace he applied himself to the translation of the *Filostrato*, a little
work found in the library of the King of Sicily, and described as
"très-piteulx et plaisant." This task he achieved "en larmoyant,"
and although he elected prose, the result was an extremely happy and
sympathetic rendering. Beauveau's French *Troilus* attracted many
readers and produced an appreciable effect on French letters. The
concetti scattered up and down in the work are the seed of which the
harvest will appear in the sixteenth century.

Chaucer preyed, so to speak, on Boccaccio, he had excellent precedent to keep him in countenance, but in both cases the fable is more or less an accident. As Bartoli observes, it is the eternal drama of man and woman that is represented in the *Filostrato*, and in treating the varying phases of human passion, fear, and joy, and despair, Boccaccio draws from a rich store of actual personal experience. In its inmost essence the poem is neither a romance nor a drama, but a lyric.

Dante, in the *De Vulgari Eloquentia*, had said, "Arma vero nullum Italum adhuc invenio poetasse." *The Teseide.* This void Boccaccio set himself to fill in the *Teseide*.[1] The poem is based in all likelihood on a late Greek or Byzantine romance now lost; but the treatment and colouring have been greatly influenced by Statius's *Thebaid*. It has often been said that just as Petrarch is the king of troubadours, so Boccaccio is the first of *trouvères*. Boccaccio, however, in dealing with a theme of this sort, adopts a method wholly different from that of the typical *trouvère*, who would have endeavoured to produce a readable and attractive tale, and multiplied incidents and adventures without troubling to ask whether his proceedings

[1] *Vide* the conclusion :—

> "Poiche le Muse nude cominciaro
> Nel cospetto degli uomini ad andare,
> Già fur di quelli che le esercitaro
> Con bello stilo in onesto parlare,
> Ed altri in amoroso le operaro ;
> Ma tu, o libro, primo al lor cantare
> Di Marte fai gli affanni sostenuti,
> Nel volgar latino mai più non veduti."

were regular.   Boccaccio, on the other hand, is always
asking himself this question.   His ambition is, not to
be popular, but to be an artist, to revive, in everything
but the language, the ancient epic.   For the attainment of this end he employs various devices.   He
interpolates reminiscences of Virgil, Statius, and even
Homer, and, to cover the nakedness of the fable, drags
in mythological digressions and descriptive passages.
Taken as a whole, the *Teseide* is an invertebrate,
inorganic composition.   The real heroes, Palemone
and Arcita, do not appear until near the close of the
second book, and for a long time Theseus remains the
dominant figure.

English versions.   Chaucer attempted two versions of the
Teseide.   Enumerating his works in the
Legende of Goode Women, he mentions—

> "Al the love of Palamon and Arcite
> Of Thebes, thogh the storye ys knowen lyte."

Of this early poem only inconsiderable fragments are
left, which, though practically useless for determining
the nature of the poem, show us at least the metre.
Palamon and Arcite was written in stanzas of seven
lines, and the rhyme-scheme was *ababbcc*.   It has been
suggested with much probability that Chaucer's first
version marked an intermediate stage between the
Teseide and his second version, the *Knightes Tale*,
which exhibits many departures from the original.
Thus, for instance, at the beginning of the affair,
Boccaccio causes Emilia, the fatal beauty, to be seen
walking in her garden by Arcita, and Arcita calls

Palemone. As Palemone, after sundry vicissitudes, is to live with her " in gioia e in diporto," while poor Arcita has to be content with a formal death-bed bridal, this ordering of matters is poetically unjust, and indeed unnatural, unless it is to lead on to a violent rivalry, such as might be predicted in the case of two youths equally enamoured of the same object. Boccaccio, however, defies common-sense by depicting those swains as constant in their mutual attachment. Chaucer, with his profound knowledge of the human heart, could not perpetrate such an absurdity, which it is hard to believe even Boccaccio would excuse, except on the ground that a poet has a right to be arbitrary. The Englishman knows better, and expresses the common feeling in the lines :—

> " O Cupide, out of al charite !
> O regne that wolt no felaw have with the !
> Ful soth is seyde, that love ne lordschipe
> Wol not, his thonkes, have no felaschipe."

To these criticisms it may be added that Boccaccio, with all his strivings to be classical, infuses, by a sort of inner necessity, a romantic tone into his dialogue. Both in the *Filostrato* and the *Teseide* the actors talk like dames and cavaliers.

In his own day, and probably with justice, Boccaccio was regarded as a poet second only to Dante and Petrarch ; but he is deficient in method, and his excellence is not uniform. He is poetical in places, but beyond and around these places stretches an arid desert of versification. In short, his poetry can hardly elude the damning epithet

Mythology.

" mediocre." His best effort was his *Ninfale Fiesolano.*
Mensola, one of Dian's train, yields to Africo's desires,
but afterwards repents and leaves him. Thereupon
the disconsolate shepherd kills himself, and Mensola
in her grief imitates him. An avenger, however,
appears in the person of Atalante, who scatters the
nymphs and drives them into wedlock. He also
founds the city of Fiesole. Bartoli remarks very
happily of this *dénouement,* that it is a parable of the
Renaissance rising on the ruins of ascetic institutions.[1]
If we except the rhetorical style, the most obvious
feature in Boccaccio's poems is the mythology. This
joy in classical legend was not affectation. Himself
steeped in ancient tradition, Boccaccio could only conceive of poetry in connection with myth. They were
as man and wife, as body and soul, and whilst he was
faithful to his own ideal of art, he could not put them
asunder.

Boccaccio's Latin writings have no high æsthetic
or psychological value, and therefore I shall not pause
Opera minora. to describe them. It may be observed,
however, that the *De Genealogia Deorum*
bears the same relation to his poetry as the *Convivio*
to the *Commedia.* It is unnecessary also to linger by
Boccaccio's backwater the *Corbaccio,* a satire against
women; nor need I again refer to his *Life of
Dante,* and what may be termed its complement, the
Comento on the *Commedia,* save only to remark that

---

[1] It is interesting to recall that in Lorenzo de' Medici's *Ambra,*
written, of course, *en pleine Renaissance,* are distinct echoes of Boccaccio's poem.

the latter is both quantitatively and qualitatively a
torso. It extended only to the seventeenth canto of the
Inferno, and is wanting in many elements of interest
to be anticipated from a *quasi*-contemporary. There
remains the immortal work so truly and aptly named
the *Commedia umana*.[1]

In 1348 a desolating plague swept over Europe.
Advancing from the East, the rumours of its approach
filled all hearts with terror, and the inci-
The Decameron. dents of its progress equalled, if they did
not surpass, the worst forebodings. A detailed account
of the horrors makes up the proem of the *Decameron*,
a singular proem due to the singular conduct of
the persons of the drama—in other words, the story-
tellers. Seven young ladies and three youths, all of
them Florentines, retire to a country house in the
neighbourhood of the city, and pass the time principally in relating tales. Each day a lady or gentleman
recounts ten stories of similar import, and the whole
performance lasts ten days. That is the origin of the
title, which, it is to be feared, is not quite such good
Greek as Boccaccio imagined.[2] As the *Decameron* has
been freely pronounced immoral, and is not a book to
be placed unreservedly in the hands of the young
person, the question is inevitable, Is there not between
the proem and the work proper, between the historical
background and the lightness and frivolity of the
imaginary actors, an inherent contradiction ? Well,

---

[1] *The Decameron: A Ten Days' Entertainment*. With Introduction
by T. Wright. London : 1872.

[2] The word should be *Dechemeron*—certainly an ugly duckling.

Villemain thinks that Boccaccio might have produced an analogy in the gaiety of the Court of Naples under the adulterous Giovanna, whose crimes transformed the city into a shambles. The analogy, however, is unnecessary. It is notorious that, in times of pestilence, misery and suspense frequently provoke a lamentable outbreak of immorality. This, as Thucydides testifies, was the case at Athens. So then, if Boccaccio's little coterie diverted themselves with dancing and repeating questionable stories, unbecoming as we may find their conduct, it was neither impossible nor improbable. Villemain is so impressed with the indecency of the *Decameron*, that he declines to sully his pages by the most distant approach to quotation. This excess of prudery argues an imperfect acquaintance with the book—though, it is true, the story of Griselda translated by Petrarch into Latin, and by Chaucer into English, cannot be termed representative. But the *Decameron*, however immoral it may be, is not immoral only. The humour of it goes a long way to excuse its indelicacy. Moreover, Boccaccio did not choose his themes because they were improper. He took them very much as they came, and if they fulfilled the indispensable condition of arousing interest, forthwith adopted them.

Villemain makes great sport of Bottari for maintaining the absolute innocence of Boccaccio's intentions—not too wisely perhaps, for in certain matters it is doubtful whether Messer Giovanni ever grasped the distinction between right and wrong. On one point, however, the critics are

Boccaccio's universality.

S

agreed. They all acknowledge the wonderful variety of Boccaccio's pantomime representing every age, sex, and condition, and under the most different lights. In this quality of breadth he is rivalled by Dante and Shakespeare alone. Like both these world-artists, he hews his materials from near and far ; but, having hewn them, treats them as his own property, alters, transforms, retrenches, amplifies, answerably to his own judgment, taste, instinct, and even caprice. The stamp of his personality is on every novel, and on every sentence, of the *Decameron*. Single stories had been wafted about the world for centuries, and having formed part of the stock-in-trade of wandering jongleur and popular preacher, might be termed old favourites, but they had never received that artistic setting necessary to fit them for a higher plane of existence. To change the simile, the chemical conditions are profoundly modified by the introduction of a fresh ingredient. To the rude and crude, if vivid and vigorous, presentments that had served hitherto, culture was added. The *Decameron* was, to all intents, a new phenomenon.

It is impossible to say of every tale from what source exactly Boccaccio borrowed it. You may *Sources.* indeed compile a learned and, approximately, exhaustive work, as Herr Landau has done in his invaluable *Quellen des Decameron*, setting forth the pedigree, antecedents, and collateral relations of the tales ; but it is needless to point out the difference between the book and the man. The *Decameron* was, as it were, a natural growth

which Boccaccio appropriated and brought to perfection, but it does not follow that he was conversant
with the botanical processes preceding the final development of every individual stamen. To take an
extreme instance, he did not, you may be sure, know
anything of Azraki's *Sindibad Nameh*. Such studies
did not belong to his day. There are, however, three
sources from which he may reasonably be supposed to
have drawn : mediæval Latin writings, *e.g.*, the *Vitæ
Patrum, Gesta Romanorum,* and *Legenda Aurea;* almost
any poetry and prose in the Romance languages;[1]
and oral traditions, respecting which last Dante supplies important evidence in the *Commedia*.[2] Besides
and beyond what may be termed the commonplace
of literature, Boccaccio imports into his work recent
and almost contemporary scandals—real people under
their real names.

Such are the tales relating to that sorry butt,
Calandrino. I am aware that the existence of this
artist, as well as that of Buffalmacco, has
been disputed ; but, so far as I can perceive,
without just cause. Those incomparable wags, Bruno
and Buffalmacco, figure not only in the *Decameron,*
but, in precisely the same character, in the pages of
Vasari and Sacchetti, while Manni in his *Veglie
Piacevoli* (ii. 33-37) claims to have proved the historical reality of Calandrino and his termagant spouse,

Butts.

---

[1] Great mistakes, however, are made even here. Thus Legrand
and Manni both imagined that the tale of Griselda was taken from
Le Parement et Triomphe des Dames of Olivier de la Marche — a
chronological absurdity.

[2] See especially *Paradiso,* xv. 125 ; xxix. 103.

Tessa, from original documents.   Another example
of Florentine gossip immortalised by Boccaccio is the
story of Giotto and Messer Forese da Rabatta, to
which Vasari alludes in his *Lives of the Painters.*

Signor Casini has pointed out, what is of the
highest interest with regard to the novels, that, from
Method.   the longest to the shortest, they are divisible into three dramatic moments: the
introduction, in which the leading personages are
brought forward, and the stage described whereon
the actions are "played off"; the development, in
which more or less rapidly, and aided more or less
by collateral circumstances, the narrator conducts
the action to the culminating point; and the solution,
in which the knot of the intrigue is, at the conclusion,
finally disentangled.   We may take as an instance the
tale of

> " The spectre huntsman of Onesti's line,
> His hell-dogs and their chase."

A young gentleman of Ravenna, Nastagio degli
Onesti, falls in love with a proud girl, daughter of
Taming a   Paolo Traversari, who disdains his offer.
lady.   In despair Nastagio is at first minded to
kill himself, but afterwards is persuaded to leave
Ravenna, and goes to live in a pine-wood, about
three miles away.   Here a strange thing betides
him.   In his solitary wandering, he fancies he hears
great weeping and loud shrieks as of a woman; and,
raising his head, he descries running towards the
spot where he is standing, dishevelled and torn by
boughs and brambles, a beautiful maid.   She cries

amain for mercy. Flanking her are two large, fierce mastiffs, who ofttimes bite her cruelly, and behind on a black courser follows a dark rider, wrathful in face, with a rapier in his hand, threatening her.

Nastagio breaks off a bough to serve as weapon, and prepares to go to her aid. But the knight, dismounting, tells him that he was called Messer Guido degli Anastagi, when Nastagio was a little boy—the similarity of their names is, and was probably intended to be, suggestive — and that what Nastagio witnesses is a punishment of slighted love rehearsed every Friday on that very spot. More horrors ensue, of which the young hermit is a passive beholder, and then Nastagio reflects. If this was an event of weekly occurrence, then he might make capital out of the affair by ordering a feast in the pine-wood, and inviting his friends, the haughty damsel included, to share in it. With some difficulty the notion is carried into effect, and just when the conviviality is at its height, everything is brought to a standstill by the uncanny spectacle of disembowelling. The lady is profoundly impressed, and as she is now fully apprised of her fate, should she persist in her contumacy, she contrives to let Nastagio know that she no longer opposes his wishes, and accordingly they wed.

It is in every way probable that Boccaccio borrowed this story either from the *Speculum Historiale* of Vincent of Beauvais, or from Passavanti's Italian version in the *Specchio della Vera Penitenza*.

Whence?

According to Passavanti's account, the ghostly cavalier

is the Count of Nevers, and the persecuted female a lady who, for love of him, has murdered her husband; and, of course, the story, as told there, is intended to have an edifying influence. Boccaccio, however, has quite other intentions, and points the moral after this fashion: "E non fu questa paura cagione solamente di questo bene, anzi sì tutte le ravignane donne paurose ne divennero, che sempre poi troppo più arrendevoli a' piaceri degli uomini furono, che prima state non erano."

This, then, appears to have been the source of the narrative, but as Boccaccio was certainly familiar with *Dante's adaptation.* Dante's portrayal of the Hell of Suicides, the following passage may be cited for the sake of comparison. Quite possibly it was adapted from Vincent:—

> "And two behold! upon our left-hand side,
>   Naked and scratched, fleeing so furiously,
>   That of the forest every fan they broke.
> He who was in advance: "Now help, Death, help!"
>   And the other one, who seemed to lag too much,
>   Was shouting: "Lano, were not so alert
> Those legs of thine at joustings of the Toppo!"
>   And then perchance, because his breath was failing,
>   He grouped himself together with a bush.
> Behind them was the forest full of black
>   She-mastiffs, ravenous, and swift of foot
>   As grey-hounds, who are issuing from the chain.
> On him who had crouched down they set their teeth,
>   And him they lacerated piece by piece,
>   Thereafter bore away those aching members."

For the idea of a pitiless maiden who cares not

what becomes of her lovers, may be compared a
fine Scots ballad, "Proud Lady Margaret."[1]
In this a damsel propounds a riddle to her
suitors. Failing to solve it, they must die.

A Scottish analogy.

> " ' And but ye read them richt,' she said,
>   ' Gae stretch ye out and dee.
>   If you should dee for me, Sir Knight,
>   There's few for ye will mean [moan];
>   For mony a better has died for me,
>   Whose graves are growing green.' "

At length a knight is successful. He is the ghost
of Margaret's brother, who rises from his grave to
warn Margaret of the consequences if she does not
mend her ways.

> " ' Leave off your pride, Margaret,' he says,
>   ' Use it not any mair,
>   Or when you come where I hae been,
>   You will repent it sair.
>   In Pirie's chair you'll sit, I say,
>   The lowest seat o' Hell;
>   If you do not amend your ways,
>   It's there that ye must dwell.' "

With regard to the merits of Boccaccio's prose,
opinions vary. He himself professes to have written
in a "fiorentino stile umilissimo." Whatever he may have intended by this apolo-
getic, self-depreciatory phrase, it can hardly be that
he aimed at a simple unaffected manner, or, if he did,
he is very far from having attained it. His prose

Style.

---

[1] The *Legendary Ballads of England and Scotland*. Compiled and
edited by John Roberts. London. P. 154.

is a tissue of Ciceronian periods which, *a priori*, most people would instantly condemn in a work of fiction, and which, *a posteriori*, indulgent critics defend on the ground that, before Boccaccio, Italian prose can hardly be said to have existed. How closely Boccaccio had studied ancient models may be seen from a comparison of his tale *The Lover in the Cask* (vii. 2) with Apuleius's treatment of the same theme.[1] In the main the tale is little else than a translation from the ninth book of the *Metamorphoses*, as such verbal coincidences as the following plainly show.

APULEIUS.

"Ego mulier et intra hospitium contenta, jamdudum septem denariis vendidi."

BOCCACCIO.

"Io feminella che non fui mai appena fuor dell' uscio . . . l' ho venduto sette."

Some writers, like Emiliani - Giudici, have proclaimed an utter distaste for the ponderosity of the style, and this particular judge does not scruple to own that he would find it no light task to read through a *giornata* of the *Decameron* at a breath. With him it is a question of "dragging oneself through all the delectable windings of the most elegant of our prose-styles." Nor is it only this literary free-thinker that has felt the irksomeness of a style that is undeniably laboured, and by the

---

[1] It is worthy of remark that, in borrowing tales from the ancients, Boccaccio Italianises them, and adapts them to existing conditions of life.

influence of which Italian prose even now is in some measure controlled. If Coleridge be right, and the best prose is, like Southey's, unobtrusive and thoroughly subordinated to the matter, then there is no more to be said, for this Boccaccio's prose is not. It resembles rather Coleridge's own style, which, as Hazlitt long ago observed, tends to be too majestic for its subject. However, a great master of our own generation—Carducci—takes up the cudgels valiantly on Boccaccio's behalf, and insists that seldom or never has instrument been adapted more perfectly to its ends. "This tongue of the Ciompi he is pleased to wind with all the cries and laments of every passion, to cause it to render with the variations of all the notes all the cries and laments of every passion, to cause it to follow with the blendings of all the tints all the adumbrations of an image" (*Discorso sui Parentali del Boccaccio*). The truth probably lies about midway between this perfervid estimate and the nihilism of Emiliani-Giudici, though even destructive criticism must, and does, recognise the grandeur of the art. The question really is, whether this art is not out of place, is not artificiality, and the answer to this question will vary with the individual and the age. Properly constructed, the period is an organism of exquisite formation, but it asks some attention ; and this the latter-day reader, not being of German nationality, refuses. The refusal is significant—but of what ? Is the abruptness of contemporary prose, the dispensing with literary ceremony, a concession to busier habits and inferior power of comprehension on the part of a wider, less educated public? Or is such impatience of form a sign of intellectual puberty, to which elaborate exposition is vexatious and almost an affront? Certain it is that prose like that of Milton is capable of a beauty and a dignity unattainable by one who writes in gasps, and yet—who can deny it?—smartness and tartness are the qualities of a good society novel. Boccaccio never thought of that. It seems to me, therefore, that Boccaccio's style is above reproach in the abstract, but is applied to an unnatural use. His masters developed that style in the forum; he imported it into the boudoir. It was a mistake.

Blunders are not always bad, least of all when they take the form of exaggerated art. If Boccaccio had *Boccaccio's triumph.* really chosen a "fiorentino stilo umilissimo," instead of achieving a most imposing reputation, he would have been nought. In these matters, as Lord Bacon has remarked, pride is a rare antiseptic, and the *Decameron* is exceeding proud. It triumphed in Italy, in Europe in the fourteenth century, and it triumphs still. Among the poets who have derived inspiration from it are Chaucer, Hans Sachs, Shakespeare, Lope de Vega (notably in his play *Servir con mala Estrella*), Molière, Dryden, Lessing, La Fontaine, and Alfred de Musset. The last-named observes in his *Sylvia*—

> " La Fontaine a ri dans Boccace,
> Où Shakespeare fondait en pleurs."

While I am forced to renounce any attempt to trace

in detail the effect of Boccaccio's labours, and more
especially of the *Decameron*, on the gen-
Disciples. eral course of things literary, it is requisite to point out the vast impulse it gave to prose-
writing in the Italian peninsula. Whereas prose had
been confined almost exclusively to sacred legend,
secular tradition, and didactic writing, principally in
the shape of translations, the second half of what has
been called the "Tuscan period" (A.D. 1283-1375) witnessed the growth of a rich harvest of original compositions—letters and sermons, treatises and histories,
novels and romances. Here I will deal only with a
trio of writers who may be claimed as Boccaccio's
immediate disciples. When the great prose-author
died in 1375, Franco Sacchetti sang:—

> "Ora è mancata ogni poesia,
> E vote son le case di Parnaso."

This was a high compliment, for Sacchetti also was a
poet, and of no mean order. Not to speak of his
sonnets, his *Battaglia delle Vecchie colle Giovane* is almost worthy of Berni. His *Novelle*, though doubtless
suggested by the *Decameron*, are composed in a different key. While there are realistic elements in Boccaccio, the natural tendency of that writer is towards
the romantic, the ideal, even the impossible, a characteristic especially noticeable in his version of the
Troilus legend. Sacchetti, on the other hand, a man
of affairs who had held important public charges, is
bent, not on creating a fancy world corresponding to
his own conceptions of *ought* and *should*, but on re-

producing the common, everyday life of his own age. His novels constitute a portrait-gallery of "marquises and counts or cavaliers, and gentlemen great and small, and also ladies, great, middling, and lesser, and people of every other sort." Many of his personages were still alive at the time he was writing of them. Sacchetti's stories partake largely of anecdote. They are short and lively, and the style is not like Boccaccio's, but simple, direct, and yet elegant—the style that is formed by the encounter of wits in society rather than by solitary pains in the closet. Of the *Trecento Novelle* only two hundred and twenty-three have come down to us, some of them mere fragments.

Of the *Pecorone* of "Ser Giovanni" and the novels of Giovanni Sercambi it is impossible to speak flatteringly. They are modelled so obviously on the *Decameron* that comparison is inevitable, and these cold and colourless, or dull and desultory, stories cannot bear the test. So far as Sercambi is concerned, his failure in this respect is partially redeemed by a vivid chronicle of Lucca, his native city.

CHAPTER VI.

THE WELL OF ENGLISH.

METRE—CHAUCER'S YOUTH—THE 'BOKE OF THE DUCHESSE'—CHAUCER
AND THE GREAT ITALIANS—PROSE TRANSLATIONS—THE INFLUENCE
OF BOETHIUS—THE 'HOUSE OF FAME'—THE 'LEGENDE OF GOODE
WOMEN'—THE 'CANTERBURY TALES'—JOHN GOWER.

IN England, as in Spain, the second half of the fourteenth century is marked by a new poetic blossoming.

Consecrated metres. Such a phenomenon has often, and perhaps
usually, its consecrated metre.   In Italy it
was *endecasillabi*, in Spain the *arte mayor*.   Chiefly
through Chaucer's example, a characteristic decasyllabic verse was destined to supplant in English favour
the heretofore fashionable short-rhymed couplets.   This
verse was not Chaucer's by invention.   It had appeared
in France as early as the *Song of Roland*, though, in
couplets, probably not much before Machault.   Such
couplets appear stragglingly in Hampole's English,
but perhaps by accident only.   Chaucer, too, employs
the "heroic couplet," but associates with its use a

stanza of seven lines—"rhyme royal." The mastery
Chaucer obtained over this form—albeit it had been
adopted before his time by both Provençal and North
French poets—renders it in a sense his own. The *arte
mayor* is found mostly in stanzas; and the growing use
of the stanza, of which evidence has already appeared
in the case of Boccaccio, and which will culminate
hereafter in the poems of Ariosto and Tasso, is typical
of the age.

It is to be remarked that Chaucer's verse differs
from the *arte mayor*, on which more will be said later,
The Craftsman. in its strictly syllabic, or perhaps one
should say iambic, character. On the other
hand, he dispensed with the observance of the fixed
cæsura, which in French and Provençal poetry invariably coincided with the conclusion of a foot, and so
introduced greater variety in the rhythms. Another
point is the order of the rhymes. Chaucer regularly
follows the system *ababbcc*, whereas his predecessors
had commonly preferred *ababbaa*. The employment
of a new rhyme, accentuating the close of the stanza,
is a peculiarly English craving, of which we find evidence in the transformation of the sonnet. It is
desirable to emphasise here and elsewhere the subject
of Chaucer's metres, because, though Chaucer himself
is much more than a master of rhyme and rhythm,
the distinguishing quality of the verse of which he
was—at any rate in England—both inaugurator and
most finished craftsman, is the art. Like Dante,
Chaucer not only dreamed but studied. He has

indeed bequeathed no treatise *De Vulgari Eloquentia*, but his grasp of the mysteries of verse is shown by the application of his ideas in practice. We have to do no more with ignorant minstrel or stupid monk, composing, as it were, by rote, but with a highly educated courtier who knew Latin, who knew French, and whose understanding was quickened by early and unbroken commerce with the world. Such a person was naturally fitted to act a leading part in a revolution—political, linguistic, literary—which, with the breakdown of royal and aristocratic prejudice, restored to the English race its place in the comity of nations.

The precise year of Chaucer's birth is unknown. It is conceivable that he himself did not know the *Birth and training.* date, since, in a deposition made by him at Westminster in October 1386, he stated that he was then "forty years and upwards," and "had been armed twenty-seven years." The word "upwards" is elastic, but, supposing it to represent "six," this would tally with other dates that have been ascertained, and make him, at his entry upon military service, nineteen years of age. His father and grandfather were wine-merchants in Thames Street, and it is not by any means unlikely that his early associations were to some extent revived in the realism of his maturer writings. The name Chaucer is Norman (chaucier = stockinger). In 1357, when he was sixteen or seventeen, he served as "squier" (or page) to the Princess Elizabeth, first wife of Lionel Duke of Clarence; and, two years later, he accompanied the expedition to France. There, taken prisoner, he was ransomed by the king for sixteen pounds. He was afterwards appointed "Valet of the King's Chamber," and married Philippa, stated to have been daughter to Sir Payne Roet, and one of the "demoiselles" in attendance on the Queen. Chaucer's connection with the Court easily explains the panegyrising and sentimental tone of his early poems, and their dependence on fashionable French models.

Appertaining to this first phase is the *Boke of the Duchese*, or *The Dethe of Blanche*. The source of the poem is Machault's *Dit de la Fontaine Amoureuse*, which has been expanded by means of allegorical accretions and learned allusions in imitation of the *Romance of the Rose*. The metre is the short couplet, as in the *Dit*, but the characteristic defect of this metre, its noisy monotonousness,[1] is reduced, as Chaucer handles it, by frequent *enjambement*. It is noteworthy that the English poet acknowledges no obligation, an omission partly accounted for by his borrowing from Machault rather the hint than the actual development of the theme. The poem commences with a personal note. Chaucer complains of sleeplessness, due, he believes, to a malady from which he has suffered these eight years, and which only one physician can remedy. To "drive the night away," he takes a book. Though he does

The Boke of the Duchesse.

[1] To realise this, one has only to read the first dozen lines of *The Lady of the Lake*.

not name the work, we know it to be Ovid's *Meta-morphoses,* and what he reads is the piteous tale of Ceyx and his true spouse Halcyone. This story Chaucer, following Machault's precedent, but writing with greater detail, narrates as a prologue and parallel to the more significant sequel.

Hardly has he finished reading this tale when he falls asleep and has a wondrous dream. It is May. His chamber is flooded with sweet bird-music, and transformed into a palace of delight. Windows and walls are all painted o'er with the Story of Troy and the Romance of the Rose. This changes to a hunting-scene, and that to the vision of a young man clad in black and sitting with his back against a huge oak. The poet greets him, and attempts to learn his thoughts, at first without success, but, persevering, draws from him an elaborate description of one whom he calls "the goode faire White." The disconsolate knight dwells on her personal charms, her accomplishments, the freshness and innocence of her character, but does not state their relationship. Moreover, it is only at the close of the poem that the fact of her death is distinctly conveyed. The vision concludes rather abruptly. On awaking the poet finds that he has still in hand the book of "Alcyone and Seys the Kynge," and mentally resolves to put the quaint dream in rhyme, and that soon.

It would be possible to read this poem without the slightest suspicion of its real intention. The dream *appears* to have grown, quite in accordance with what we know of dreams, out of the tale; but, in point of

T

fact, it was evolved out of the circumstances in which the English Court then found itself. All *The intention.* were lamenting the death of Blanche, daughter and heiress of the Duke of Lancaster, and wife of John of Gaunt; but the only words in the *Boke* which plainly refer to her are those already cited, "goode faire White." By inditing this poem, which so delicately enshrines her memory, Chaucer claims the position of poet-laureate of the Plantagenets. But, with all his delicacy, he is not very well suited to the position. In this early, technically by no means perfect, composition, the dramatic quality of his genius begins to peep. Instead of concentrating his efforts on a threnody, he drops almost insensibly into dialogue. To be sure, the speeches are inordinately spun out.

To the same phase, or period, as the *Boke of the Duchesse* belongs the *Compleynte of the Dethe of Pité*. *The Compleynte of the Dethe of Pité.* Here we have fully described the "sickness" at which he had hinted in the former work. The germ of the poem is discoverable in the *Romance of the Rose*. Chaucer, "ful of busy peyne," had written a letter to Pity, but, on running to deliver it, finds her dead, and buried in a heart. As the poet cannot hand the "bill" to Dame Pity, he passes it to the reader instead. The allegory is rather bare. The *Compleynte* is in "rhyme royal," and probably the first instance of the employment of this metre in the English tongue. A stanza may be quoted in illustration of both metre and symbolism :—

"Aboute hir herse there stoden lustely,
Withouten any woo, as thoughte me,
Bounté, parfyte wel araied and richely,
And fressch Beauté, Lust and Jolyté
Assured-maner, Youthe and Honesté
Wisdome, Estaat, Drede and Governance,
Confedred bothe by honde and alliance."

An example of an eight-lined stanza, very similar in form except for the splitting of the couplet by inter-position of a *b* rhyme, occurs in Chaucer's A.B.C., an invocation of Mary translated, at the desire of the "goode faire White," from Deguilleville. In some minor pieces, artistically constructed after French models, we have, it may be, the remains of Chaucer's youthful lyric.

In 1369 Chaucer was present, with Petrarch and Froissart (who mentions a certain "Joffroy Chaucier"),

Chaucer and the great Italians. at the marriage of Lionel, Duke of Clarence, with Violanta, daughter of Galeazzo, Lord of Milan. He was again in Italy in 1372-73, and a third time in 1378. The effect of these visits was to set him in touch with the Italian Renaissance, and he used his opportunities for his individual bene-fit and for that of his native literature. With his return to England after his first Italian tour begins a new artistic phase of which the dominant notes are inspired by Dante, Petrarch, and Boccaccio. So far as Dante was concerned, there could be no question of personal relations—he had long been dead—but in Chaucer's verse is found ample evidence that the English poet had made careful study of Dante's works. Let us take, first of all, a composition produced at this

time—the *Secounde Nonnes Tale*—and compare the
following passages :—

> "Vergine Madre, figlia del tuo Figlio,
>   Umile ed alta più che creatura,
>   Termine fisso d' eterno consiglio,
> Tu se' colei che l' umana natura
>   Nobilitasti sì, che il suo Fattore
>   Non disdegnò di farsi sua fattura."
>
> —*Paradiso*, xxxiii. 1-6.

> "Thou mayde and moder, daughter of thi sone,
>   Thow welle of mercy, synful soules cure,
>   In whom that God of bountes cheese to wone,
>   Thou humble and heyh over every creature,
>   Thow nobeledst so ferforth oure nature
>   That no disdeyn the maker had of kynde
>   His sone in blood and fleissch to clothe and wynde."

We miss here the vigorous phrasing "fattore—farsi
—fattura" (for which compare "Amor, che a nullo
amato amar perdona," *Inf.*, v. 103); but Chaucer felt
its force, since in the following stanza he seeks to
copy it in the words "creatour of every creature."
The English writer, in this place, does not mention
Dante, though the imitation is too close to admit of
the least question.   In a rather similar instance—the
section of the *Monkes Tale* entitled *De Hugilino Comite
Pise*—the obligation is avowed :—

> "Of this tregede it ought ynough suffise ;
>   Who-so will hiere it in a lenger wise,
>   Rede the grete poet of Itaile
>   That highte Dante, for he can it devise,
>   Fro poynte to poynte nought oon word wil he fayle."

This passage, however, contains something more than

an acknowledgment. The manner shows how profoundly, though perhaps in a certain degree unconsciously, Chaucer's style has been influenced by the *Commedia*. The free unconventional allusion to an earlier prophet necessarily recalls the lines :—

> " Ma leggi Ezechiel, che li dipigne
>   Come li vide dalla fredda parte
>   Venir con vento, con nube e con igne ;
> E quali i troverai nelle sue carte
>   Tali eran quivi, salvo ch' alle penne
>   Giovanni è meco, e da lui si diparte."
>   —*Purgatorio*, xxix. 100-105.

Thus it becomes manifest that Chaucer was familiar with parts of the three *cantiche*, and from the fact *A doubtful argument.* that he, in each case, recollects or translates from concluding cantos, it may perhaps be deduced that he was familiar with the poem as a whole. Sir Harris Nicolas judges otherwise, and contends that Chaucer was blandly ignorant of Italian. He says, "That Chaucer was not acquainted with Italian may be inferred from his not having introduced any Italian quotation into his works, redundant as they are with Latin and French words and phrases." The true inference from this omission is not what Sir Harris Nicolas suggests, but that Italian would have been unintelligible to the vast majority of Chaucer's readers. I cannot lump together all the proofs of Chaucer's knowledge of the *Commedia*. Of these more will be cited later. That he knew it well is certain, and the most feasible explanation of such knowledge is that he obtained it from a personal perusal of the poem.[1]

What is true of Dante is true, in a less degree, of Petrarch, one of whose sonnets (*S' amor non è, che dunque è quel che sento?*), expanded into three stanzas, is embedded in *Troilus.* With regard to their literary, and perhaps personal, relations the *locus classicus* is in *The Clerk of Oxenfordes Prologue :—*

The "laureat poete."

> " I wil yow telle a tale, which that I
> Lerned at Padowe of a worthy clerk,
> As provyd by his wordes and his werk.
> He is now deed and nayled in his chest,
> Now God give his soule wel good rest !
> Fraunces Petrark, the laureat poete,
> Highte this clerk, whos rethorique swete
> Enlumynd al Ytail of poetrie."

These lines have suggested, and suggested very naturally, that, during one of his visits to Italy, Chaucer obtained the story of Griselda from Petrarch's own lips. It is a fact that Petrarch was keenly interested in the story, and translated it from Boccaccio's Italian into Latin.   The incident is one that, apart from any

---

[1] Into the quarrel between poet and patrician, which was so vital a matter to the Guinicellian school, Chaucer did not feel called upon to enter.   If he had, he might have been found ranged on the side opposite to that of Dante.   Nevertheless, in a theological rather than sociological sense, he expounds the doctrine of true nobility :—

> " Ful selde upriseth by his branches smale
> Prowesse of man, for God of his goodnesse
> Wol that we claime of him our gentilesse :
> For of our elders may we nothing claime
> But temporel thing, that man may hurt and maime."
>
> (*Wif of Bathes Tale ;* cp. *Purg.*, vii. 121.)

question of dates, might probably have occurred, and it is consistent with Chaucer's practice to shroud his personality under the mask of a fictitious character. That is about all that need be said on the subject, though the topic occupies several pages in Sir Harris Nicolas' biography, and leads him to indulge in violent and quite unnecessary invective against Godwin. Whether or not there was ever an interview between the poets, it is incontestable that the *Clerkes Tale* is based upon Petrarch's version. The moral of the tale is expressed in the following words:—

> "That every wight in his degré
> Shulde be constant in adversité,
> As was Grisild; therefore Petrarch writeth
> This story, which with high stile he enditeth."

The allusion, of course, is to Petrarch's Latin style, which Chaucer was good enough scholar to admire, though not to imitate. That defines his attitude to Petrarch generally. The words "high stile" are convertible with "rethorique swete," which, as we saw, is his description of Petrarch's verse. Both phrases imply a certain distance. The two poets had, in fact, very little in common. As regards mental constitution —the distinction is trite, but may serve once more— Petrarch is *subjective*, Chaucer *objective*. If we come to metre, even when Chaucer writes lyrics, he employs, not the sonnet, but current French forms, and that is proof that he had not succumbed, or only partially and temporarily, to Petrarch's charm.

The contrast between Petrarch and Chaucer is very marked in their posture towards Latin. Petrarch was,

at heart, a literary oligarch. Latin was his fortress;
Latin, his bodyguard. His motto is, "Odi
profanum vulgus, et arceo;" and he confides
his most precious thoughts, nearly all of his inner life
that does not concern his lady, to the Latin language.
He loves to figure as an ancient Roman born out of
due time. With these sentiments Chaucer has, apparently, no sympathy. He does not oppose himself
to the tendencies of the age, and those tendencies
include the free use of the vernacular, not only in
verse, but in prose. Chaucer aided this development
by a series of translations, of which, however, only
one has been handed down intact. His version of
Innocentius' *De Contemptu Mundi* is represented by
fragments inserted in his later poems; his version of
Origen's homily *De Maria Magdalena* has perished
utterly. The character of these translations may
perhaps be inferred from the rendering of Boethius' *De
Consolatione Philosophiæ*. In spite of occasional errors
of no great importance, this version is a faithful reflex
of the original, but it does more than translate—it
interprets. Sometimes this is accomplished by a
periphrasis, sometimes by interpolating a gloss. Here
is an illustration :—

Translations.

"Who so that the covertures of her veyn apparailes
myght strepen of thise proude kynges, that thou seest
sitten on heyghe in her chayeres, glyterynge in
shynynge purpre, envyroned with sorweful armures,
manasyng with cruel mouthe, blowynge by woodnesse
of herte—he sholde se than that thilke lordes beren
withinne hir corages ful streyte cheynes. For leccherye

tormentith hem on that oon syde with gredy venyms
and troubable Ire, that araisith in hem the floodes of
troublynges, tourmentith upon that other side hir
thought, or sorwe halt hem wery or ycaught, or slidyng
and disseyvyng hope tourmentith hem.   And ther-
fore syn thou seest oon heed—that is to seyne oon
tyraunt—bere so many tyrauntis, than ne doth thilke
tyraunt nat that he desirith, syn he is cast doune with
so many wicked lordes—that is to seyn with so many
vices, that han so wicked lordshipes over hym."

Compare with this the conclusion of the passage in
the original (iv., Metr. 2):—

> " Hinc enim libido versat
>   Avidis corda venenis,
>   Hinc flagellat ira mentem
>   Fluctus turbida tollens,
>   Mæror aut captos fatigat,
>   Aut spes lubrica torquet.
>   Ergo, cum caput tot unum
>   Cernas ferre tyrannos,
>   Non facit, quod optat, ipse
>   Dominus pressus iniquis."

This translation of Boethius, diffuse and disfigured,
like Wiclif's more famous translation of the Bible, by
frequent Latinisms, proves that since the days of
Alfred, the first translator, English prose has made
by no means the same strides as English verse.   In
fact, it is still infantile.   For the production of good
prose a more or less advanced civilisation appears to
be a necessary condition.   Nevertheless such efforts
—and in this connection we must not forget Trevisa's
translation of Higden's *Polychronicon*—to employ prose

as a vehicle, whether successful or otherwise, are extremely significant, attesting alike the growing prosperity of the middle and lower orders, and the participation of the learned class in the general European literary movement towards prose.

Chaucer could not translate a work like Boethius' *Consolation* without being profoundly influenced by
Philosophy.
the thought, if indeed interest in the thought did not occasion the translation. The interest and influence are visible in two ways. First, in modifying Chaucer's conceptions of love—in substituting for the chivalrous notion expounded in his earlier works the more philosophic idea of love as a chain binding earth and sea, as a universal, all-pervading bond of union. Secondly, in inducing a sort of scepticism. How is it possible to reconcile the freedom of the human will with the fact of Divine providence? The problem is insoluble, and so Chaucer found it. It is poor Troilus that discusses the point—

> " 'For certeynly, this woote I wel,' he sayde,
> 'That forsyght of devyne purvyaunce
> Hathe seyn alwey me to forgon Criseyde,
> Syn God seth every thynge, out of doutance,
> And hem disponeth thorugh his ordinaunce,' " &c.[1]

This discussion of the prescience of God and necessity is evidently founded on the fifth book of the
Troilus and Cryseide.
Consolation of Philosophy, and the theme of the poem is man in relation to Fortune. Although the story of *Troilus* is borrowed from

[1] *Troilus and Cryseide*, bk. iv., stanza 134 *et seqq.* For Chaucer's philosophy of love see the same poem, bk. ii., stanzas 243-245.

Boccaccio, and, indeed, based on the *Filostrato*, Chaucer, when writing it, was still under the spell of Dante. The style, the landscapes, prove this, and in the envoy Chaucer translates a terzine of the *Paradiso* literally :—

> " Quell' uno e due e tre che sempre vive
>   E regna sempre in tre e due ed uno,
>   Non circonscritto, e tutto circonscrive."

> " Thow One, and Two, and Thre ! eterne on live,
>   That raignest ay in Thre, and Two, and One,
>   Uncircumscript, and al maist circumscrive."

Towards the close the poet speaks as though conscious that he had not yet achieved his mission. He terms his " litel boke " a tragedy, and expresses the hope that God will vouchsafe that he may compose, ere he dies, some comedy. It is probable that he uses this word " comedy " much in Dante's sense, and that he is alluding to the *House of Fame*, of which he had already conceived the plan, and in which Dante's influence is still more apparent. We, however, with our knowledge of what was to befall, are tempted to read into this utterance a prophecy of the *Canterbury Tales*.

It seems to be generally accepted that the Glasgow fragment printed in some editions as part of *The Romance of the Rose.* Chaucer's translation of the *Romance of the Rose*, is not that which procured for him Deschamps' well-meant but woefully inadequate compliment, " Grant translateur, noble Geoffroy Chaucier." The fact of the translation is rendered absolutely certain by his own allusions and the

evidence of his immediate successors.   It belonged to
the period of recreancy in which he half-abjured his
old faiths and ideals.   What attracted him in the
Romance was Jean de Meung's satirical turn and
attacks on women, and in the prologue of the *Legende
of Goode Women* the God of Love takes him to task
for the achievement :—

> " Thou mayst it nat denye,
> For in pleyne text, withouten nede of glose,
> Thou hast translated the Romaunce of the Rose,
> That is a heresye ayeins my lawe,
> And makest wise folk fro me withdrawe."

Closely connected with the translation of the
Romance of the Rose are two occasional poems—*The
Complaynt of Mars and Venus* and *The
Parlement of Briddes* (or, The Assembly
of Foules).   Both are allegorical renderings of court incidents, and the first, oddly enough,
is a poetical version of a scandalous intrigue.   Neither
John of Gaunt nor Chaucer himself were persons of
strict morals, and it would appear that the Duke of
Lancaster had watched with Pan-like satisfaction the
progress of an adulterous game, in which the principals
were Isabella, the younger sister of his wife, Constance
of Castille, and John Holland, a great-grandson of
Edward I.   The injured husband was his own brother,
Edmund, Earl of Cambridge.   The *Complaynt* consists
of three divisions : (i.) an Introduction, supplying what
purports to be the history of the affair; (ii.) the *Complaynt of Mars ;* (iii.) the *Complaynt of Venus*.   The
last-named division is practically a distinct poem,

dating from a later period, and translated from Oto
de Granson. The whole concludes with an envoy.
The metre is varied with each new departure. The
Introduction is in "rhyme royal." Next we have a
nine-lined stanza (*aabaabbcc*), an extension or development of "rhyme royal," while Venus complains in a
seven-lined stanza augmented by a refrain, which
changes after each set of three stanzas. The envoy
approximates to the Old French and Provençal forms,
from which "rhyme royal" was evolved, and runs
aabaabbaab.

The *Complaynt* opens with an address to the birds,
with whom Chaucer, in his capacity as songster, identifies himself. He quotes very solemnly the
speech of a certain biped, from which it
results that the date of the *Complaynt* is St Valen-
tine's Day. This circumstance forms a connecting
link between the allegory of Mars and Venus and the
Parlement of Briddes, which is throughout in "rhyme
royal." The real subject of the latter poem is the
wooing of Princess Ann of Luxemburg by Richard II.
The English king was opposed by the rivalry of two
German princes, and the negotiations were protracted
over a year. At length the object was attained, and
the young couple were married on the 14th of January
1382. As with the *Boke of the Duchesse*, so here
Chaucer finds inspiration in an old-world story. This
time it is "Scipio's Dream," of which he gives an
account based, no doubt, on Macrobius. Then follows
the inevitable "swevene," which contains reminiscences of the Divine Comedy. Chaucer's guide is,

The Parlement
of Briddes.

not Virgil, but Scipio Africanus, who conducts him to the gate of a park enclosed by walls of green stone. Over this gate are two inscriptions, one of which is contradicted by the other:—

> "Thorgh me men goon into that blysful place
>   Of hertes hele and dedely woundes cure," &c. ;

says one, and

> "'Thorgh me men goon,' thanne spake that other side,
>   'Unto the mortale strokes of the spere,'" &c.

These inscriptions recall, and made be said to parody, that famous writing over Hell-gate:—

> "Per me si va nella città dolente,
>   Per me si va nell' eterno dolore,
>   Per me si va tra la perduta gente," &c.[1]

The idea of this Garden of Love was almost certainly suggested by the description of a like place in the first part of the *Romance of the Rose,* where Nature is introduced as God's vicar. In the *Parlement of Briddes* this divinity is endowed with qualities elsewhere attributed to Love:—

> "Nature, the vyker of thalmyghty Lorde,
>   That hoot, cold, hevy, lyght, moiste, and drye
>   Hath knyt, by evene noumbre of accorde."

Nature holds on her hand a "formel [*i.e.*, female] egle," who is in want of a mate, and, so to speak, she invites applications for her. A royal eagle advances his claim, but two other tercels profess to love her

---

[1] *Inferno,* iii. 1-9.

better. This "cursed pleading," which lasts from morn to sunset, is resented by the other birds, who make the place ring with their cries, "Kek, kek, kukkow, Quek, quek, hye!" They afterwards express their sentiments in more articulate fashion. Finally Nature yields the choice to the lady most chiefly concerned. The "formel egle" is modest:—

> "I wolle noght serven Venus ne Cupide
> Forsoth as yet, by no maner weye."

Nature thereupon puts off the decision for a year, bidding the rival tercels meanwhile be of good heart, and strive to render themselves worthy. As for the other birds who have got suited, they are dismissed amidst great jubilation, and, according to custom, sing in honour of their patroness a roundel "maked in Fraunce." The "debate" was a form so common in mediæval literature that it is needless, and might be useless, to quest for the immediate model of the *Parlement*. The real sources of the poem have been already indicated. It may perhaps be added that, although the idea of the Garden was suggested by a French prototype, it seems on a comparison extremely probable that Chaucer was indebted for much of the detail to descriptive passages in the *Teseide*, which poem, as we have seen, furnished material for *Palamon and Arcite*.

The *House of Fame* is introspective. In it Chaucer reviews his life and his aims, and the work affords evidence of some discontent. Apart from books and dreams, the world is a dismal waste. From what is

said later it is plain that, under this similitude, he
The House alludes to the dry ciphering which occupied
of Fame.   him in his official post.   At the date of the
composition of the poem he had just come back from
a pilgrimage, from mingling with his kind; and, fresh
from the delights of society, he seems to have asked
himself, with reference to his wearisome toil and fine-
spun ideal world, "What profit?"   Chaucer, moreover,
had not been happy in love, and it is for that reason
that the walls of the Temple of Venus are glum with
the story of Æneas, and more particularly with Dido's
martyrdom.   The poet needed distraction.

Like the *Divine Comedy*, of which the *House of Fame*
is a palpable copy, Chaucer's vision is divided into
three parts, and the first part represents the *Inferno*.
Of this intention a hint may be found in the allusions
there made to the pains of hell, in which Dante is
mentioned by name.   From the brittle, unsatisfying
pleasures of youth, which are his to celebrate, not to
enjoy, Chaucer is raised by the spirit of philosophy,
here symbolised as an eagle "with fethres as of gold."
This artifice is undoubtedly taken from the *Purgatorio*.
The very wording shows that—

> "In sogno mi parea veder sospesa
>   Un' aquila nel ciel con penne d' oro,
>   Con l' ali aperte, ed a calare intesa."

> "Me thought I sawgh an egle sore
>
>   .   .   .   .   .   .
>
>   Hyt was of golde and shone so bryght,
>   And somewhat downwarde gan it lyght."

At the same time it is to be remembered that Chaucer,

like Dante, hardly ever owed everything to any one
source or suggestion. His reference to Icarus and
Ganymede (ii. 61) is a proof and illustration of con-
verging influences. The eagle of the *House of Fame* is,
in truth, a composite being. Something he has in
him of the bird of burden just mentioned, something
of Dante's Virgil, something, and much more, of the
beatified Beatrice, since he imparts to Geoffrey, whilst
they are yet in mid-air, weighty moral and astronomical lessons. The House of Fame, whither they now
arrive, is formed of a mountain of ice, the sides whereof are covered with names. Chaucer observes with
dismay that many of these names are in process of
being erased, and he finds that this is due to the
action of the sun. On the north side the inscriptions
are as fresh as when first graven. This, however,
brings no consolation, since it is only a symptom of
the caprice of Fame, own sister to Fortune. An important share of the third part of the poem is devoted
to the throwing into relief of this hateful characteristic.
Desert goes for nothing; all depends on what " me
lyst." Fame's messenger is Æolus, the god of wind,
and he has two clarions, Clere Laude and Sclaundre.
It is the blast of Sclaundre that requites the good
deeds pleaded by meritorious suppliants. The palace
where Fame dwells is spoken of as a castle. Beneath,
in a valley, is a wooden house with innumerable doors
always open, whence speed all manner of tidings.
"Fama" in Latin signifies "rumour," and this postscript was doubtless suggested by a well-known passage in the *Æneid*. The general outlines, however—

U

the castle on the hill, and the house in the valley, the latter crowded with shipmen and pilgrims, pardoners and couriers and messengers—bear an astonishing resemblance to the prologue of *Piers Plowman*.

With regard to the significance of the poem, it seems quite inaccurate to suppose that Chaucer here teaches himself the lesson of resignation. *The moral.* Nothing was further from his thoughts. While the *Commedia* is the fruit of disappointment, the sense of the futility of things earthly, the *House of Fame* embodies an aspiration—I may say, a hope—to share more fully than hitherto these very things. In the parable it is Jupiter that lifts him out of his irksome groove; but all the while he is thinking of Richard II. of England, and, by dint of allegory, he contrives to acquaint the king with his desires. He wants leisure, and this he can obtain only by being relieved of the active duties of his office. Chaucer's hints were neither ignored nor misunderstood. On the 25th November 1384 he was granted a month's leave; and on the 17th February following he was allowed to appoint a permanent deputy. For these favours he was indebted, there is reason to believe, to the intercession of Queen Ann; and this circumstance accounts for the fact that before, or contemporaneously with, the production of the *Canterbury Tales*, he applied himself to the making of a poem which savours rather of the Temple of Venus than the Pilgrimage to Saint Leonard.

From the prologue of the *Legende of Goode Women* it would appear that Chaucer had been treated to

much unkind criticism, and that perhaps was the
The Legende of reason why he had dwelt, at the conclusion
Goode Women. of the *House of Fame*, on the universality
of false reports. Like Milton, he had felt the sting
of "evil tongues." In the *Legende of Goode Women*
Chaucer at once states the case for the defendant, and
makes the *amende honorable*. In certain of his earlier
poems he had assailed the credit of the sex and
ridiculed the "great passion." Now, as an act of
complaisance to his benefactress, he recants his errors,
and sings in moving strains the constancy of true
womanhood. Once more he owes the frame, the broad
outlines, of his poetry to Boccaccio, who had written
in Latin prose a cyclic work *About Famous Women*.
But Chaucer's scholarly attainments enabled him to
have recourse to the fountainhead—to more than one
fountainhead; and this he seems to have preferred
to slavish dependence on what may be termed "classical dictionaries." He consults a late mediæval work,
the *Trojan History* of Guido of the Columns, for whom
he has discarded his former mentor, Benoît de Sainte-
More; but apart from this, his sources are Livy, Florus,
Virgil's *Æneid*, Ovid's *Fasti* and *Metamorphoses*, and,
above all, Ovid's *Heroides*. A characteristic of the
Early Renaissance is the intermingling of Christian
and pagan elements; and so, while fetching his
material, or most of it, from classical authors,
Chaucer squares and fashions it into a *legendarium*
or martyrology.

The most interesting portion of the *Legende* is, in
many respects, the prologue, which bears witness to

an agreeable change in the poet's condition. He no
longer wastes tiresome hours in casting up
Daisy-worship.   accounts, but spends the whole day, from
sunrise to sunset, amidst the carols of the birds and
in the worship of the " emperice and floure of floures
all," the daisy. In the evening he hies home, and
lays him down to rest in a little arbour, so that
he may be abroad betimes to see the flower open,
and with this thought he falls asleep. Anon he
dreams a dream, wherein the God of Love appears
to him, leading by the hand a queen "got up" as
a daisy :—

> " And she was clad in real habite grene ;
>   A fret of gold she hadde next her heer,
>   And upon that a white corowne she beer.
>   .   .   .   .   .   .
>   The white corowne above the grene
>   Made hire lyke a daysie for to sene."

The stage-name of this beauteous lady, in whose
honour Chaucer is constrained to indite a hyperbolical
ballade, is Alcestis, who, according to Froissart, was
turned into a daisy; but " goode Queen Alceste " is
but a symbol of another queen, to whom Chaucer is
to deliver his book, when finished, " at Eltham, or at
Sheene." It is a notable coincidence that Chaucer
wrote in all nine legends—a total corresponding to
the number of years that Queen Ann survived. His
martyrs are Cleopatra, Thisbe, Dido, Hypsipile and
Medea, Lucrece, Ariadne, Philomela, Phyllis, and
Hypermnestra. He himself speaks of this task as a
penance, probably intending the expression playfully ;

but the themes, as remote from that realism for which his soul yearned, and precluding the exercise of his gift of humour, were not specially congenial, and at last he seems to have wearied of them. Something of this weariness appears in the perfunctoriness of the concluding tales, which, as compared with the preceding narratives, exhibit an appreciable falling off. Although Dante is cited, the *Legende of Goode Women* indicates a waning of his influence before the seductions of Ovid and Virgil, whose words Chaucer—not always accurately—translates. But the chief significance of the poem lies in this—that, whilst its contents may be deemed in a certain sense reactionary, its outward form marks another stage in the direction of the *Canterbury Tales*. The *Legende of Goode Women* is, in fact, the first example in English of a connected series of short versified tales in decasyllabic couplet. *The Seven Sages* (to seek no further) is, though much earlier, in octosyllables.

In the *House of Fame* Chaucer had reverted to the short couplet as more suited than "rhyme royal" for the purpose of narration. During this excursus he had apparently felt anew the disadvantages of octosyllabic verse,[1] and in the *Legende of Goode Women* he employs a compromise—heroic couplets, of which his successors were destined to make so large a use, but which now appear for the first time in English literature. The earliest application of this metre may perhaps be criticised as

Metre.

---

[1] Chaucer's, however, are splendid octosyllables, the first really good, and among the best to this day.

inopportune, as out of accord with the tenderness and pathos of the subject ; but, whatever we may think of its handselling, the value of the metre, its aptness for humour and characterisation, is at once realised on reaching the *Canterbury Tales*.

It is fairly certain that the germ of the *Canterbury Tales* is to be sought in actual experience. We know *The Canterbury Tales.* from the *House of Fame* that Chaucer had gone a-pilgrimaging, and that this transient glimpse of the world had left a deep impression on him. Probably it was at this time that the idea of describing such a journey laid hold of his imagination, though he may have been previously acquainted with the account of the pilgrimage to Saint Truth in the vision of *Piers Plowman*. A motley company of pilgrims meet at the Tabard in Southwark, and on the proposal of mine host each agrees to tell a story in going to, and returning from, the shrine of St Thomas at Canterbury. This programme, so far as the record is concerned, was never carried out. There are twenty-nine pilgrims, and only twenty-four tales, so that, assigning one tale to each pilgrim, five would be required to make up the promised number of stories during the journey *to* Canterbury. The whole of the remainder of the work—the stay at Canterbury, the tales told during the journey from Canterbury, and the prize - supper which the company was to "stand" the winner — remains a blank. Not only was the plan of the *Canterbury Tales* never completed, but there are indications that, with the progress of the work, the plan itself underwent modifications. For instance, in the general prologue the host stipulates—

> " That ech of yow to schorte with your weie,
> In this viage, schal telle tales tweye,
> To Caunturburi-ward, I mene it so,
> And hom-ward he schal tellen other tuo."

In the prologue of the *Persones Tale*, the host observes, on the contrary—

> " Now lakketh us no tales moo than *oon*,"

and adjures the parson—

> " Ne breke nought oure play,
> For every man, save thou, hath told his tale."

Another difficulty respects the number of the pilgrims. In l. 24 of the general prologue Chaucer states plainly that there came into the Tabard

> " Wel nyne and twenty in a companye ";

but immediately upon this he proceeds to enumerate, himself included, thirty-one. It has been proposed to surmount this difficulty by rejecting ll. 163, 164—the latter, at any rate—as interpolated; but Chaucer's inconsistencies do not end here, and rather than disturb the text on non-textual grounds, it will be better to regard these contradictions as due to vacillation on the part of the writer, who, distracted by the untoward and unlooked-for bulkiness of his task, either forgot or neglected to reconcile those passages in which his change of purpose is betrayed.

The poet's inclusion of himself is significant in two

ways. First, in his own eyes he figures no longer as *Self-por-* a recluse, but as a citizen of the world. *traiture.* With that frankness, however, which is one of his most engaging qualities, he recognises that he has not yet acquired the style and address of a man of affairs. There is that about him which testifies to his abode in Faëry—something uncanny. The other characters in the play are minutely described in the general prologue. For obvious reasons Chaucer could not very well take this course with himself; but in the prologue of *Sir Thopas* he makes the host criticise his appearance, and that worthy performs the duty with a plain-spokenness leaving nothing to be desired. Secondly, it may be remarked that Chaucer's self-consciousness, distinguishing him from the crowd of adapters, usually but not invariably nameless, is a sign that he has correctly estimated his importance as an artist. Appropriation of the laurel is a feature in the three great Italians; but while Dante, Petrarch, and Boccaccio openly formulate their claim, the Englishman's dry humour causes him to prefer another method. Instead of asserting his superiority to the despicable race of minstrels, he affects to fraternise with them, to be no better than they, knowing full well that thus his merits will shine forth more conspicuously. By putting into the mouth of a layman (and such a layman!) blunt condemnation of rhyme as opposed to alliterative verse and prose, he as it were calls attention to the whole subject, and by parodying the kind of rhyme hitherto in vogue—rhyme without reason—he enhances the effect of his own studied composition. More generally, his object was to pass a sweeping condemnation on the whole class of what were, for the most part, vulgar travesties of a moribund art.

Turning to the substitute, there are excellent reasons for surmising that the *Canterbury Tales* were projected not without mental reference to the *Decameron*. Already Chaucer had borrowed so many hints from Boccaccio that it is idle to suppose the coincidence accidental. Ocular reference is another matter, and it is likely that Chaucer, though he had probably read the *Decameron*, himself did not possess a copy. Otherwise it is extremely odd that hardly any, perhaps none, of the *Canterbury Tales* can be traced to Boccaccio's work; and this circumstance, so far as it goes—and, taken singly, it seems to go a long way—undoubtedly supports Sir Harris Nicolas's contention that Chaucer knew little or nothing of Italian. We may take as a crucial instance the not very edifying *Reeves Tale*. Here Tyrwhitt is unquestionably right in surmising that, whereas the story had been referred to the *Decameron* (D. ix., N. 6), "both Boccace and Chaucer have taken whatever they have in common from an old *Fabliau* or *Conte* of an anonymous French rhymer, *De Gombert et des deux Clers*." This is awkwardly expressed, and the *fabliau*, anonymous in one version, was the work of Jean de Boves. Still Tyrwhitt is right in the main. Further investigation proves, beyond any possibility of mistake, that Chaucer did not base his story on the *Decameron*, but on the *fabliau*. Of the *fabliau* itself there exist two versions, one con-

The Canterbury Tales and the Decameron.

tained in Legrand's (iii. 102) and the other in Barbazan's collection (i. 238). These versions differ in certain particulars—*e.g.*, in one the victim is a miller, in the other a host—and, to make an end of controversy, Chaucer follows the former, Boccaccio the latter account.

All this, however, does not prove that Chaucer had never seen or studied the *Decameron*, and it is not at all improbable that the English poet, in the maturity of his powers, deliberately attempted an improvement. The inconvenience of harping on one string had been brought home to him in the case of the *Legende of Goode Women*, and, indeed, nothing is more obvious than that, when the narrators are ten young people equal in rank and education, a certain monotony is inevitable, or, at least, only to be avoided by violating dramatic probabilities. The dramatic instinct was not Boccaccio's strong point, and Chaucer was a dramatist in everything but form. Boccaccio was fully alive to the need of variety, but, in order to obtain it, reduced his *dramatis personæ* to mere puppets. There are no puppets in the *Canterbury Tales*. The persons of the play are actual breathing types, men and women whose appearance, calling, and mental idiosyncrasies contribute not a little to the effect of their recitals. Instead of belonging to the same set, they are taken from every class of society except the very highest and the very lowest. The limitations are important, in that they reveal the true artist resolved not to impair in any degree the accuracy of his presentment.

The players.

In other words, he excludes from his group those whose presence would have clashed with everyday experience of life. As it is, the list is quite varied enough, and embraces a knight, a squire, a yeoman, a prioress, three priests, a merchant, an Oxford scholar, a barrister, a draper, a cook, a physician, a ploughman, a miller, and many more.

Ten Brink, in his admirable chapters on Chaucer, is fond of calling him a *Weltkind*. This expression is accurate enough, in so far as it denotes *Worldliness.* complete emancipation from ecclesiastical prejudice; but Chaucer was not, and he recognised that he was not, a typical worldling. If you compare him with Langland or Wiclif, he seems a worldly sort of person, because he does not permit himself to be carried away by moral indignation or passion for reform. But the world, I think, finds a much truer representative in Boccaccio, whose anti-religious bias is unmistakable. Chaucer cannot properly be described as an enemy either of religion or of the Church. Just as he declines to mix himself up with the political controversies of the day, so likewise he studiously holds aloof from ethical and doctrinal disputations. In all causes, religious and civil, he steadily refuses to take sides; he is not a citizen but an *elf*. The result of this neutrality, this purely observant attitude, is seen in the absolute fairness and fidelity of his portraiture, even though, as might be expected from his elvishness, he betrays a roguish enjoyment in contemplating life's comedy. Those "lymytours," for instance—how differently Langland would have written of them, what rough epithets he would have cast at them! But Chaucer simply and serenely records a *phenomenon*, concluding with an innocent jest, and leaving it to others to draw the moral. Yes, Chaucer is very innocent. His irony is of the kind that only provokes a smile, and when, as in the *Man of Lawes Tale* or the *Prioresses Tale*, he treats of Christian legends, he does not, as Boccaccio would have done, denaturalise them by imparting to them a satirical or comic turn. The gentle irony vanishes, and all is reverence and tender sympathy. This is good art, but it is not, in any sense, affectation. It is part of Chaucer's endowment to be able to enter at will into other men's lives, to surround himself with their atmosphere, to see things from their point of view. This Protean faculty, frequently exercised, causes him to lose sight of himself, and entirely precludes the adoption of any one cry. Hence the many surprising contrasts of the *Canterbury Tales*. The truth of these remarks can be best shown by quotation.

In the *Wyf of Bathes Tale*, the scene of the story is shifted from Sicily, as we find it in Gower, to *Fairyland.* Britain, in the time of King Arthur. Whatever motive may have dictated this transplanting—a wish to differentiate the narrative from Gower's version, or the sense of having become the poet of his nation—certain it is that the incidents are entirely in accord with old-world traditions. It would seem that legend and myth were much in Chaucer's thoughts at this time. The Host, describing him, observes—

> " He semeth elvisch by his countenaunce,
> For unto no wight doth he dalliaunce."

And the *Wyf of Bathes Tale* sets out with an arch contrast between past and present :—

> " In olde dayes of the Kyng Arthour,
> Of which that Britouns speken gret honour,
> Al was this lond fulfilled of fayrie ;
> The elf-queen, with hir joly compaignye,
> Dauncede ful oft in many a grene mede.
> This was the old oppynyoun, as I rede ;
> I speke of many hundrid yer ago ;
> But now can no man see noon elves mo.
> For now the grete charité and prayeres
> Of lymytours and other holy freres,
> That sechen every lond and every streem,
> As thik as motis in the sonne-beem,
> Blessynge halles, chambres, kitchenes, and boures,
> Citees, burghes, castels hihe and toures,
> Thropes, bernes, shepnes, and dayeres,
> That makith that ther ben no fayeries.
> For ther as wont was to walken an elf,
> Ther walkith noon but the lymytour himself,
> In undermeles and in morwenynges,
> And saith his matyns and his holy thinges,
> As he goth in his lymytatioun.
> Wommen may now go saufly up and down,
> In every bussch or under every tre
> There is non other incubus but he,
> And he ne wol doon hem no dishonour."

It is unnecessary to point out how much there is in these introductory lines, so blithe in tone and so delicate in fancy, to remind us of *A Midsummer's Night's Dream*. Indeed, the whole narrative is essentially a fairy-tale retold for adults.

Reserving for the moment the poet's relations with Gower, from whom he borrowed the idea, and who

Sources.   was perhaps his sole authority for the outline of the story, it is important to notice Chaucer's varying and independent treatment of his material. Sometimes, as in the case of his "moral tale vertuous," which is a simple translation of *Le Livre de Melibee et de Dame Prudence,* he adheres closely to the original; sometimes he departs so widely from it that it is hard to decide which of two writings has served as model. Thus, it is open to question whether the *Tale of the Nonne Preste* is founded on the fifth chapter of the *Roman de Renart* (" Si come Renart prist Chantecler le coc ") or on a *lai* of Marie de France ; but in all cases, even where no original has been traced,[1] it may, I think, be safely assumed that Chaucer did not *vom Grunde aus* invent the story. Having found it, he subjects it to any changes he may deem advisable. The *Knightes*

---

[1] The source of the *Marchants Tale* seems to have baffled Tyrwhitt. He adduces an elegiac Latin poem of one Adolphus, dating from the year 1313, but a more probable source is the *Cento Novelle Antiche*, in which God and St Peter take the parts which Chaucer has assigned to Pluto and Porserpina. In the Italian version, however, the woman excuses herself by saying, "S' io non avessi fatto così con costui, tu non avresti mai veduto lume," while May maintains that it was an optical illusion. The latter explanation, in a wholly different setting, occurs in Garin's *fabliau, Du Prestre ki abevete.* All known Pear-tree Stories have been carefully collected in the Chaucer Society's *Originals and Analogues.*

Tale is an instance of curtailment; the *Tale of the Nonne Preste*, of expansion.

The wonderful *Wyf of Bathes Tale* suggests an important observation. A poet by nature, Chaucer was by education a theologian, and when he listed, could preach excellently. In the *Tale*, the curtain lecture of the old crone, so soon to become a radiant young bride, is worthy of a school divine, and even Ten Brink admits the incongruity of her discourse, whilst excusing it on the ground of poetical necessity. But the learning of the old crone, incongruous as it is, must be considered with reference to the narrator. The wife of Bath herself is a portent of erudition, which circumstance is accounted for, in her case, by the fact of her fifth husband being a clerk of Oxenford. However, it is useless to deny that Chaucer is, as we judge, far too ready to parade his acquirements. The Merchant's allusions to Seneca, Theophrastus, Ovid, and the " poete Marcian " certainly betray forgetfulness of the speaker. But, as in the case of Shakespeare's anachronisms, earlier generations were in this respect less critical than our own, and there is an easy and obvious explanation of Chaucer's insistence on his clerkliness. It was scholarship, intellectual attainments, that made all the difference, both social and literary, between himself and the uneducated minstrel.

Temptation.

The *Wyf of Bathes Tale* is one out of several proofs of the rivalry that existed at this time between Chaucer and Gower. To the " moral Gower " and the " philosophical Strode " Chaucer had waggishly dedicated

Troilus and Cryseyde, but Gower had not then entered the field of English composition, in which his younger contemporary, having rightly interpreted the signs of the times, was winning his laurels.   Thus Chaucer may be likened to Dante and Boccaccio, while Gower resembled Petrarch in that he failed to discern the importance, with respect to his own fame, of the changes that were going on in the world.   He began his career in letters with the making of French ballades which, whatever may be said about the position of the cæsura, are good enough to be criticised as French poetry.   Gower was a man of family, so that French, in a sense, was his native tongue.   Perhaps some ten years older than Chaucer, he was—partially for that reason — more strongly attached to manners and customs fated to become obsolete.   Gower's conservatism shows itself in several particulars.   His long avoidance of English for literary purposes is, of course, the most notable.   When at last the force of circumstances, rather than personal inclination, caused him to adopt the English speech, he employed grammatical forms— *e.g.*, the present particle in *ende*—which were no longer current, and which Chaucer at least had definitely discarded.   Again, his metre is the short couplet, not any of the metres that Chaucer had introduced.   Herein, it must be allowed, he displays good judgment.   Not only is this simple form exactly suited to his poetical range, but he handles it with an ease never before attained by English versifier, not even by Chaucer. In the last place Gower is thoroughly aristocratic.

The right attitude of the people, in his eyes, is " obei-
saunce under the reule of governaunce." Chaucer, as
we have seen, was no politician, but he exhibits much
sympathy with common life, and in the *Persones Tale*
gives utterance to sentiments rather Christian than
courtly.

The *Cinquante Ballades*, save that they are in
French, may be compared with Chaucer's early poems.
The Cinquante They treat of platonic love. There are
Ballades. May-scenes and birds' minstrelsy. Allegory
also, and old-world instances. But the cleavage between Gower and Chaucer is perceptible from the
very beginning. Not only is Gower more learned,
but he is more didactic. Already he is earning his
epithet "moral." The justice of this epithet is established by later works—the *Speculum Meditantis* and
the *Vox Clamantis*. From the titles it might be inferred that these writings were in Latin, but Gower
had a weakness for Latin superscriptions. Even his
English poem must be known as *Confessio Amantis*.
It was a symptom of incorrigible pedantry. The
Speculum Meditantis, long lost, has been recovered,
but is not yet accessible in print. Like the *Cinquante
Ballades*, it is in French.

The events of the year 1381—the memorable year of
Wat Tyler's rebellion—were the occasion of Gower's
The Vox third experiment, which not only bore a
Clamantis. Latin name, but was actually a Latin poem.
If Gower's temper and point of view had not been so
hopelessly mediæval, we might have seen in this an
earnest of the Renaissance. The style and versifica-

X

tion, despite some palpable false quantities and excess of word-play, are based on Virgil and Ovid, and testify to much power of assimilation. The influence of those writings, however, was purely formal. The spirit of the work is derived from the old Hebrew prophets, and especially from the Book of Daniel. There is that in the *Vox Clamantis* which suggests *Piers Plowman.* But Gower is not, like Langland, a born dreamer ; and the form of the vision is limited to the first part of the poem, where men are represented as beasts. Gower regards national distress as punishment for national sin, and he is particularly severe on the clergy ; but he betrays no sympathy with the Lollards, and in his later Latin poem vehemently assails the sect. This, the so - called *Tripartite Chronicle,* is in leonine hexameters, and directed against the fallen Richard.

The *Confessio Amantis* was undoubtedly called forth by Chaucer's *Legende of Goode Women.* It is probable that Gower thought that here *Gower and Chaucer.* his friend was attempting something he could do very much better himself. The *Legende,* it will be remembered, was the fruit of Chaucer's Latin period, and Gower had good reason to deem himself the finer scholar, while he was not yet convinced of his inferiority as a poet. Gower evidently regarded his contemporary with disapproval, perhaps even with some contempt. He advises him to cease writing on love-topics, as unbefitting a man of his years. This allusion provoked Chaucer's remarkable outburst in the *Prologue of the Man of Lawes Tale,* in which he retorts that he, at any rate, had not treated incestuous themes like "Canace" and "Apollonius of Tyre."

The fable, or, as it may perhaps be called, the setting, of the *Confessio Amantis* is taken from two sources. In the *Romance of the Rose* Jean de Meung had made Genius the chaplain and confessor of Nature. Gower makes Genius the priest of Venus, and Genius receives the confession of the lover. Hence the title of the book. But Gower owes something to Chaucer also. In the prologue of the *Legende of Goode Women* the God of Love appears, and is full of wrath with the poet, while good Queen Alceste intercedes for him. In the *Confessio Amantis* it is Venus who acts the part of mediator between her son and the lover. The confession covers a very wide field. Altogether there are about thirty thousand lines in the poem, and its multifarious content includes dissertations on various branches of science and philosophy, as those terms were then understood. Clearly a work of this sort cannot be read through, and as "skipping" must be indulged in, the most sensible course is to peruse only the tales.

These tales are introduced nominally as *exempla*, though, in many instances, Gower ignores the true moral and drags in an application which does *Antecedents.* not tally ; but that is one more reason why the context should be neglected. Gower borrows his stories, for the most part, from mediæval Latin authors.[1]

---

[1] Gower's *Tale of the Coffers* was based directly or indirectly on *Barlaam and Josaphat.* It is commonly regarded as derived from

He was, of course, familiar with the *Gesta Romanorum*
and the *Seven Wise Masters*, versions of which had appeared in English; and he may have been influenced
also by the attempt of an English Dominican,
Thomas Walleys, about 1340, to "moralise" Ovid's
Metamorphoses, as well as by the similar attempt of
Chrétien le Gouais, at the beginning of the century.
The best of his stories is perhaps that of Florent, of
which the source is unknown.   It is roughly identical
with the *Wyf of Bathes Tale*, and Chaucer, it may be
surmised, felt the admirable style of the narration as
a challenge.   In general, Gower is not comparable to
Chaucer.   He is a great pedant, and at heart a monk.
The *Confessio Amantis*,[1] however, is of considerable
importance as the first collection of "novels" in
English, and it is highly probable that its publication
assisted, even more than the *Decameron*, in determining the form of the *Canterbury Tales*.

the *Decameron* (x. 1), or from Vincent de Beauvais' *Speculum
Historiale*, but these are points which cannot be determined with
certainty.   Not long before Jean de Condé had written his *Dit dou
Roi et des Hiermittes*, of which the fundamental idea is the same;
and it is superfluous to remind the reader of Shakespeare's caskets in
the *Merchant of Venice*.   As *Barlaam and Josaphat* was originally
composed, about A.D. 800, in Greek, it will be seen that this was
linguistically a well-travelled fable.

[1] The *Confessio Amantis* is much in need of complete re-editing.
Pauli's edition is not regarded as satisfactory.

CHAPTER VII.

TIME AND SPACE.

DINO COMPAGNI—THE VILLANI—FROISSART—LOPEZ AYALA—RAMON
MUNTANER—MARCO POLO—SIR JOHN MAUNDEVILLE.

IT is a sign of the solidarity of European letters that
you cannot talk about Chaucer without talking in
the same breath about Boccaccio. In dis-
Dino Compagni. cussing the *Canterbury Tales* I have not
quitted Boccaccio, and therefore cannot be said to
return to him; but other comparisons render it
necessary that I should take leave, at least for a
spell, of Chaucer. From Boccaccio and his brother
novelists, from Franco Sacchetti especially, to Dino
and the Villani is but a step. Sacchetti paints his
times, and so does Dino Compagni. The great difference between them is that Dino lived earlier, and did
survive to witness the apotheosis of the novel—in
his day a slight, unimportant class—under the hand
of Boccaccio. He was forced to depend, therefore,
on such patterns of Italian prose — rude chronicles,
translations, treatises—as might then be had. But

neither Sacchetti nor Compagni can be regarded strictly as professional writers.   Both were men of affairs.

Dino's *Chronicle of the Things that Happened in his Times,* whether you consider it with reference *An important* to its external fortunes or in respect of *controversy.* its matter, has much the interest of a romance.   The reputed author of an uninspired allegorical poem, the *Intelligenzia,* and of certain lyrics about which a similar verdict must be entered, Compagni figures in his own narrative as a Florentine of mark.   Other historians do not convey quite this impression.   Indeed, they are silent concerning him. For three or four centuries he was a lost name, a vanished memory.   All at once, after this long oblivion, his fame began to grow, until now, among literary folk, he is one of the *lares et penates* of his native city.   Not to know Dino Compagni argues yourself ignorant of an exciting and sanguinary controversy, the end of which is not yet.

The celebrity of the man is bound up with that of his chronicle, which, in 1640, underwent a resurrection.   In that year its existence was notified by Federigo Ubaldini, but the MS. remained unprinted until the next century.   In 1858 Pietro Fanfani sounded the signal for the fray by uttering in his review *Il Piovano Arlotta* the ominous word "apocryphal."   Dino found a champion in M. Hillebrand, who, in answer to Signor Fanfani, published a book entitled *Dino Compagni, étude historique et littéraire sur l'Époque de Dante.*[1]   A new assailant, however,

[1] Paris, 1862.

appeared in Herr Scheffer-Boichorst, whose damaging
researches threatened a speedy end to poor Dino's
precarious fame. Then a most able and patient
Italian scholar — Signor del Lungo — came to the
rescue, and in a monumental work, *Dino Compagni e
la sua Cronica*,[1] succeeded in refuting some grave
objections, but not perhaps in establishing the *Cronica*
in an absolutely safe and impregnable position.

Is the *Cronica* an original composition, finished in
1312, or is it a forgery of later date, a compilation,
a sort of mosaic? Dino's implacable foe,
The problem. Scheffer-Boichorst, who as a matter of
course espouses the latter theory, can give reasons
for the faith, or non-faith, that is in him. He can,
that is to say, put his finger on sundry passages
which exhibit so close a resemblance to other writings
—*e.g.*, a commentary on Dante, and the *Cronica* of
Giovanni Villani, produced later in the century—as
to leave in most candid minds a moral certainty of
something like plagiarism. Villani, it is important
to note, is not above citing his authorities; but he
does not cite Dino Compagni. This is a great difficulty, from which, however, there exists a way of
escape by supposing an authentic nucleus of which
Dino was the author, but in which, by the caprice
of some copyist, or as the effect of accident, there
have been intercalated foreign elements. The utter
collapse of all linguistic, and of many historical, objections ought certainly to induce a spirit of caution
— a disposition not to emphasise too strongly an

[1] Florence, 1879-80.

argument which, on the face of it, appears decidedly formidable.

I have not attempted, in these paragraphs, to record at all fully the vicissitudes of the dispute, which has engaged some of the best intellects, but the reader will be at no loss to understand the occasion of so much stir. Here is a history purporting to be written by a contemporary of Dante—not only a contemporary but a fellow-citizen; not only a fellow-citizen but a member, and an active member, of the same political faction. Doubtless, if the work is a pretence, it must be rigorously proscribed, but it is easy to defend some amount of warmth on the part of those who, sincerely believing in its authenticity, are unwilling to surrender what they regard as a priceless relic of the Trecento, on, as they opine, wholly inadequate grounds.

Assuming that the *Cronica* is genuine, at any rate as respects its main elements, Dino Compagni expresses the sentiments of the well-to-do *popolani*, since the disfranchisement of the nobles and great men the preponderant force in Florentine politics. He, like Dante, is of the Bianchi, and describes, from their point of view, the events of his time down to the year 1312, though he appears not to have died until the 26th of February 1324. Dino, whose existence can be proved from authentic documents, was a good, honest, peace-loving man, preaching patriotism and concord to a generation of vipers. His own sentence, " Niente vale l' umiltà contro alla gran malizia," might be

The man.

chosen as the motto alike of his life and of his work. However, he is a devout believer in the providential government of the world, and although, in 1301, the wicked (the Neri) triumphed over the righteous (the Bianchi), he is assured that their victory is not for long. The coming of Henry, in 1312, is to him, as to Dante, the coming of a deliverer; and he opportunely lays down his pen in an hour when circumstances seem to promise well for his cause.

There was a tendency at one time to overestimate Dino, to credit him with having repeated, in another *Merits and* sphere, the transcendent success of Dante. *defects.* And, indeed, he resembles him in one thing —he can paint. He seizes for artistic purposes the psychological moment, as, for instance, when he shows Corso Donati riding through the streets, and the people shouting after him, "Viva il barone!" But mere picturesqueness will not suffice. Other qualities go to the making of an historian, and in Dino Compagni these qualities are not present. Clearness and completeness are essential to the perfection of the art, but Dino is often confused, often desultory. Although his *Cronica* is devoted to the feuds of the Donati and the Cerchi, of which he recounts the origin, he, while mentioning the restoration of the Cerchi, says nothing about the return of their rivals, an omission for which it is hard to find any plausible excuse.

Such faults are enough to depose Dino from the elevation to which injudicious admirers have exalted him, but they are not enough to provoke or justify any general depreciation. Dino should be read rather as a Pepys than as a Robertson. We constantly meet with such expressions as "io feci," "io andai," "io dissi." In fact, he communicates just what has interested himself. Regard him in this light, and you will say, not that he is an insufficient historian, but that he is a diarist who has outgrown the form, without renouncing the spirit, of the diary. He is, and feels himself to be, a typical man of his age, and with what warmth of sentiment he contemplates the ever-unfolding drama! So far as intentions go, we are simply compelled to trust him. Speaking of the death of Corso Donati, of whose personal appearance, accomplishments, and character he has just given a striking portrait, he refers to a vulgar rumour that he had been slain by Messer Rosso della Tosa and Messer Pazzino de' Pazzi—a suitable assassin, we might think, this last—but Dino exonerates the knights. "And I, wishing to search out the truth, searched diligently and found it to be true as I said"—namely, that he was killed by a foreign soldier, "così vilmente !"

If I may not call Dino a great historian, the title can hardly be refused to Giovanni Villani. Doubtless Villani is, for some purposes, in the *Villani.* swaddling-clothes of the Middle Age; but he knows what is expected of an historian, and, in a large measure, responds to that expectation. Villani was a merchant, and interested in a banking concern, which, as having lent large sums of money to the Kings of England and Sicily, broke; and the chronicler, who was also a politician, was for some time in prison. Now these facts are important. It is comparatively easy to write a personal narrative; but history, in the proper sense of the word, implies *education.* Not the education simply which is gained from books—that was the great mistake of the Middle Age—but the education which results from wide experience of affairs, like that attained by practical statesmen in the present day. It may sound strange, but in the fourteenth century none occupied so nearly the position of a modern statesman as an Italian merchant in a democratic community like Florence. And this may be postulated, not only of his public life as alderman or mayor of a free town,[1] but also of his professional life, which rendered him acquainted with the financial side of government, gave him insight into character, initiated him into the arts of diplomacy, and necessitated extensive travel in foreign countries. Such a training tended to produce a man of the kind described in the opening lines of the *Odyssey,* and that was the kind of man that alone could indite modern history in mediæval times. But Villani, as I have intimated, is not wholly modern. He is a colossus of brass with feet of clay. His book is a compromise. The keen-sighted man writes part; his age, the rest.

Villani's *Cronica* was conceived at Rome at the nominal date of the *Commedia,* in the year of the Great Jubilee. The impression made on strangers, particularly on the countless pilgrims journeying to

[1] In this context a remark of M. Baret may be worth quoting: "Pour écrire l'histoire, il faut être libre, comme Thucydide, ou avoir connu, comme Tacite, l'usage de la liberté."

the "limina apostolorum," by the sights of Rome,
Origin of the Cronica. may be judged from two Latin works which, considering the period, had a vast circulation in the twelfth, thirteenth, and fourteenth centuries — the *Mirabilia Romæ* and the *Graphia Aureæ Urbis Romæ*. The former, at any rate, was translated into Italian during the thirteenth century, and in that shape may have become known to Villani.

Moreover, there existed at this time a venerable legend, which may be read in the *Libro Fiesolano,* as well as in the pages of the *Cronica,* regarding Florence. According to this legend, the foundation of the city was closely connected with the Catilinarian War, in which a noble Roman named Florinus had the misfortune to be killed, and, by way of recompense, was chosen eponymous hero of the new city. The builders of Florence were five Roman signiors — Julius Cæsar, Macrinus, Albinus, Gnæus Pompeius, Martius; and they laid her out on the model of Rome, with walls, and aqueducts, and Capitol. This beautiful work of civilisation was destroyed by that dog's son Attila, and Florence remained a heap of ruins until Charlemagne, in despite of Fiesole, restored her.

Apparently this legend was as gospel to the Florentines, and Villani, who was not without a tinge of *Point of view.* superstition, no doubt accepted it as true. The spectacle of the Eternal City and the memory of the legend, uniting, gave birth to the *Cronica,* which, however, was long in arriving at maturity. The inevitable proem having been finished,

Villani turned his attention to real events. Concerning these he writes either from personal knowledge or from oral tradition supported by State documents, to which, in his official capacity, he had access ; and he handles his material, not indeed with the insight of a philosopher, but with the shrewdness of a man of the world, and the sobriety of a father of a family. The object of his work is the instruction of his fellow-citizens in the lessons of the past—"acciocch' eglino si esercitino adoperando le virtudi e schifando i vizi, e l' avversitadi sostegnano con forte animo a bene e stato della nostra repubblica,"—and that no part of the narrative may lack its appropriate moral he appends to each chapter the conclusion, whatever that may be, which the topic suggests. Like Dino, Villani believes in portents and miracles, and in one place [1] goes out of his way to interpolate a story—borrowed from Marco Polo —of a cobbler who by his prayers removed a mountain, and so converted the Caliph. He regards every calamity as a punishment or purgation of sin ; and his favourite proverb is an old adage in a new dress—" A cui Iddio vuole male gli toglie il senno."

It is due perhaps to the material insignificance of Florence that Villani, anticipating a view of history which largely prevails to-day, devotes considerable space to the statistics of everyday life. Villani himself was a *popolano,* and he writes a history of the people. Thus, in furnishing an account of the taxes imposed to meet the cost of the war against Mastino

[1] vii. 46.

della Scala, lord of Verona, for the possession of
Lucca, he interrupts the recital with a remonstrance
addressed to the lords of Florence, and concludes with
the words, "Temperate, carissimi, i disordinati desiderj
e piacerete a Dio e non graverete il popolo inno-
cente!"[1] But, for all that, he does not behold with
approval the rise of artisans and the humbler sort of
people from their natural position in society.

Perhaps then, in a political sense, I might almost
call Villani a Whig. In the terminology of his time
Guelfism. he was certainly a Guelf, and he rejoices
over the discomfiture of the enemies of
the Church. So confirmed is this leaning that, strong
as is his sentiment of justice, he cannot bring himself
to pronounce a categorical or unqualified censure on
oppressors fortunate enough to be protected by "the
cloth." The case of Brother Venturino at Avignon
may be cited in proof. Villani is greatly tempted
to take his side. "E questi sono i buoni meriti c'
hanno le sante persone da' prelati di Santa Chiesa."
But, quickly recollecting himself, he adds : "ovvero
che fu giusto per temperare la soperchia ambizione
del frate, tutto ch' adoperasse con buona intenzione."

The way the book ends is dramatic in the extreme.
Villani was describing the ravages of the plague,
Finis. which, as we have seen, was the occasion,
or pretended occasion, of the *Decameron.*
The last date is the 11th April 1348, and the concluding words are: "e duro questa pistolenza fino
a . . ." This sentence Villani, himself a victim of

[1] xi. 91.

the pestilence whereof he writes, never lived to complete. The *Cronica* was continued, however, by his brother Matteo and his nephew Filippo, and ultimately extended to the year 1364.

With reference to the original and most important instalment, its value lies in the serious spirit which

Gallicisms.

animates it, and which induced its author to look carefully at the facts. This great virtue, however, was not accompanied by any fine sense of style. Villani's prose is simple, and, for the purpose he has in view, effective, but it is also not seldom uncouth. A curious feature in the work is the presence of a large number of Gallicisms. The circumstance has been explained as arising out of Villani's commercial relations with France; and it is possible, and probable, that these relations exercised some influence on his diction. But Villani possessed an acquaintance with French literature — for example, with the Breton romances. Anyhow, it is interesting to find this early writer guilty of the very fault afterwards laid at the door of Alfieri and Manzoni. The continuation by Matteo Villani exhibits the same qualities and defects, save that the style is rather less vigorous and natural. In conclusion, the charge of plagiarism from Ricordano Malespini may be considered finally disproved, Villani's chronicle being undoubtedly the older.

It would be difficult to conceive a greater contrast than exists between Giovanni Villani and Jean Froissart. It is hardly too much to say that one is everything that the other is not. In turning from the elder to the younger—Froissart was fifteen years

Froissart. old at the death of Villani—we are sensible, not merely of a change of persons, but of a change of epoch. From modern and democratic conditions, intolerant of individual eminence, we are cast back into a state of society in which the governing and essential principle is personal ascendancy. Villani, it is true, was not exempt from class prejudice, but Froissart takes the aristocratic point of view for granted. He always thinks and writes *en gentilhomme.* Thus he rejoices exceedingly over the defeat of Philip van Arteveldt and his Flemings, because their success would have been fatal to the existing order of things. This is how he speaks: " Aprés cette victoire, qui fust tres honnourable et tres prouffitable pour toute chrestïenté et pour toute noblesse et gentillece, car se les villains fuissent la parvenus a leur intentïon, oncques si grans crüaultez ne horribletez ne advindrent en ce monde que il fust advenu pour les communaultez qui par tout se fuissent rebellez et destruit gentillece."

One way of distinguishing between Villani and Froissart— for comparison is inevitable—is to assert

Talent and that the former has talent ; the latter, *genius.* genius. Froissart writes neither as servant of the public nor in the manner bred of public service. He writes because he finds pleasure in the practice, and, as time passes, his enthusiasm waxes rather than wanes. " Plus j'y suis, et plus y laboure, et plus me plaist, car aussi comme le gentil chevalier et escuyer qui aime les armes et en persévérant s'y fortifie, ainsi en labourant sur cette matière, je m'habilite et me délite." He is really and truly a chronicler by vocation, and his chronicles may be termed a vast biography of himself. Not only is he a frequent and interesting figure in his pages—often an interlocutor —but on all of them he impresses the stamp of his personality. Suppress his opinions and sympathies he cannot. Moreover, by virtue of his intimacy with many of the leading actors, he has succeeded in identifying himself with the events of the age, so that there might be some propriety in re-christening his work, *Froissart and his Times.* Were there space to attempt an analysis of the *Chronicles*—omitting the introductory section from 1325 to 1356—it would be delightful to trace the chief episodes of a life which, though not the life of a student, was wholly dedicated to the historical calling. " Je suis un historien."

In speaking thus, I do not forget that Froissart was a poet also, but, compared with his greater achievements in prose, his verse naturally appears *Diplomacy.* as a graceful accomplishment, a *parergon*, if not as a means to an end. With his poems he puts the various courts he visits into good humour. They form a bond of union between himself and the great people. For instance, he meets with a patron in Wencelas, Duke of Brabant. This feeble prince has a *penchant* for literature. He writes poetry. By a master-stroke of policy Froissart, who can versify with most French poets of the day, touches up the composition, and having added other poems of his own, forms the whole into a romance entitled

Méliador, or *Le Chevalier au Soleil d'Or*. Anon
Froissart finds himself at Béarn, at the court of
the Count de Foix, and—

> " Là, toutes les nuits je lisoie
>   Devant lui, et le solaçoie
>   D'un livre de Méliador,
>   Le Chevalier au soleil d'or,
>   Lequel il ooit volontiers ;
>   Et me dist : ' C'est un beaus mestiers,
>   Beaus maistres, de faire tels choses.'
>   Dedans ce romanc sont encloses
>   Toutes les chançons que jadis
>   Féit le bon duc de Braibant,
>   Dont l'âme soit en paradys ! "

At Avignon he loses his purse, and forthwith he writes
a witty poem—*Le Dit du Florin*—in lieu of a begging-
letter. Again, in England, he presents the ill-fated
Richard II. with a copy of *Méliador*. The volume,
both outwardly and inwardly, was worthy of the
King's acceptance. "Car il estoit enluminé, escript
et historié, couvert de velours vermeil à dix clous
d'argent dorés, avec roses d'or au milieu et deux
grands fermails dorés et richement ouvrés de roses
d'or." The king inquires the subject of the work,
and Froissart answers, "Love!" Richard, delighted
at this response, at once dips into the book, while he
bestows on the poet substantial tokens of his favour
in the shape of a heavy goblet, silver-gilt, and a
hundred nobles. Froissart, then, employs his poetical
talents as leverage, as a sort of enchantment, by dint
of which he procures his own advancement, and, at
the same time, provides himself with opportunities for

carrying on his great work under the most auspicious circumstances.

Froissart's master in history was Jean le Bel, canon of Saint Lambert, at Liége, who wrote a chronicle ex-

Froissart's master. tending from 1326 to 1361.[1] It is worthy of remark that this worthy priest initiated Froissart into the art, not only of history, but of life. Here we have to do with no minstrel or *jongleur* eking out a precarious existence by recitations, and approximating in his condition to sheer mendicancy. Nothing of the kind. Le Bel, according to a contemporary, Jacques de Hemricourt—author of *Le Miroir des Nobles de Hesbaye*—lived in lordly style, with rich habits, horses, serving-men, and squires; and, finally, 'tis said of him, " Si ly fist Diex la grasce qu'il vesquit tot son temps en prospériteit et en grant santeit et fut ancien de quatre-vingts ans ou plus quant il trespassat." What Hemricourt says of Le Bel serves as a reminder of Froissart's account of his own journeys in Italy, where, after the wedding of Lionel Duke of Clarence, he travelled " en arroi de suffisant homme." In every sense, therefore, Jean le Bel may be regarded as harbinger of Froissart, whom he even preceded in a visit to that " terra incognita "—Scotland.

Froissart, it seems, was born in 1337 at Valenciennes. The chronicler did not set much store by local ties. He is, in fact, more truly cosmopolitan than almost any writer that can be named ; but this circumstance

---

[1] The complete MS. of this chronicle was discovered, as lately as 1862, by M. Paulin Paris in the library of Châlons-sur-Marne. *Méliador* also has only recently been discovered, by M. Lougnon.

does not in any way detract from his debt to a neighbourhood rich in literary associations, where, on festal
days, "la vraie fleur de chevalerie" assembled in the
great halls of Mons, of Valenciennes, of Beaumont, to
listen to recitations in prose or verse. Froissart tells
us nothing about his parentage, and considering his
general garrulity, it is hardly surprising that the suspicion has occurred to some minds that he was ille-
gitimate. Like so many masters of prose, Froissart
began with poetry; and in his poems may be found
a picture of his youth either as it was or as it fashioned
itself in his dreams. Not less gay than his predecessor,
he was fond of "caroles" and tourneys, but he had not
yet attained the age of twenty when an event occurred
which struck his imagination most powerfully, and
made it impossible that he should devote his talents
solely to love-lyrics. In 1356 was fought the battle
of Poitiers. Five years later the treaty of Brétigny
enabled Froissart to proceed to London, where he was
received in audience by his exalted countrywoman,
Philippa of Hainault, Queen of England; and to her he
presented a book he had written on the heroic events of
the war just terminated. This book is lost, and nothing
is known respecting its character. M. Kervyn thinks
it was in verse; M. Paulin Paris, in prose. One thing
is certain—that, as a novice in history, Froissart followed timidly in the footsteps of Jean le Bel. After
the year 1361, at which Le Bel's chronicle ends, Froissart has to trust his own resources, or, in his own
words, "vole désormais de ses propres ailes."

Although this dependence on the older writer was

not ill-advised, seeing that Le Bel possessed a first-
hand acquaintance with many of the in-
The "editions."
cidents, Froissart appears to have felt the
obligation as irksome; and in his later recensions,
when personal inquiry had given him greater assur-
ance, he exerted himself to eliminate from his work
this incommodious foreign element. It will be well
to deal with these successive "editions," or, as they
may be termed, "rifacimenti," consecutively. The
Chroniques have not come down to us in anything
like a simple form,—in a form, that is to say, finally
approved by the author. They consist of four principal divisions. The first, which is also by far the
most important, extends from 1325 to 1378; the
second, from 1378 to 1385; the third, from 1385 to
1388; the fourth, from 1388 to 1400. The whole
is contained in manuscripts of the age of Froissart,
but, as between these manuscripts, there exist many
noticeable variations. These variations are no mere
textual errors attributable to carelessness or stupid-
ity in the copyists. They are changes deliberately
introduced by Froissart himself, who, at three different epochs, undertook a complete revision of his
work. By "work" must be understood mainly Book
the First. The matter is rendered yet more complicated by the fact that the first "edition" reveals
three "phases," or, if you prefer, is composed of three
instalments—the original nucleus (1356-60), to which
he added, between 1369 and 1373, the events that had
happened since 1360, together with the earlier period
treated by Le Bel; and, afterwards, the events of the

six years from 1372 to 1378. Some MSS. do not extend beyond the year 1372, while in others the sections dealing with the first and third epochs have, without being entirely recast, been retouched in certain details. The "second edition" was produced, there is little doubt, between 1380 and 1383; and the "third edition," which is a mere fragment stopping at the death of Philip of Valois in 1350, at some date posterior to 1400, since it contains a reference to the assassination of Richard II. of England.

A cynical explanation of these "editions," to which the case of Joinville or Villehardouin offers no analogy, is to say that they are adaptations of the *Chroniques* to the circumstances in which Froissart found himself—that they represent the mutations of Fortune both individual and national, as regards himself and as regards England and France. Stated baldly, this account of the matter might be a trifle unjust to Froissart, whose motives would thus appear purely venal, whereas his change of tone may be more accurately ascribed partly to temperamental causes, such as a genial, sympathetic, impressionable nature, and partly to increased knowledge inevitably leading him to modified opinions of men and causes. No doubt, however, Froissart was by choice, as well as by habit, a courtier.

The first "edition" was wholly favourable to the English, and this predilection is explained both by the martial renown of the people and by Froissart's residence in the country as a pensionary of Queen Philippa, and afterwards at the court of Robert of

Namur, a warm partisan of Edward III. and the
Black Prince.   Later, Du Guesclin revives the lustre
of the French arms, and Froissart's new patrons, Duke
Wencelas and the Count de Blois, are pro-French in
their sympathies.   The chronicler gains fresh information about Crécy and Poitiers, and is brought to see
things in an altered light.   The result is a second
" edition."   This second " edition " is notable for its
linguistic changes.   Froissart was born on what may
be called " debateable ground," with Germany on one
side, France on another, and England separated by not
many miles of sea.   In his *Dit du Florin* he informs
us that he knows three languages—French, English,
and " Thiois " (*i.e.*, German, *deutsch*).   His mother-
tongue was, of course, French, and his *Chroniques* are
written in that language ; but the second " edition "
contains a good many variants—such as *w* for *b* or *v* ;
ch for *c* soft, and *c* hard or *k* for *ch*—smacking of
Walloon.   The third edition is also, in a large measure, Walloon ; and in it Froissart's estrangement from
the English, who had fallen on evil days and murdered
the grandson of his former patroness, Queen Philippa, is
complete.   Further, as has been already observed,
Froissart in this third version " sheds," so to speak,
Le Bel.

With regard to this writer, it is necessary to say
that there is not one Froissart, but three Froissarts.
A matter of taste.   As the name is to some extent a variable
quantity, it is important to determine in
what sense it is to be used, or, more definitely, which
of the three " editions " is to be accepted for general

purposes as authentic. Contrary to the ordinary usage
in such cases, M. Siméon Luce [1] has assigned the preference to what he terms "the first edition revised,"
and, in so doing, he has exercised a wise choice.
While, as regards most histories, the latest edition
would represent the mature results of additional years
of study and research, Froissart's alterations consist in
the substitution of one *ex parte* statement for another.
Dispassionate criticism has no bias in favour of
French, as opposed to English, evidence, so that the
question is removed from the court in which historical
disputes are wont to be adjusted, and instead of a
tribunal of Truth we set up a tribunal of Taste.

If Froissart's reputation depended on accuracy
in matter of fact, it would very soon collapse, and

Difficulties.

what wonder, seeing that he relied for
his information on oral testimony? It
was not Froissart's fault. He never slackened in
searching for, and comparing, this higher gossip.
Already stricken in years, he travelled to Bruges
on purpose to acquaint himself with the affairs of
Portugal and Castille. Whilst there, he learns that
a counsellor of the King of Portugal is in Zealand.
Accordingly, he goes in quest of him, and spends
several days examining him. To appraise the value
of such testimony, a good way is to interrogate
the oldest and ablest inhabitants of a district about
past events. The discrepancies will be startling.
Carelessness, lapses of memory, prejudice, levity, and

[1] In the edition of the "Société de l'Histoire de France," begun in
1869.

malice are some of the causes tending to invalidate
the evidence of a single witness, or even of several
witnesses, unconfirmed by documentary proof. Now,
with regard to documentary proof, Froissart occupies
a singularly unfortunate position. His predecessors
had no occasion to trouble themselves about state
archives, which—until, at least, the twelfth century—
could hardly be said to exist. It follows that, in the
majority of cases, it is impossible to "check" the
assertions of the chroniclers. After the sixteenth
century, the invention of printing led to the multipli-
cation of "pièces officielles," and the historians make
good use of these sources. During the middle period
Froissart and his brethren, though the precious
documents existed, were none the better for the
circumstance. The documents embodied state secrets,
and the merely curious investigator could not be
permitted to investigate them. To-day, this caution
being no longer necessary, students can examine and
compare at their leisure. What is the result? Why,
that Froissart appears either as an elaborate liar or as
a systematic blunderer. So far as particulars are
concerned his credit is largely gone.

Nor is this deficiency redeemed by a sound and
clear understanding of the phenomena of the age.
A personal Froissart's aristocratic sympathies are in
limitation. part to blame. The rise of a substantial
middle-class, the discontent and revolutionary temper
of the peasants, would not be treated by an ideal
historian as immaterial, or simply as causes of alarm.
By an ideal historian the shifting of the political

schwerpunkt would be observed with profound attention, and recorded with extreme care. But Froissart's preoccupations are entirely opposed to such procedure. It would be paying far too much respect to the *canaille*. In the year 1355 King John II., under pressure of an expected invasion by the English, convoked the estates of the realm in the halls of the Parliament of Paris, the object being to procure supplies, both men and money. Each of the three orders replied through its speaker that they were "appareillés de vivre et de mourir avec le roi," but that the consent of all three estates was necessary in respect of each proposal. In other words, the despised "tiers état"—the citizen element in French society—had now risen to equal importance, collectively, with the clergy and nobility. Froissart summarises these proceedings in the unmeaning assertion that the estates "placed their persons and property at the service of the king." [1]

---

[1] A corrective of this partial mode of presentment may be found in the *Grandes Chroniques de France*, which furnish the official version, interlarded with authentic documents, and were drawn up, first by the monks of St Denis and afterwards by secular writers appointed by the king. From these *Grandes Chroniques* it is possible to glean a large amount of information concerning the "liberal movement" of the fourteenth century. Still more interesting is a *Chronique Anonyme des Quatre Premiers Valois*, extending from 1327 to 1393, and therefore as nearly as may be covering the ground of Froissart's *Chroniques*. Two features characterise this anonymous chronicle. One is its remarkable agreement with official declarations, which it may often be employed to supplement. The other is its rejection of the old feudal, aristocratic spirit, and the sympathy shown for Etienne Marcel and the party of reform in their efforts to establish a free government. The Norman author of this chronicle is the historian of the "tiers état."

Froissart, then, is neither an accurate transcriber nor a philosophic interpreter of the events of the time. He errs in matters of detail, and he com-

A great artist. pletely misses the import of vast social and constitutional changes. "Je suis historien," he says of himself; but there is a disposition on the part of critics not therefore unfriendly, to contest this claim. One calls him a "troubadour," another a "chronicler," but, perhaps, it would be more reasonable to style him a great "prose-poet." He is almost without rival in word-painting, and though he may confound one village with another, he brings before us in torrents of colour the broad features of the age. It is true that he deals mainly with the superficial aspects of contemporary life, with courts and camps, with fightings and feastings, that he is fairly absorbed by pride and pomp, by beauty and gallantry; but this limitation should not be made a reproach to him. His onesidedness gives a sort of unity to his work. Whether he favours French or English, he is always, as regards principles and criteria, himself. Froissart is the finest exponent the world has ever had of the chivalrous idea as it shaped itself in practice; and therefore his *Chroniques* possess general truth which it would be folly, were it possible, to barter for trustworthy particulars. As to these, Froissart was perfectly versed in the arts and the usages, in the thousand and one minutiæ, of that side of life he undertook to depict.

And he is a faithful witness. In all history probably no incident has ever impressed the imagina-

tion of childhood more than the devotion of the six
citizens of Calais, who offered themselves *hart au
col* to the tender mercies of Edward III.

Fidelity.

The incident we owe to Froissart, and
though he does not express any sympathy for the
"great merchants" in their hour of trial, he narrates
the story so fully and explicitly that we can supply
our own commentary.   The peaceful character of
the proposed victims, the strong emotions of their
neighbours—all Calais seemed to be in tears—in-
tensify our sense of the barbarity of the command,
for there is no doubt that Edward meant to execute
the entire party.   He "moult haïssoit les habitans
de Calais," says Froissart; and when they appear,
"il commanda qu'on leur coupast tantost les testes."
The admirable courtesy exhibited by the Plantagenets
to King John is not extended to his subjects, and
it is only the compassion of Queen Philippa, and perhaps her imminent maternity, that saves these sheep
from the slaughter.[1]   So far as Edward is concerned,

[1] The passage is worth citing in full, and it will lose none of its
effect if given in the fine old version made by Lord Berners.   When
Sir Walter Manny, we are told, "presented these burgesses to the
king, they kneeled down and held up their hands, and said, 'Gentle
king, behold here, we six, who were burgesses of Calais and great
merchants, we have brought to you the keys of the town and of the
castle, and we submit ourselves clearly into your will and pleasure,
to save the residue of the people of Calais, who have suffered great
pain; sir, we beseech your grace to have mercy and pity on us through
your high nobless.'   Then all the earls and barons and other that were
there wept for pity.   The king looked felly on them, for greatly he
hated the people of Calais for the damages and displeasures they had
done him on the sea before.   Then he commanded their heads to be
stricken off.   Then every man required the king for mercy, but he

it is pardonable to conclude that Froissart considered him above criticism. Master of the situation, he had a right to be barbarous. To us, on the contrary, such conduct reveals the utter hollowness—in the last days, if not in the first—of chivalrous professions. Froissart, however, is so in love with the martial and magnificent that he is prepared to condone anything but cowardice and obscurity. The Count de Foix had murdered his own son, yet Froissart terms him, complacently enough, " excellent prince." He is a warm admirer of Du Guesclin, and so, when that intrepid

would hear no man on that behalf. Then Sir Walter of Manny said, ' Ah, noble king, for God's sake, refrain your courage ; ye have the name of sovereign nobless, therefore do not a thing that should blemish your renown, nor to give cause to some to speak of your villainy ; every man will say it is a great cruelty to put to death such honest persons, who by their own wills put themself into your grace to save their country.' Then the king wried away from him, and commanded to send for the hangman, and said, ' They of Calais had caused many of my men to be slain ; wherefore these shall die in like wise.' The queen, being great with child, kneeled down, and sore weeping, said, ' Ah ! gentle sir, sith I passed the sea in great peril, I have desired nothing of you : therefore now I humbly require you, in the honour of the son of the Virgin Mary, and for the love of me, that ye will take mercy of these six burgesses.' The king beheld the queen, and stood still in a study a space, and then said, ' Ah, dame, I would ye had been as now in some other place ; ye make such request to me that I cannot deny you ; wherefore I give them to you to do your pleasure with them.' Then the queen caused them to be brought into her chamber, and made the halters to be taken from their necks ; and caused them to be new clothed, and gave them their dinner at their leisure ; and then she gave each of them six nobles, and made them to be brought out of the host in safe-guard, and set at their liberty." (The translation undertaken by Bourchier Lord Berners " at the high commandment" of Henry VIII. was reprinted in 1812 by E. V. Utterson, in two quarto volumes, and is accessible, with some omissions, in a cheap edition by G. C. Macaulay.)

soldier commits an act of perfidy by conniving at the assassination of Don Pedro, Froissart raises no note of indignation.

The same episode is described in the chronicle of Froissart's Spanish contemporary, Pedro Lopez de *A Spanish version.* Ayala, and in much the same way Ayala also is completely impassive, and records the ghastly affair with business-like precision. While he states with reference to "Mossen Beltran" that Don Pedro put himself deliberately in his power, he recognises no obligation as resting on Du Guesclin, and it is one of Du Guesclin's knights that says to King Enrique, "This is your enemy," thus inaugurating the bloody scene. It is evident that, with both Froissart and Ayala, treachery and cruelty are commonplaces so familiar that it would be ridiculous to exclaim about them. Don Pedro, no doubt, met with his deserts. Surnamed "the Cruel," he had, it is said, put many persons to death in his realm, "por lo qual le vinó todo el dano que aveys oido," and so his untimely end was a nemesis.[1] But this, it is needless to observe, is no excuse for Du Guesclin's breach of honour, or for the way justice was done on the unworthy monarch.

In using these terms of a king who had killed, among others, his five brothers and his wife, I might seem to be on perfectly safe ground, and only setting down the unanimous verdict of humanity. But just

---

[1] The same remark applies also to Trastamara. Chaucer, in his *Monkes Tale*, naturally sides with King "Petro," as an ally of the Black Prince.

as there has been a disposition of late to "white-
" White- wash" Henry VIII. of England, so in the
washing." seventeenth century there is visible a reaction in favour of this monster, for whom Moreto
and Calderon in their dramas put forth brilliant,
but ineffectual, apologies. In our own age this
process of "white-washing" has been revived, and
littérateurs with pronounced democratic sympathies
have done their best to elevate Don Pedro into a
popular hero, a champion of the poor against the
oppressions of the grandees. But facts are stubborn
things. The character of Don Pedro is of importance for Ayala in two ways. The historian was
originally his follower, but when, in 1366, Pedro left
Spain and sought an asylum at the English Court at
Bordeaux, Ayala went over to the side of his rival
Trastamara, who made him his chancellor, and whose
successors he continued to serve during several reigns.
In the second place, it is to be noted that Ayala's
penetrating analysis of the character of Don Pedro
is a new phenomenon in Spanish historical literature.
Ayala, having thus described the life and morals of
Pedro the Cruel, was himself described with equal
impartiality by his nephew Fernan Perez de Guzman,
and it is interesting to observe that his kinsman, in
his generally laudatory account, censures him for a
frailty which Ayala attributes, though without censure, to Pedro. "Fue mucho amador de mugeres," says
the *Crónica;* "Amo mugeres, mas que à tan sabio
caballero como el convenia," say the *Generaciones y
Semblanzas.* Perhaps the sense of personal imper-

fection may help to explain the *insouciance* with which Ayala records the vilest crimes

Ayala is a very remarkable figure in the literature of Spain, and, on account of his versatility, I shall again have occasion to mention him in the *Latin influence.* succeeding chapter. Here he will be dealt with as an early and prominent representative of the classical tendency, one of the characteristics of the period which extends from the time of Pedro I. to that of Ferdinand and Isabella. A symptom of this tendency is the host of translations of Latin authors, accomplished sometimes by the way of French and still oftener by that of Italian "middlemen"; and, in this context, it may be noted that Boccaccio, director of the humanist movement, is already raised to the rank of a classic. Ayala's chief contributions to this popularisation of learning consist in translations of the *History of Troy*, of Boccaccio's *Casus Principum* (*Caida de Principes*), and the first, second, and fourth Decades of Livy. It is the last circumstance that I desire to emphasise. The classical tendency showed itself nowhere more strikingly than in the field of history. Attempts are made to emulate the Latin period, and these attempts not infrequently realise the position of "vaulting ambition which o'erleaps itself."[1] There is other evidence of ambition. It appears that Ayala's translation of Livy was undertaken at the instance of Enrique III. Possibly, therefore, the insertion of fictitious speeches in the Chancellor's

[1] This criticism, however, does not apply to Ayala's style, which is simplicity itself.

chronicle was dictated by a wish to propitiate that monarch; but however that may be, it cannot be doubted that the innovation is due to the influence of the Latin historian. The older *Crónicas* are quite innocent of anything of the sort, and content themselves with a simple narration of facts. As an historical expedient, fancy orations are not free from exception. They constitute an artificial and more or less arbitrary element in what, by its nature and profession, ought to be rigorously truthful and scientifically precise. Nevertheless, at a certain stage of human development the artifice may be useful, as enabling the reader to enter more adequately into the complexities of a situation, just as is done in an historical play or novel. The fictitious speech, therefore, with its *pros* and *cons*, may be regarded as a stepping-stone from a primitive, puerile, unintelligent stringing together of events to the philosophical probing of a mature historical method.

These chronicles relating to Castile are written in the Castilian variety of the Spanish language, the *Catalan* classical dialect for prose. The neighbour-*histories.* ing kingdom of Aragon exhibits a similar condition of things. In the sphere of history we come upon the "four pearls" of Catalan literature —the *Libre dels feyts esdevenguts en la vida del molt alt senyor rey En Jacme lo Conqueridor*, which, there is reason to believe, was penned by Jacme himself; and the chronicles of Bernat Desclot (which exists only in a Castilian translation), of Ramon Muntaner, and of Peter IV. of Aragon. This last was supposed,

Z

until quite lately, to have been the work of Peter
IV.; but documents found in the archives of Aragon
render it certain that Bernat Desclot, counsellor and
treasurer of John I., drew up the record, which extends from 1335 to 1387, under the direction of Peter
IV. Taken together, these writings throw abundant
and continuous light on the state of affairs in Aragon
during the fourteenth century; but the only work of
which it is necessary to say anything in particular is
the Chronicle of Ramon Muntaner. Unlike the rest,
it bears a personal impress, and is, in various senses,
an actual work of art. It abounds in vivid touches
and local colour only attainable by a sympathetic
observer of the events described. Hence it is that
Ramon Muntaner has been styled, not inaptly, the
Catalan Froissart.

It is not clear whether this Chronicle was begun in
the year 1325 or 1335, but it concludes with the
Ramon Muntaner. coronation of Alfonso III. in 1327. Muntaner's account of the way he came to
undertake it is characteristic alike of the man and
the age. His career as a soldier was ended, and he
was asleep in his castle of Xiluella, when the vision
of an old man clad in white appeared to him and
bade him make a book of the great marvels he had
witnessed, and that God had wrought in the wars
he had been in. Muntaner did not at once comply,
and the vision was repeated. Thereupon he hesitated
no more, but began his task, " that he might draw
down the blessings of God on himself, his wife, and
his children."

As we have already seen, Catalan literature was the offspring and heir of the literature of Provence, suppressed by the brutalities of bigots and hypocrites. The kingdom of Aragon comprised at the beginning of the thirteenth century Provence, Béarn, Gascony, and the towns of Carcassonne, Béziers, and Montpellier; and Muntaner, in his Chronicle, traces for us the nature of these relations which must, of necessity, have produced a great effect on the intellectual development of Aragon proper. Unquestionably, however, the chief interest of the book lies in the story of the Aragonese in Greece. The Emperor Andronicus Palælogus hired a company of Catalan troops to oppose the advance of the Turks. Under their valiant commander, Roger de Flor, they succeeded in delivering Andronicus, but the emperor, after creating Roger high admiral and conferring upon him the title of Cæsar, caused him to be perfidiously assassinated at his own table. The Aragonese manifested their resentment by ravaging the country, and finally established themselves as masters of the duchy of Athens. All this is described by Muntaner in a vein of ardent patriotism, combined with much shrewdness and sufficiency of literary style. In this last respect, it is inevitable that his work should be compared with the history of the same expedition by a very elegant Spanish writer some three centuries later. Such a comparison, however, is not likely to affect prejudicially the reputation of Ramon Muntaner. It is Don Francisco de Moncada who is on his trial, and who, often enough, does little more than substitute for the racy Catalan of his pre-

decessor the pure and polished Castilian exacted by
the times.

Muntaner may be regarded—partly on account of
the personal note, partly from the fact that the most
interesting portion of his narrative con-
Travellers.
cerns a foreign and an eastern land—as
a connecting link between historians proper and the
class of explorers of which Marco Polo and Sir John
Maundeville are the worthiest representatives. The
former was born at Venice in 1254, and he came of
an adventurous stock. When he was still an infant,
his father, Niccolò Polo, and the second of his uncles
set out for Mongolia on a mercantile expedition.
They were well received by Koubilaï Khâan — a
name rendered familiar to us by Coleridge — and,
in 1266, he permitted them to return home with a
proposal to the Pope that he should send mission-
aries, and if they could prove the superiority of
Christianity to all other forms of religion, he and
his people would be converted. Two preaching friars
were accordingly despatched on this errand; but when
they had got as far as Armenia, their hearts failed
them and they turned back. It was otherwise with
the Polo brethren. In 1271 they determined to re-
visit the East, and this time took with them Niccolò's
son, Marco, who had now attained to man's estate.
"Par les maus temps que il orent et pour les granz
froidures," they occupied in the journey three years
and a half.

Marco Polo's exile in the East lasted seventeen years.
During that time he found such favour with the Khan

that he was appointed governor of a province in which

Marco Milioni. were twenty - seven towns; and he appears to have visited, mostly in an official capacity, China, India, Tonquin, Ceylon, the coasts of Coromandel and Malabar, &c. With his father and uncle, he returned home, in 1295, by way of Persia, the Black Sea, and Constantinople; and they had become so altered in appearance and manners that they could hardly be recognised. Naturally, they came laden with treasures, and the house in which they lived was called " Corte dei Milioni." It is, however, not quite certain that this term has anything to do with "millionaires." It seems that Marco was surnamed " Milioni " in ridicule. The Venetians would not believe his wonderful stories, and as the word " million " was constantly on his lips, he became known as Marco Milioni.

Soon after his return to Europe war broke out between Venice and Genoa, and Marco was taken

His book. prisoner in a sea-fight. In the dungeons at Genoa he made the acquaintance of a Frenchified Italian, " Messire Rustacian," who has been identified with a certain Rustichello, the author of a prose-version in French of the legends of the Round Table. " Messire Rustacian " did not know French very well, but he employed it again for the *Livre* of Marco Polo. He seems to have been guided in the choice by the consideration that the use of that language afforded greater scope for publicity. In its original French the *Livre* is something of a translation, for the traveller, who dictated it, though versed in Mongolian, Chinese, Persian, and Arabic, seems to have possessed no knowledge of French. In old copies the work is entitled *Le Devisement du Monde* or *Le Livre des Merveilles du Monde*. In Italy, however, which very soon acquired an excellent version, the author's nickname attached itself to his book, which was styled *Il Milione*.

For a long time the name " Marco Polo " was treated as synonymous with " liar," and the book which he *fist retraire*, though translated into all the languages of Europe and eagerly devoured by all classes of readers, was generally disbelieved. Modern researches, however, have tended to heighten its credibility, so that, in both these respects, the mediæval traveller may be compared to Herodotus. In regard to style, for which he can hardly be held responsible, Marco Polo is by no means on a par with the old Greek writer, or with his own contemporary, Froissart. The interest of the book lies in the facts it records, not in the way the facts are recorded, and one can only regret that the fashions of the time precluded Froissart, or some author of equal charm, being sent on a roving commission to the Far East by an enterprising Parisian journal.[1]

Somewhat later Italy produced travellers who availed themselves of their native speech. Between the years 1346 and 1349 Fra Niccolò da Poggibonsi visited the Holy Land and recorded his *impressions*

---

[1] The best recent edition of Marco Polo is *The Book of Ser Marco the Venetian*, newly translated and edited by Colonel Henry Yule. 2 vols. London : Murray, 1871.

de voyage on a pair of tablets carried at his side, ultimately forming them into his *Libro d'oltramare.*

Italian books of travel. Another traveller was Lionardo Frescobaldi, who, in 1384, was the envoy of the Republic of Florence to Count da Barbiano at Arezzo. Whilst thus engaged, he conceived the idea of journeying to Palestine, and, on his return, published an account of his travels. Simone Sigoli, of whom nothing more is known, composed an independent version. These works do not call for any special characterisation. Any one who has read Hakluyt's *Voyages* knows tolerably well what to expect in the way of " travellers' tales," and these *Viaggi* appear to have aroused only local, or, at most, " national" interest.[1]

Very different was it with *The Voiage and Travaile of Sir John Maundeville* — to give to the book its *Maundeville.* English title — which is of European importance. Here again we are confronted with a question of language. The work has been claimed as properly French, and the authorship assigned away from the English knight to a physician of Liége, one John of Burgundy or John of the Beard. On this point it is to be remarked that, while the French *relation* may have been, and probably was, older than any English version, the book in its English dress acquires an interest which in fortuitous French it is altogether without. For it is the first attempt in English to handle prose as Chaucer handles

---

[1] See C. Gargiolli, *Viaggi in Terra Santa di Lionardo Frescobaldi e d'altri del secolo xiv.* Firenze : Barbera, 1862.

verse—with freedom and independence. The identity
of the translator is as obscure as that of the author.
Critics discriminate between these twain; but, after
all, it is just conceivable that they were one and the
same. The English "Maundeville" says (p. 5), "And
yee schulle undirstonde, that I have put this boke
out of Latyn into Frensch, and translated it agen
out of Frensch into Englyssch that every man of
my nacion may undirstonde it." The book purports
to have been written in 1356. The first printed
edition was, perhaps, that of Pietro de Cornero, of
Milan, in 1480:' "Tractato delle piu maravigliose
Cosse e piu notabili che si trovano in le parte del
mondo vedute . . . del Cavaler Johanne da Manda-
villa." The first English edition was printed at
Westminster, in 1499, by Winkyn de Worde, and
was entitled: "A lytell Treatise or Booke, named
John Mandevyll, Knyht, borne in Englande, in the
towne of Saynt Abone, and speaketh of the wayes
of the Holy Lande toward Jherusalem, and of the
Marvyles of Ynde and other diverse Countries." The
best English edition is that of London, 1725, *The
Voiage and Travaile of Sir John Maundeville, &c.,*
reprinted by J. O. Halliwell, in 1839, and based on
the Cotton MS. (Titus, C. xvi.) in the British Museum.
This version is in the Midland dialect.[1]

Notwithstanding its brave introduction, which

---

[1] Mr Warner's edition, undertaken for the Roxburghe Club, though
difficult to obtain, should also be mentioned. Mr E. B. Nicholson,
of the Bodleian Library, Oxford, is in great request as an authority
on Maundeville.

seems to have "honesty" inscribed on the face of
Nature of the it, the question has been asked whether
contents. as traveller, or only as author, Maundeville was an historical, or, contrariwise, a legendary,
typical personage. Well, the doubt is excused by
the circumstance that the book is certainly, in some
measure, a compilation. Whereas Marco Polo is
content to describe what he has himself heard and
seen, Maundeville makes his work an *olla podrida*
of mediæval fancy and tradition, which help to
supplement his own observation. Has he availed
himself of the prerogative accorded to all travellers,
and imposed on human credulity in those sections
purporting to deal with facts ? There are two
reasons which would lead us to think otherwise.
One is his simple, frank, unpretentious style, and the
other an occasional proviso, as, for instance, when he
tells us, though he describes its marvels, that he has
himself never been to the Earthly Paradise. It is,
moreover, quite possible that the more outrageous
stories of giants, monsters, and devils may have been
added by copyists. It is worthy of note that the
English traveller covered the same ground as his
Venetian predecessor, and one result of his writings
was to familiarise his countrymen with the notion of
the Far East, hitherto a land unknown. Philologically,
his book is of great value, since the variety of the
subject-matter entails a corresponding variety in the
vocabulary.

As regards intrinsic worth, it would be absurd to
compare Maundeville's *Voiage* with the *Commedia*,

but it has this quality in common with it, that it is
the representative European work of its
A guide-book. class. It is the culmination of a literature, the literature of pilgrimage. This circumstance,
even more than the quaintness of the book itself,
explains its wide diffusion, not only in England but
in Continental countries. Marco Polo was popular;
Maundeville was, if anything, more popular. Germany, for instance, had at least two translations, one
by Michel Velser, the other by Otto von Diemeringen;
and the influence of this precedent is seen further in
original German *Pilgerreisen*.[1] Holland could boast
its *Reysen van Jan van Mandeville;* and Denmark also
had a translation. In addition to these vernacular
works there were many Latin renderings. In fact,
"the book named Mandevyll" obtained every distinction the age could bestow.

[1] See Röhricht and Meisner's *Deutsche Pilgerreisen nach dem
heiligen Lande*, Berlin, 1880.

CHAPTER VIII.

ALLEGORY, MYSTICISM, AND REFORM.

ITALIAN ALLEGORIES — SPANISH AND JUDÆO - SPANISH MORALISTS — ARABIAN CULTURE — 'PIERS PLOWMAN' — RELIGIOUS POETRY — THE 'FIORETTI' OF ST FRANCIS—ITALIAN PREACHERS—ST CATH-ERINE OF SIENA—GERMAN MYSTICS—JEAN GERSON—JOHN WICLIF.

ALTHOUGH in the literature of this period allegory is to be found apart from mysticism, mysticism apart *The World and* from reform, and reform apart from alle-*the Church.* gory, still there is a tendency on the part of each pair to coalesce; sometimes, indeed, all three characteristics are united. This circumstance renders it expedient, if not imperative, to study these develop-ments in a single chapter, in order to show their interaction, notwithstanding a certain incongruity in associating the purest and most spiritual effusions with the leavings of Provençal animalism. Even this, however, is not quite so incongruous as might at first appear, seeing that, in this matter, the Church borrowed from the World, and the World from the Church.

So far as allegory is concerned, in the Italian peninsula the preponderant fact is the influence of the *Roman de la Rose*. On this point I have already touched in relation to Brunetto Latini, whose position with regard to Dante made it desirable to introduce him earlier in the work than would otherwise have been the case. Strictly his place is here. Concerning him I shall only add the remark that his poem the *Tesoretto*, especially as viewed in connection with his French work the *Trésors*, illustrates the tendency of didactic verse to become allegorical in character and encyclopædic in range. It is very true, as M. Aubertin observes, " on est facilement enclin à tout embrasser quand on ne peut rien approfondir." The continuation of the *Roman de la Rose* itself, by Jehan de Meung, is, of course, an exemplification of this truth.

One great fault of the *Roman de la Rose*, particularly of the later contribution, is its discursiveness. An Italian imitation, *Il Fiore*, which, in

Il Fiore.

form, is a garland of two hundred and thirty - two sonnets,[1] avoids this defect, partly, no doubt, on account of the compendious nature of the sonnet, which precludes the admission of more than a limited amount of matter and does not easily transfer its surplus stock to its successor. The general term *fiore* is kept throughout, there is no specific mention of the rose, and this is only one indication out of many that the work is not a translation, properly so

---

[1] The employment of the sonnet as a stanza is a proof of the early date of the poem; it probably belongs to the last twenty years of the thirteenth century.

called, but, like many other mediæval productions, examples of which have been quoted, an adaptation. It might perhaps be better named an appropriation, for, in a passage corresponding to that in which Guillaume de Lorris inserts his name, we met with the name Ser Durante, which occurs also in two other places. Ser Durante was probably a real personage, who "flourished" at the end of the thirteenth and at the beginning of the fourteenth century, and was a Florentine notary.

Ser Durante appears to have been formed rather in the mould of the satirical Jehan than the soft and dreamy Guillaume, but he is the slave of neither. He thinks, indeed, less of his models than of his readers, for whose tastes he endeavours to cater; and he seems to have been animated by contempt and dislike for the all-powerful middle class, which in Florence at this time had gained a monopoly in public affairs.

The influence of French literature is visible also in the *Intelligenzia*. The reason for attributing the *In-*

The Intelli-   *telligenzia* to Dino Compagni is the circum-
genzia.   stance that one of the two oldest MSS., the
Magliabecchiano, has, written by a later hand and half-erased, the words "Questo si chiama la 'ntelligienzia, lo quale fecie Dino Chompag. . . ." The poem, which consists of three hundred stanzas in *nona rima*—practically the *ottava*, with the addition of a ninth line rhyming with the sixth—exhibits a convergence of several literary movements. In Stanza V. we find an allusion to Guido Guinicelli's thesis regarding Love and the Gentle Heart.

On the other hand, the poem opens with a description of Spring conceived quite in the Troubadour style, and the two first lines are, as Nannucci has pointed out, directly translated from the Provençal. The great bulk of the work is taken up with a minute account of the jewellery worn, and the palace inhabited, by a lady of whom the poet feigns himself enamoured.

The significance of the poem is certainly not self-evident, but we are not left to the illumination of our own unaided understandings. The conclusion of the work shows that the Lady is a personification of Universal Intelligence, her palace is the soul of man, her summer and winter rooms are the liver and the spleen; the kitchen is the stomach; the paintings and sculptures are pleasant memories, and the chapel is faith in God. This is sorry stuff, and were it not that the *Intelligenzia*, in respect of its symbolism, is a fit representative of the age, it would not be worth while to bestow so much space on it.

This scholastic idea again presents itself in Francesco da Barberino's *Del Reggimento e Costumi di Donne*, com-

Francesco da Barberino. pleted between 1318 and 1320. The writer claims that this is the first attempt ever made in verse to improve the morals of females. The work is concerned with the externals of morality, the proprieties, and is, in fact, a manual of etiquette. Some of its precepts, inculcating lying and deception, cannot be reconciled with the highest form of morality, though the prevailing character of the poem undoubtedly favours correct behaviour. Francesco includes in his survey all sorts and conditions of women, from the empress to the serving-maid, and is prolific of advice to wife and widow, nun and marriageable girl.

The composition of *Del Reggimento* reminds us of Tupper. The lines are of varying length, they are without rhymes, and intermixed with prose; indeed, these *versi sciolti* are never far from prose. The prose proper consists of moral tales, simple and rather tame, which are used to exemplify the instructions given in the versified portions.

Francesco's other work, the *Documenti d' Amore*, is interesting mainly as one of the links between Italian and Provençal literature, and appears to have been sketched and, for the most part, written during the author's residence in Provence (1309-1313). About twenty years before Matfre Ermengau had composed his *Breviari d' Amor*, a work in many respects similar, but Francesco seems to have based his poem, not on this, but on other Troubadour writings now lost. The title is at first rather misleading. "Documenti" means lessons, but the lessons Love teaches are not those usually associated with the whispers of Cupid. Love is here regarded, in agreement with the familiar Provençal theory, as the source of both wisdom and virtue, and this view finds expression in the opening lines of the poem—

> " Somma virtù del nostro sire Amore
> Lo mio intelletto novamente accese."

The original MS., which is preserved in the Biblioteca Barberini at Rome, includes not only draw-ings, but a Latin translation of the poem and a full commentary, which is of the utmost service for the light which it throws on Provençal and early Italian literature.[1]

From Italy we turn to Spain, where we meet with the same didactic tendency, and, though less evidently, the same tendency to symbolism. For chronological and other reasons it behoves us to deal, in the first instance, with a very remarkable personage—Juan Ruiz, Archpriest of Hita. Before Juan Ruiz the last important poet was Gonsalvo de Berceo, who wrote at a time when Spain was still suffering from the effects of her struggle with the Moors. This was now past, and the country everywhere showed signs of prosperity. The farming and mercantile classes were thriving, and the art of reading became generally diffused. Even the Archpriest's man-servant could read; if he read badly, perhaps it was his own fault. The result was that the Juglar lost nine-tenths of his consequence, even among the lower orders, though in the fourteenth century he still practised his *cazurrias* and sang his *dulces cantares*. Folksong, however, did not share in the Juglar's fall, and, indeed, gradually acquired greater regularity. For this commodity a market was still to be found in Jewesses and Moorish women, blind persons, and serenading scholars; and a whole host of lyrics, *danzas* and *troteras*, was composed by Juan Ruiz. Out of these only four scholar-ditties

Spain.

Juan Ruiz.

[1] See A. Thomas, *Francesco da Barberino et la Littérature provençale en Italie*, &c. Paris, 1883.

have been—rather by accident than intention—preserved.   Probably all his poems that he thought
worthy of preservation were included in his *Libro de
Buen Amor*,[1] one of the most amazing productions
of that or any other age.   It may be compared, in
certain respects, to the *Vita Nuova*, since it is partly
in verse and partly in prose, and the thread that
runs through all is the writer's personality and love.
The work begins with hymns to God and Mary; with
hymns it continues, and with hymns it ends.   Between these sacred effusions lies a mixed medley,
which is of the world worldly, and what edification it
contains proceeds rather from the pervading irony
than from direct admonition.   Ruiz is essentially too
frivolous to offer himself as an "awful example," but
he makes a present of his own experiences and observations to any more seriously disposed who may
chance to read his book.   Some of the tales are allegories without disguise; but, from the preface, it is
clear that the writer intended the whole work to be
in some sense an allegory.   "Beware," says he, "of
holding this for a frivolous and lying book; believe
not that it speaks only of trifles: just as goodly coins
are hid in vile leather, so a jesting work may conceal
goodly knowledge.   The grain *axenus*, outwardly
blacker than porridge-pot, is inwardly whiter than
ermine; a vile cane conceals white sugar; on a twig
of thorn blows the noble flower of the rose."

A striking feature of the work is a brilliant re-
setting of a mediæval Latin comedy *Pamphilus de*

[1] So he calls it in the Epilogue.

2 A

Amore, in which the central figure is a bawd Trota-conventos, and other actors are Juan Ruiz himself (under a pseudonym), a Moorish woman, and a nun. Interspersed are charming apologues and burlesque pastorals (*cánticas de Serrano*).

The irony of Ruiz might be illustrated by his verses on the power of money, or by the nun's tale. The *The Nun's Tale.* tale was originally advanced as an argument against yielding to temptation. It is to this effect. In the " Tierra sin Justicia " were many robbers, and the king sent his officers to suppress them. One robber, who had been punished with the loss of his ears, said to himself: " I am already betrothed to the rope; next time I shall be married altogether." Before, however, he had completed his repentance, a devil came, that he might not lose him; and robber and devil signed an agreement, the former pledging his soul on condition that the devil would never forsake him. Soon after the robber was captured, and called on his protector to redeem his promise. The devil was as good as his word, and, bidding him take courage, tells him: " When you are brought up for trial, draw the *alcalde* aside, and, putting your hand in your bosom, give him what you shall find there." This proved to be a gold cup " muy noble de preciar," and the criminal was discharged. The same ruse was tried on many subsequent occasions, and was never found to fail. At last, however, the devil grew weary, and the robber, on putting his hand into his bosom, drew forth a long rope as a present. The judge at

once ordered him to the gallows.   The robber was
seriously alarmed ; but the devil was not going to
desert him yet, and, though he was apparently hanged,
supported him on his shoulders.   When the execu-
tioners had left, the devil bade the criminal open his
eyes, and tell him what he saw.   What he saw was
the devil's feet torn and bleeding, in his hand a number of hooks, and hanging from the hooks a company
of cats.   The devil is not long in explaining that
these cats are the souls of those whom he has en-
snared, and that his feet are blood-stained through
hunting for them.   Already he had informed the
wretched man—

"Non puedo mas sofrirte, ten lo que mereçiste ;"

and, his discourse ended, he drew himself away, gave
a leap, and left his friend high and dry in the noose.
The moral is—

"El que con le diablo fase su crianza,
    Por mucho que se tarde el galardon alcanza."

Captivity is a circumstance connecting Ruiz with
Lopez de Ayala, already mentioned in his quality of
Spanish   chronicler.   Ayala was taken prisoner by
Bunyans.   the English at the battle of Nareja, 1367,
and in England he passed a dolorous confinement.
There, perhaps, he wrote a didactic work entitled
Rimado de Palaçio, comprising his experiences of life,
and offering good advice to all and sundry.   Ayala does
not speak very flatteringly of his predecessor, calling
him indeed "a priest of Satan," but it is clear that

the *Rimado* was composed, as it were, in full view
of the Book of Good Love.   The Alexandrine metre
is used in the satirico-didactic portions, while, in the
lyrical pieces, the *versos de redondilla* are employed
for preference.   Ayala is not equal to the Archpriest
of Hita as a poet, and he has nothing of his charming
irony, which is replaced by puritanical earnestness.
According to the twofold dating of the epilogue, Juan
Ruiz put his book together in 1330 and added some
pieces in 1343, whilst undergoing imprisonment at
Toledo by order of the Archbishop, Gil Alborniz—
an imprisonment which lasted thirteen years.

The *Rimado* was composed at different times between 1378 and 1385, and the connection between the
parts is often extremely loose.   At the end of the work
is an appendix, including complaints, hymns to Mary,
and prayers, a good deal of it dated back.   Most of
these lyrics are either in Alexandrines or in some form
of court verse.   It is worthy of note, as marking a new
departure, that two complaints of the Great Schism,
added in 1398 and 1403, are in the metre of the *arte
mayor*, a rough form of decasyllabic verse characteristic of the period now opening, just as the carefully
measured *cuaderna via* was of the preceding.   As
Alexandrine verse disappears with Ayala, he may
be regarded as bridging over the chasm between the
old and the new state of things, as the poet of the
transition from the Portuguese to Castilian court
poetry.

The employment of the *arte mayor* is one of the
features the Spaniards admire in the *Danza de la*

Muerta of a contemporary of Ayala, Rabbi Don Santo [1]

The Arte   de Carrion—*el maestro de buen nombre.* It
Mayor.   may therefore be well to explain in the
first place what this *arte mayor* is. It corresponds
to an Old-French form of decasyllabic verse—which,
however, was seldom used—with the cæsura after the
fifth syllable. In Old Portuguese it appears chiefly
in the dance song. In Castilian, on the other hand,
it is rarely found in lyric poetry, though it is a
favourite metre for longer compositions, generally in
eight-lined stanzas. The effect, which is often that
of four amphibrachs ($\smile - \smile$), may be gathered from
the following strophe by one of the greatest masters
of this verse, Juan de Mena :—

> " Mientra morian y mientra mataban,
>   De parte del agua ya crescen las ondas,
>   Y cobran las mares soberbias y hondas
>   Los campos que ante los muros estaban ;
>   Tanto, que los que de allí peleaban,
>   A los navíos sí se retraian,
>   Los aguas crescidas les ya defendian
>   Tornar a la fustas que dentro dejaban."

The fifth and sixth lines, which begin, the one with
a trochee and the other with two spondees, show that
there is nothing obligatory about the nature of the feet
except a certain equivalence, and this freedom is further
emphasised by the presence of what may be termed
enclitic syllables—*e.g.*, *y* in lines 1 and 3.

Rabbi Don Santo is doubtless the most remark-

---

[1] Santo, not Santob, is the Judæo-Spanish form of the Hebrew
Sem Tob (or Shem-Tob ?). This is proved by the rhyme, as well as
by the writing of Santillana, and therefore to be retained.

able example of Jewish influence on early Spanish
literature, but it did not begin with him.

Jewish converts.

More than two centuries before, a Jew
called Moses had been baptised at the age of forty-
four into the Christian faith, and received the names
Petrus Alphonsus, after the saint on whose day
the ceremony was performed, and King Alfonso of
Aragon, the god-father. After his conversion Petrus
Alphonsus wrote in Latin a work which he entitled
Disciplina clericalis, addressed not so much to priests
as to persons of education, and designed as a guide
to right living. It was a collection of fables, anecdotes, stories, and proverbs, supposed to be communi-
cated by father to son; and it represents a curious
mixture of Oriental and European elements, the latter
being derived almost exclusively from common life.
It has to do, not with knights and ladies, but with
merchants, farmers, artisans, and pilgrims. This
Disciplina clericalis is a work of European importance.
It was early translated into French under the title
of *Le Castoiement ou Instruction d'un Père à son Fils*,
and either in the Latin original or through the French
version became known to Boccaccio, who included four
of the tales in the *Decamerone*. The *Disciplina* was
translated into Catalan in the thirteenth, and into
Castilian in the fourteenth, century.

There is a certain parallelism between the lives of
Petrus Alphonsus and Rabbi Don Santo. Both were
converted Jews, and both were more or less directly
connected with Spanish courts. While, however,
Petrus Alphonsus justified his change of creed by a

book of Christian evidences, the Rabbi began with a
work more in the style of the *Disciplina clericalis*—
namely, his "Counsels and Instructions," dedicated to
Peter the Cruel.   These counsels deal with the
commonplaces of politics and morality, thrown together without any definite plan, and exhibit a marked
tendency to repetition and prolixity, said to be characteristic of Hebrew doctors.   The book is written in
the old redondilla verse.   Santo seems to have been
aware of the incongruity of a Jew giving lessons in
Christian morality, but he knows how to excuse
himself.

> " Por nascer en espino
>   La rosa, ya ne siento
>   Que pierde, ni'l buen vino
>   Por salir de sarmiento,"—

so likewise the author is none the worse for sleeping
in a nest of mud, nor good doctrine for passing through
the mouth of a Jew.

The style and versification of the " Counsels and
Instructions " are both good, but this first work is of
The Dance   far less interest and importance than Rabbi
of Death.   Santo's "Dance of Death," which, as I
have said, is a specimen of the *arte mayor.*   Every
nation in Europe has its "dance of death," the period
at which the idea was most prominent to the imagination of the peoples being the fifteenth century, the
era of the Black Death, though, at present, it is
perhaps most familiar through the great allegorical
painting of Holbein.   Holbein found the tradition
painted on the walls of a churchyard at Basle, and it

is probable that Santo's *Danza* is based on a French
original. In neither case is the circumstance material.

The Dance is actually a moral dramatic allegory,
or, if you will, a morality, an allegorical play, of
which the personages are Death, a preacher, and
people of every age, sex, and condition. There is a
brief introduction containing a sketch or summary
of the whole, and then Death opens the ball by
stating who he is and the summons he has come to
deliver. He is succeeded by a preacher who, at
considerable length, commends a virtuous course of
action as the best preparation for the inevitable
dance. Death glances round on the crowd and bids
two pretty young girls. They would like to avoid
him, but they cannot — they are his brides. After
that he bids all sorts and conditions, and the
method of the poem is as follows: In the first
octave the victim is summoned by Death to the
dance; in the second the person summoned bewails
his bitter lot; in the last are expressed the resignation and pious resolves of the victim. This *Danza
de la Muerte,* from its exact and vivid portraiture,
has great historical value as a mirror of the age,
and, in the opinion of the Spaniards, it combines
with the wise reflections of Lopez de Ayala the
humorous touches of the Archpriest.

Besides Jewish influence we find operating in the
peninsula that of the Arabs. This was the natural
El Conde   result of the Moorish conquest and settle-
Lucanor.   ment. During the reign of Alfonso the
Wise a translation was made, and included in his

Siete Partidas, of Mobaschir's sentences under the title of *Bocados de oro*, or, to give it its full description : *El libro llamado Bocados de oro el qual hizo el Bonium Rey de Persia*. The Mouthfuls of Gold are an epitome of the wisdom of the East as culled by an imaginary King Bonium, who is represented as journeying to India expressly for this purpose.   But far more significant than this thirteenth-century translation is the *Conde Lucanor* or *Libro de Patronio* of Don Juan Manuel (1282-1348), nephew of Alfonso the Wise, and uncle of Alfonso XI., whose guardian he was.   The princely author led a stormy life, being always at war either with his quondam ward or with the national foe. Although he defeated the Moors at the battle of Guadalhorra, Juan Manuel knew how to profit by their culture. *El Conde Lucanor* contains other ingredients, but its chief ultimate source was the *Pantscha-Tantra*, a Sanscrit work written in the remote past by a pundit Wischnou Sarma for the sons of an Indian sovereign, his pupils.   A descendant of the *Pantscha-Tantra* was the *Hitopadesa* produced in the sixth century of our era and translated by a physician, Barzouyeh, into Pehlvi or Old Persian.   Hence, in the eighth century, it was translated by Abdallah-ben-al-Mokaffa, at the command of the Khalif Mansour, into Arabian, under the title of *Calilah and Dimnah* —the two jackals whose adventures are related in the work.

It is not improbable that Juan Manuel possessed a first-hand acquaintance with this Arabian version. He certainly understood the language, as the *Conde*

Lucanor in general, and the story of Al Hakem King
of Cordova in particular, contains many Arabian
quotations. But there is another possibility. In the
eleventh century Rabbi Joel is reputed to have
translated the *Calilah and Dimnah* from Arabian into
Hebrew; and, in 1261, this Hebrew version was
translated — by order, it is believed, of Alfonso
X. — into Castilian. The name Lucanor, which is
suspiciously like Lokman, appears to have been taken
from the prose Tristan, but Lucanor doubtless represents Juan Manuel himself. The nobleman, who
is no longer very young, and gets his full share of
the troubles of life, has recourse, on every emergency,
to his friend Patronio, who clothes his advice in
parables. These parables, by no means invariably
of Eastern origin, are told charmingly, and probably
from memory. *El Conde Lucanor* is in prose, but
here and there are signs of a poetical vein, and the
moral is regularly presented at the close of each
recital in a couplet, *e.g.* :—

> " Si por vicio et por folgura la buena fama perdemos,
>   La vida muy poco dura; denostados fincaremos."

The work is at the same time what it was intended
to be—a thesaurus of good sense and practical philosophy.[1] A general feature of these Spanish treatises
is the absence from them of the cant of chivalry.
This was to come in the period now beginning.

---

[1] *Count Lucanor : or, The Fifty Pleasant Stories of Patronio*, first
done into English from the Spanish, by J. York. Westminster :
Pickering, 1868.

Many of the traits observed in Italian and Spanish allegories and works of instruction reappear in a notable English poem—the *Vision of* (*i.e.,* "*concerning*") *Piers the Plowman.* The writer, probably named William Langland, or Langley, must have been born—tradition says, at Cleobury-Mortimer in Shropshire—about 1332; and he died about 1400. *Piers Plowman* belongs to the category of poems occupying a lifetime; and, like Froissart's *Chroniques*, it exists in three different versions or "editions." The first version seems to have been composed, near the Malvern Hills in Worcestershire, in 1362, and to have been inspired by the events of the preceding year, when, for the second time in the reign of Edward III., England had been ravaged by the plague. On the 15th January 1362 a new calamity befell in the shape of a devastating tempest, which filled all hearts with terror, and seemed to usher in the Last Day. The moment therefore was favourable to any one desiring to lift up his voice against prevailing corruptions in Church and State.

Although Langland chose for his poem rhymeless alliterative verse, he, like all other educated Englishmen, knew French, and certain French compositions exercised a powerful influence over his imagination. It is superfluous to mention the *Roman de la Rose*, and, besides this, he may probably have read one of its sources — the *Tournoiement d'Antéchrist* of Huon de Méri. He was certainly acquainted with Robert Grosseteste's *Castel d'Amour*, translated about half a century earlier.

Piers Plowman. (margin note)

Sources. (margin note)

The Castle of Love, which is the bosom of the Holy
Virgin, has suggested the "Tour on the Toft," and
Grosseteste's four daughters of the Most High King
are quoted in the *Vision* as Mercy, Sothfastnes, Righ-
wysnes, and Pees.   Grosseteste was indebted for the
idea to a homily of St Bernard, and it is possible that
Langland drew from the same source.   Anyhow, he
was well versed in Holy Scripture and the great
Latin Church Fathers.

The Prologus gives the *cadre* of the poem—a wonderful vision of a castle, and a dungeon, and a field
full of people.   From this general description Langland proceeds to pass in review the various orders
that made up the realm of England—bidders and
beggars, pilgrims and palmers, bishops and bachelors
of divinity, barons and burgesses, bakers and butch-
ers, tailors and tanners, masons and miners, dykers
(ditchers) and delvers, cooks and taverners, and
many more.

What is the meaning of this spectacle ?   A lady
with a beautiful face descends on purpose to inform
The meaning.   him.   The "Tour" or castle (as we should
probably say) is the Truth of God; the
"Dungun" (dungeon) is the Castle of Care, the
abode of Wrong.   The field full of people is, of
course, the "world."   "Of other heuene than heer
holde thei no tale," he says of the busy crowd.   But
who is the lady herself ?   "Holi churche Icham,"
she replies, and at once William is down on his
knees, beseeching her to pray for the pardon of his
sins, and to teach him to believe on Christ.   After

further discourse, he begs her to instruct him in
the art of detecting lies, and is told to look on his
left hand. He sees there a woman gorgeously arrayed, who, he learns, is Meede (bribery), and
with her are two companions, Fals and Favel. The
name Fals speaks for itself ; the meaning of Favel
is not so obvious. According to some, it is derived
from the Old French *favele* (Lat. *fabula*), signifying
"idle talk," and is here employed figuratively for
Flattery. Occleve certainly uses it in this sense—

> " But *favelle* taketh all another parte,
>   In wrong preisynge is all his craft and art."

There is, however, another slightly different explanation. The word is sometimes spelt *Fauvel*, and this
suggests a connection with the French *fauve* (*i.e.*,
"fallow," as used in "fallow deer"). In the *Roman
de Fauvel*, both parts of which date from the commencement of the fourteenth century, the beast so
named personifies the vices rampant in the Church
and in society. Although the name is stated to be
compounded of *fauls* and *vel*, the *couleur fauve* of the
animal is distinctly emphasised. The progeny of
Fauvel are Flaterie, Avarice, Vilenie, Varieté, Envie,
and Lascheté, the initials of which compose the name
Fauvel. I have laid more stress on this point than it
would otherwise deserve, because it brings into prominence a French work which may not improbably
have influenced Langland, just as Langland in turn
must have influenced the English poets of the succeeding century.

Curiously enough, the protagonist has no part in the first vision, which seems to have been designed *The second* for the special benefit of King Edward III. *vision.* The second vision again shows us the field full of people, but now Conscience appears in their midst, and, cross in hand, begins to preach. He tells them that the pestilences and the south-west wind, which on a Saturday at even tore up trees by the roots, were sent as punishment for sin and a reminder of "domesday." His efforts were supported by Repentaunce, whose eloquence "made William to weope watur with his eyen." The contrite sinners set out on a pilgrimage to "Seynt Treuthe," but lose their way. Meeting a palmer, who had travelled far and wide in the East, they ask him to direct them, but he has never heard of such a saint. At this juncture a ploughman comes forward with the information that he knows the saint well, and has worked for him these fifteen winters. He offers to show them the way.

Who is Piers the Plowman? Well, there is no doubt that in the later developments of the poem *The "hero."* Piers is none other than Christ himself. In the First Epistle to the Corinthians (x. 4) St Paul speaks of the rock smitten by Moses, from which water gushed out for the Israelites in the wilderness, and, referring to its spiritual significance, he adds, " and that rock was Christ." Langland builds on this passage ; " Petrus id est christus," he says in the *Vision* (xv. 206). The question, however, may fairly be raised whether this interpretation is not really an afterthought. At his

first entrance Piers suggests rather a good honest man
leading a true Christian life, and serving as contrast
and rebuke to the whole tribe of ecclesiastical hypocrites satirised in the prologue. In any case, there is
no absolute inconsistency, as, in Langland's belief, the
essence of Christianity lies in practice. This is the
conclusion reached at the end of the *Visio de Petro
Plowman* in its first shape. In 1377, however, Langland revised and extended his poem.[1] In this second
" edition " is elaborated, more fully than in the first,
the *Visio de Dowel, Dobet et Dobest secundum Wit et
Resoun*—actually three visions in which the nature
of virtue is set forth. Dowel is the personification
of a godly life, and the way to its attainment is shown
in the conversion of one Hawkyn, " the Active Man,"
a minstrel. The central idea of Dobet is love, the
essence of which is explained to the poet in a dialogue
with Anima (the soul), according to the principles
laid down in the thirteenth chapter of the First
Epistle to the Corinthians, and other passages of
Holy Scripture. There is a striking coincidence in
the sentiments here expressed with regard to the
disastrous results of the *dos ecclesiæ* of Constantine
and those of Walther von der Vogelweide, Dante,
and Juan Ruiz, while the psychomachy of the last
vision may well remind us of the *Libro de Buen Amor*

[1] A third version was produced between 1380 and 1390. The three
versions are distinguished as the A text, B text, and C text. Professor Skeat has edited the poem, with his customary skill and learning, for the Clarendon Press. *Piers Plowman's Creed* (contained in
Wright's edition) is a Lollard satire dating from the end of the fourteenth century, and thought to be by another hand.

of the Spanish Arch-Priest. Dobest signifies the ideal
ministry of the ideal Church.

To resume. The interest of the *Vision of Piers
the Plowman* is twofold. It supplies a picture of
contemporary England, and it unfolds to
us the moral and religious ideas of an
educated layman. The first aspect has been dealt
with by Mr J. W. Mackail in a charming paper contributed to the *Cornhill Magazine* for 1897, which
thoroughly deserves reprinting.[1] The remarkable
thing about Langland's allegorical personages is
that they are evidently drawn from life. Take
Covetyse, for instance. He is beetle-browed, blear-
eyed, his cheeks flap like a leathern purse, and he wears
a torn and threadbare tabard twelve winters old. He
relates how he served Sim at the Oak, and was his
pledged 'prentice, and learnt to lie. At his master's
bidding he went to the fairs at "Winchestre and Wych"
(Weyhill, in Hampshire), where he cheated; and he
alludes to his wife at Westminster, who cheated too.
The whole account suggests a living prototype, or, at
least, an intimate knowledge of the trading classes and
their ways.

At the same time, it might be going too far to make
Langland a popular bard. The wedding of Meede the
Maiden, with the elaborate court-scenes, suggests that
the poet was familiar with "high life," though, it is
true, his tone is not very courtly. The allegory of
Conscience, who is one of the king's knights, renders
it evident that Langland was not specially incensed

Realism.

[1] M. J. J. Jusserand's studies also are of great merit and interest.

against the great people, or against greatness, but he much desired, for great and small, a moral reformation combined with the reign of reason.

The prophecies will naturally remind the reader of the famous foretelling in Dante's first canto—that *Prophetic literature.* of the *Veltro*, who may have been Can Grande or possibly Uguccione. But a circumstance which is far less widely known is that Italy in the fourteenth century rejoiced in a whole literature of such prophecies composed in the vague and rambling style of the French *fatrasie*, and allied in many cases with the old political *serventese*. A notable example of the sort, predicting all manner of dreadful things for the year 1369, was fathered on Jacopone da Todi, the religious enthusiast of the preceding century, and bore as title *Prophetia fratris Jacoponis*. In general these seers, like our modern Moores and Zadkiels, are shrewd enough to avoid perilous precision. The majority of them were friars, and this rage for prophesying was the outcome of a misguided zeal. It is especially noticeable that the prophets—some of them, anyhow—do not drive poor mortals to despair by representing their destiny as fixed, but intimate, like Jonah, that timely repentance may avert the otherwise impending calamities.

Dramatic literature will no doubt be fully dealt with in the succeeding volume, but it is permissible to point out the remarkable similarity between the later visions of *Piers Plowman* and an early morality —the *Castell of Perseverance*. Those spiritual combats, I cannot but think, were inspired by the well-

2 B

known passage in the *Epistle to the Ephesians* (vi. 12):
"We wrestle not against flesh and blood, but against
principalities, against powers, against the rulers of the
darkness of this world, against spiritual wickedness in
high places."

The literature of religion in the fourteenth century
exhibits the same general traits we have been accus-
Religious tomed to note in other departments—*e.g.*,
writings. by a gradual transition from verse to prose.
The subjects of the narrative poems, and this is true
also of other metrical compositions, are mostly conventional, and the same in all European languages.
Many, indeed, are derived from a common source, such
as the *Aurea legenda* of Jacobus a Voragine.

Though nobody is known to have essayed a poetical version of the whole Bible, portions thereof, and
especially the Psalter, were frequently rendered into
verse.   The *Psautier lorrain* and the Northumbrian
Psalter are specimens.   In this connection may be
mentioned some remarkable homilies in the Northumbrian dialect, to which also belongs the *Cursor Mundi*
or *Cursor o Werld*, an immense poem describing Old
and New Testament history, variegated with mediæval
legends.   Much relished by contemporary Englishmen, the work is worth reading by their descendants,
now that it is at last accessible.[1]

From works like this it is but a step to edifying
compositions, many of which surpass it in vast extent.
Such are a number of prodigious visions, of which the
three *Pèlerinages* of Guillaume Deguilleville, com-

[1] E.E.T.S.   7 vols., ed. Morris, 1874-1892.

posed about 1330, are, perhaps, the best known.   The
climax is reached in the 71,000 lines of the *Méta-
morphoses d'Ovide moralisées*, by Philippe de Vitry,
Bishop of Meaux.   This attempt to transfigure Ovid
—strangest metamorphosis of all—into an angel of
light will strike most readers as sufficiently bold and
original, though, in reality, it does not lack countenance from the practice of contemporary pulpiteers.

Allusion may here be made to the Church hymns,
many of which at this period were given a dress in
Church hymns. the vernacular.   Thus, in England, about
the year 1330, William Herebert, a Fran-
ciscan friar, translated — obviously that it might be
sung in divine service — the Latin *Popule mi, quid
feci tibi*.   Versions of the hymns *Stabat Mater* and
Dies est lœtitiœ, in Dutch, pertain to this age, as,
in all languages, an abundance of Christmas carols,
some macaronic.   An interesting example of the class
has been preserved in a German hymn commencing,
Syt willekomen, Heirre Kirst.   This carol is found in
a copy of the Gospels belonging to the Emperor Otho
III., with musical accompaniment for one voice ; in
a manuscript of the year 1389 it appears with an
arrangement for three voices.   It was sung, during
Christmas-eve, by the civic authorities in the minster
at Aix.

The whole subject of *leise*, of which this is one, is
most attractive, but can only be dealt with briefly
Leise. here.   The word is derived from the recurring *Kyrie eleison* of the litany, which
was pronounced by the lay-people.   Gradually their

share in the service was expanded by the insertion
of strophes, of which *Kyrie eleison* was the refrain.
In 1349, when Europe was being decimated by the
Black Death, the flagellants sang these hymns in
their processions and voluntary castigations.   Perhaps, however, the most striking application of the
leis was its use on the field of battle.   The king
sang the words of the hymn, and his followers re-
sponded *Kyrie eleison.*   A favourite hymn, which
was sung in military expeditions and crusades, as
well as on ordinary pilgrimages, was one beginning
In gotes namen varen wir.   Apart from these extraordinary occasions, there is ample evidence that the
singing of vernacular hymns formed a regular part of
divine worship, the laity being incited thereto, at the
close of the sermon, by the announcement of the opening words of the canticle.   We have also some reason
to surmise that hymns were sung *before* the sermon ;
indeed, so far as the fifteenth century is concerned, the
fact is assured.

Hymns, however, were only the lowest and most
general form of the religious lyric, which was cultivated by knights and gentlemen, and by
Religious lyrics.   spiritual   persons.   Among   aristocratic
poets composing in this vein were Oswald von Wolkenstein, Count Hugo von Montfort, and Count Peter
von Arberg.   The most noteworthy production of the
kind was certainly a *Marienlob* of Bruder Hans vom
Niederrhein.   It consisted of five books, comprising
each a hundred strophes, whereof the initial letters
make up the Latin words of the Angel's salutation.

The model of this poem was Bonaventura's *Laus beatœ Virginis*. A sixth book was added, full of rhythmical caprices, which afford convincing proofs of Bruder Hans' dexterity, and including variations in French, English, and Latin. Notwithstanding these features, and the narrative and didactic portions, the work is lyrical in character, and the feelings of the writer are freely laid bare.

Just as the music of the mass was borrowed or adapted from popular airs, so in Germany a whole category of religious verse was based on the *tagelied* and *tanzlied* of Minnesong. The Bridal of the Soul with Christ and the Annunciation to the Virgin were the points of contact ideally, the result being that indubitably profane songs were translated into religious poems, and there sprang up a crop of *contra-facta*, or spiritual parodies, designed to oust the secular originals. What is true of Germany is true also of England; the erotic element in literature, while preserving its outer shell, was transformed and spiritualised. This tendency, which finds its fullest expression in the prose of some Continental writers, is in England represented chiefly by certain poems. Those of William of Shoreham on the Seven Sacraments, the Ten Commandments, the Seven Deadly Sins, &c., are distinguished by thought and learning, while they reveal that inclination to allegory which may be termed natural to the mystic temperament.

English poems.

William of Shoreham, of Kentish extraction, spent a considerable portion of his life as vicar of Chart,

near Maidstone. As a poet he is much inferior to a
noted Yorkshire recluse, Richard Rolle of Hampole.
The term "recluse" is used here in its most literal
signification, since the person in question does not
appear to have filled any ecclesiastical office, his early
career being that of a mendicant preacher. The fruits
of his study and meditation are seen in his realistic
Pricke of Conscience, wherein he describes the Fall of
Man, the Judgment, Hell, and Heaven, agreeably to
orthodox conceptions, and in a less certain but more
poetical body of lyrical work, as well as in prose.
Another clerk who endeavoured to correct the vices
of the age was Robert Mannyng of Brunne, who
translated into English, in the year 1303, William
of Waddington's *Manuel des Pechiez*, under the title
of *Handlyng Synne*. It is requisite to say "translated," but the translation is uncommonly free. Indeed, so many are the divergencies that the work
may fairly be reckoned independent. One way in
which it differs from the French original, or, perhaps,
pattern, is that it contains a far greater abundance
of concrete examples. This is not, as might be supposed, a dry book. Mannyng dearly loved a tale, and
the more bizarre it was, the better. He distributes
his censures broadcast, but the worst offenders, from
his point of view, are the women, who, he pleasantly
observes, do no wrong except all day.

It has been said that, in England at this period, the
tendency to mysticism was most conspicuous in
poetry. To this statement there is one notable exception—the *Ayenbite of Inwyt*, or, in modern phrase,

Remorse of Conscience. Its author was Dan Michel of Northgate, who describes himself as a "brother of the cloister of St Austin of Canterbury"; and the work was a very unintelligent translation of a favourite French treatise, the *Somme des Vices et des Vertus* or *Somme le Roi*, written by the Dominican Frère Lorens in 1279, and dedicated to Philippe le Hardi.[1]

The most obvious trait in the mystic literature of the fourteenth century is its frank adoption of the *Vernacular theology.* vernacular. The great writers of the preceding age — Bernard of Clairvaux, and Hugh and Richard of St Victor, in France ; Bonaventura, in Italy ; and Ramon Lull, in Spain—had recorded their thoughts in Latin, though it is worthy of note that Lull (better known as a wayward comet of scholasticism) probably owed much in this respect to the collaboration of his disciples. At any rate, the quality of some of his writings is so poor as to suggest, in the case of the remainder, revision by a more competent hand.

The causes of this extraordinary change from the official language of the Church to "dialects" understanded of the people are not far to seek. It is, in the first place, part of a general phenomenon affecting, in a greater or less degree, all branches of literature. With regard to theology, we see here the effect — somewhat postponed it may be, but, nevertheless, inevitable—of the rise of the great preaching orders.

---

[1] *Handlyng Synne*, and the *Ayenbite of Inwyt*, have been edited for the Roxburghe Club (the latter also for the E.E.T.S.) ; and the *Pricke of Conscience* for the Philological Society.

The missionary zeal of St Dominic and St Francis
could not be perpetuated solely in the verbal utterances of their perfervid followers; it was bound to
germinate in a literature. Accordingly, it has been
remarked that about the year 1260 the Order of St
Dominic underwent a transformation. The Black
Friars, to give them their popular name, grew more
learned, appropriated the formulæ of the schools, and
addressed themselves to various kinds of science.

A third cause lay in an increased regard for the
mental and spiritual welfare of women, who, as a sex,
were supposed to be ignorant of Latin. Towards the
end of the thirteenth century the cure of souls and
task of preaching among the nuns had been confided
to members of the Dominican fraternity, and it was in
the warm devotional atmosphere of the convent that
the style of speaking and writing afterwards so common blossomed into maturity. We have documentary
proof of the care bestowed on female religious culture
in a Rule of St Benedict and a sermon in praise of
pious virginity—both English, and dating from this
period. The sermon, like most of the compositions
before noticed, had a Latin original, which may be
traced to Ailred of Rievaux. The activity of the
Dominicans, however, was not confined to nuns. Num-
bered among their auditors were secular clerks, and
even layfolk. Out of these heterogeneous elements
arose in Germany a sect of people calling themselves
Friends of God, who were principally to be found in
the large western cities — Cologne, Strasburg, and
Basle.

It is doubtful whether this wave of mysticism can be properly described as an intellectual movement. *The essence of mysticism.* Perhaps it is best compared to the Evangelical revival of the last century, which incredulous observers, like Horace Walpole, loved to designate as "enthusiasm." The truth is, however, that the movement had several phases, and comprehended all of religion which is not purely outward and ceremonial. The great articles on which it insisted were a striving after and union with God, renunciation of the world, and the cultivation of an inner and spiritual life. Merely to specify these points is to convey but a faint notion of the exalted passion with which they were embraced and held fast, and in which lay the real significance of the movement. The essence of mysticism was not a cold assent of the reason to certain abstract propositions, but feeling and imagination, the perception of a divine beyond invisible to the eye of flesh, and the glowing response of the heart to the abysmal love of God.

It is in the land of St Francis that mysticism shows itself in its most winning form. The artistic sense of the Italians, now beginning to assert itself *The Fioretti.* in the portraiture of Cimabue and Giotto, was opposed alike to crude theorising and reckless exaggeration in practice. The career of the great saint himself has been aptly described as a "life-poem," and though we find in it passages which appear quaint and childish, they possess the quality of their defect. His preaching to the birds, for instance, was a *Benedicite* in action, and bespeaks the tenderness and universal

sympathy of his nature.   As years rolled on, the
image of this son of Assisi, graven on the popular
fancy, lost nothing of its attractiveness, and the
Fioretti di San Francesco testify to the influence and
the charm exercised on succeeding generations by his
truly angelic spirit.   At one time regarded as an
original composition, this has since been shown to
be an anonymous fourteenth-century version of a
Floretum by a certain Frate Ugolino di Monte Santa
Maria.   Mirrored in the work are the doings of St
Francis and his early disciples — not all historical
perhaps, for already *Aberglaube* has tinged them with
a hue as of sunset.   Tales like the Conversion of
Brother Wolf, though told with delightful *naïveté*,
impose too great a strain on modern credulity.
Compelled to reject them, we reject them not as
mendacity, but as myth.[1]

If it were a question of selecting from among the
contemporaries of Dante, who were also his countrymen, the man that most resembled Francis

Fra Giordano.

of Assisi, I should be tempted to name Fra
Giordano da Rivalto.   It is true he founded no order,
yet, as a preacher, he was " in labours more abundant."
At Florence master of theology in the monastery
of Santa Maria Novella, he would hold forth as often
as five times in a single day, and not only in the
churches, but in the public squares.   It is possible
that these stupendous efforts brought him to his untimely end.   The sermons he has left, like the sermons

---

[1] The latest edition of the *Fioretti* is that of Monsignor Leopoldo
Amoni.   Rome, 1889.

of Robertson of Brighton, are of necessity mere fragments, and lack the crowning effects of the speaker's
presence.   Judging, however, from the loose notes
that have come down to us, it would appear that Fra
Giordano's discourse (for example) on the City of
God is just such a sermon as St Francis might have
preached, full of love and full of ecstasy.

It has been thought by some that Fra Giordano,
despite his cognomen, was originally of Pisa.   From
this quarter came another Dominican, of
" Devilling."   even greater fame, Domenica Cavalca.
Pisan historians write in extravagant terms of this
friar's literary aptitudes; but it would be unfair to
deny that there is much merit in his compositions,
and, accordingly, some reason in their eulogies.
Cavalca is deserving of esteem for the easy flow,
the unaffected style, the lucidity of his prose; his
verse, like Bunyan's, is of no great value.   His works,
which are many, are divisible into two sets : compilations and translations.   The personal rectitude
of Fra Domenico is doubtless not open to suspicion,
yet his reputation, it would seem, is based in some
degree on the toil of others.   The practice of
" devilling," to use a vulgar but expressive term, is
familiar to all students of literature, the classical
instance being that of Pope's " Homer."   Probably in
Cavalca's day this convenient, but not too praise-
worthy, method of delegating pains was not consciously in vogue, and it was the dishonesty of
circumstances, rather than any fault of his own,
that formerly attributed to Fra Domenico a trans-

lation of the Bible, known as the *Bibbia Volgare*.
This is now ascertained to have been the work of
several hands. Fame has been equally kind to him
with respect to the *Vite de' Santi Padri*. By temperament Cavalca was mild and pacific, but a righteous
indignation spurs him now and again to strong denunciation of ecclesiastical abuses.

The sternness which has been noted in Cavalca
as a passing mood reveals itself in Jacopo Passavanti
Lenten as an abiding characteristic. His most
literature. important work — indeed the only work
which can with safety be attributed to him—is his
Mirror of True Penitence. Of this rather celebrated
book the author himself has given us an account in
the Prologue. It appears to have originated in
Lenten discourses delivered at various times, but
principally in the year 1354, to Florentine con-
gregations. Of necessity they were given in the
vernacular, in which form they partook, it would
seem, of an impromptu character. Passavanti, however, declares that he " wrote the same things, word
for word, and in Latin, for the clerks." This was
a concession to learned prejudice. So customary
amongst clerks was the use of Latin that high dig-
nitaries in the Church and at the Universities professed themselves scarcely able to understand " dialect,"
or, at least, to speak it with difficulty. Younger
scholars, however, would frequently attend the expositions of popular preachers, whose sentences they
turned into Latin as they proceeded, unless, as sometimes happened, a racy proverb was introduced which

baffled their search for a substitute. When Passavanti reduced his sermons to writing in Italian as well
as in Latin, such action was indicative of a change.

The *Mirror* concludes with a series of disquisitions
on Pride, Humility, Vainglory—and Dreams. This
last section deals in a curious and instructive manner
with magic, the belief in which was so universal and,
I may add, so fatal. Paracelsus, who threw all his
medical works into the fire, confessed that the only
persons that knew anything were those luckless and
hated beings, the witches. As for Passavanti, his
favourite instrument for persuading people to reform
was the terrors of the law, the threat of Divine retri-
bution; and, like other moralists of the age, he breaks
off from his exposition to adduce some " example " from
the lore, religious or profane, of the past. The story
of Count Giuffredi and Dame Beatrice, albeit a borrowed one, loses nothing in his telling, and, repeated
orally, must have fallen with horrifying effect on the
ears of any adulterers or adulteresses who might have
listened to it.

However suitable to the season of Lent, this style
of preaching was not characteristically Italian. It
belonged rather to the gloomy regions of the North,
whence came the Voyage of St Brandan, the Vision of
Tundale, the Purgatory of St Patrick, and similar compositions. When, however, an Italian did apply himself to the task of heaping up horrors, it became apparent that the comparative paucity of such writings
in the southern literature sprang not so much from
incapacity as from disinclination. For Passavanti is

equalled, if not excelled, in his gruesomeness by a
younger monk, Fra Filippo da Siena. The latter, an
Augustinian, wrote a book, *Gli Assempri*, which treats
of the wiles of the Devil, and of wicked cavaliers, vain
women, naughty priests, German soldiers, and others,
who become his prey.

This is mysticism on its lower side; the sublime is
never far from the ridiculous. From such grotesque
St Caterina manifestations it is a relief to turn to the
da Siena. lofty inspiration, combined with shrewd
common-sense, of that noble woman, St Caterina da
Siena, who, though in reality much more, exhibits
the attributes of a mediæval Elizabeth Fry. The
same *Aberglaube* which has veiled in solemn mist
the truth of St Francis' ministry, has included in its
folds the record of Caterina.

Though a masculine intellect qualified her to inter-
vene in public affairs, the glare and glamour of the
world never diverted her thoughts from the immutable
background, before which actors on the terrestrial
stage flitted like phantoms, and the pomp and page-
antry of life disclosed their emptiness. I have
already observed how potently the imagination was
affected by the emblems of the Heavenly Bridegroom
and the high espousals that await the souls of the
redeemed. Of no one was this more true than of
Caterina da Siena. In one of her letters she describes
how she attended a condemned prisoner in his last hours,
and on the scaffold. The weakness and shrinking of the
man, in view of the terrible prospect, are recorded, and
Caterina's comforting expressions, almost audible in

their music. And the refrain is always the same,
"*Giuso!* to the wedding, my sweet brother!"

In such a life, replete with kind deeds and zeal for
the public good, authorship could have but a subordinate part. It seems rather incongruous, therefore,
to subject her composition to rules of criticism proper
enough for professional and self-conscious artists, but
wholly out of place with regard to persons writing
under a sort of spiritual afflatus.[1] Another point
worthy of being remembered is, that she learnt to read
quite late, and, as she believed, by a miracle, while it
was not until 1378 that she acquired the art of
writing, and she died in 1380. Thus the whole of her
literary activity was compressed into two short years.
In view of these facts, the facility she displays is
nothing less than astounding, and this facility a
passionate tenderness, intense and always present,
transmutes into eloquence. No wonder then that so
much of her work has survived the wreck of Time,
while that of lifelong students has been cast to the
winds. Even Caterina, however, has cause to com-

---

[1] St Caterina's figures are forcible and expressive, but homely, and
some would even say, vulgar. She calls the wound in the Saviour's
side "una bottiga aperta piena d'odore, intanto che il peccato vi di-
venta odorifero." Then again as to her metaphor of "eating." Sometimes she intends by this satisfying one's longing for God, and this,
we can very well see, may have been inspired either by the words of
our Lord or by the practice of the Church in Holy Communion.
Virtues are "cotte al fuoco della divina Carità e mangiansi in su la
mensa della Croce, cioè con pena e fadiga s' acquista la virtù." Sometimes she means by "eating" a ravenous desire to win souls for the
Kingdom. Her followers are to be "gustatori e mangiatori delle
anime per amore di Dio."

plain of this enemy of human industry; her treatise on the Gospels has perished utterly. On the other hand, there have been left as souvenirs a long dialogue on Divine Providence, the words of the saint as she lay a-dying, certain prayers, and, above all, her incomparable epistles. These letters, addressed to all sorts and conditions of people, are both numerous and important, containing a full revelation of herself and shedding some light on the age.[1]

The philosophy of mysticism during this period is represented by Meister Eckhart and his followers.

Meister Eckhart. Born at Hochheim in Gotha, he was first prior and provincial - prior, then master and professor of theology at Strasburg, and later at Erfurt, where he died in 1327. Eckhart's Latin writings are noticeable for two things—his adoption of the formulæ of the schools, and the influence of neo-platonic ideas, which have come to him through the medium of St Augustine. It is, however, his German works, his *predigten* and *traktate*, that chiefly interest us. In these popular expositions the language clothes itself, for the first time, in a philosophic diction, and a theory is set forth which is barely distinguishable from Pantheism. In his desire to banish anthropomorphic conceptions of God, Eckhart revels in paradox, indicating man's rightful attitude to the Supreme in such crabbed phraseology as the following: "Comprehend nothing of the unspoken

[1] The best edition of her letters is that of N. Tommasèo: Florence, 1860. On the doctrines of these writers the reader should consult F. Falco, *Moralisti Italiani del Trecento:* Lucca, 1891.

God.   Thou shouldst all at once sink from thy thine-
ness and melt in His Hisness, and thy thine should
become a mine in His Mine, so fully, that thou comprehend with Him evermore His uncreated Isness
and His nameless Nothingness."

The distinction between words like these and downright blasphemy, except on the score of intention, is
evidently rather fine ; torn from their context, they
might be quoted with deadly effect against their user.
It is therefore scarcely matter for surprise that the
Archbishop of Cologne should have instituted proceedings against him.   In reply, Eckhart denied the
competence of the tribunal, and, at the same time,
appealed to the Pope.   Before the decision was an-
nounced, the philosopher recanted by declaring at the
close of a sermon that he had always eschewed errors
of faith, and offering to retract anything that might
be pointed out to him as partaking of that character.
Soon after he died.   Two years later a papal bull was
published in condemnation of twenty-six theses which
Eckhart allowed having taught, and two more that
had been attributed to him, while the fact of his recantation was duly noticed.   Nevertheless, the dis-
semination of his opinions went on unchecked.
Sermons and treatises by Meister Eckhart, *dem got
nie niht verbarc*, were multiplied beyond number.
How many were authentic it is impossible to say,
but a considerable share was received into editions of
his collected works.   As a proof of appreciation in
days not far removed from his own, it may be mentioned that about the middle of the century Hermann

von Fritzlar, projector and part author of a Book of
Holy Living, suggested to Giselher von Statheim the
preparation of a sequel. Giselher accepted the task,
and whilst inserting a few of his own lucubrations,
did not forget Meister Eckhart, some of whose discourses here find a place.

Eckhart, as before implied, was the founder of a
school. Among those who had heard him at Cologne
Heinrich Seuse. were two young Dominicans, Heinrich
Seuse and Johannes Tauler, who in different ways carried on his teaching. Both were
born about the year 1300. Seuse spent the chief
part of his life in a monastery at Constance, dying,
however, in 1366, at Ulm, where his last years
were passed. He was the poet of the movement.
The story of his inner life, taken down from his
own description by a Swiss nun, Elsbeth Stagel,
and revised by himself, has been well named a
spiritual *Vita Nuova*. In it there is much to remind
us of the secular Minnesong, on which Seuse draws
freely both for phrase and phantasy. He has a " *hohe
Minnerin* " in the Eternal Wisdom, which appears to
him, " sometimes as a wise monitress, sometimes as a
buxom mistress." On New Year's Eve, when ordinary
lovers repair to their sweethearts' and sing for a garland, he, Seuse, before the image of Mary with the
Child, sings and speaks the praises of the Eternal
Wisdom. When May comes, he sets up a spiritual
Maypole, the Cross, and celebrates it in a lovely ode
above all flowers, above all the songs of birds, and
above all the deckings that ever graced a Maypole.

In the midst of these ecstasies he cherishes a grateful feeling towards his master, who, indeed, has shown himself to him since death and affirmed his old teaching. These epiphanies, of which we shall have another example presently, are a great stumbling-block to those who insist on a plain and literal interpretation. It is evident, however, that minds like Seuse's are carried up into a state in which common experiences are left behind, and all is dissolved in rapturous contemplation. In such a mood anything is possible.

That the best sort of mystics, among whom we may surely reckon Heinrich Seuse, were guilty of *Doctor Johann* intentional deceit, is, I think, out of the *Tauler.* question; but it seems necessary to admit that some of them possessed eminent gifts of imagination. It is requisite to add that they were not all of this soaring spirit. Eckhart's other chief disciple, Tauler, represents the severely moral aspect of the religious life, and he is sternly opposed to exaggerations such as may be found in a *Book of Spiritual Poverty*, once falsely assigned to him. It is to be observed that for most purposes Tauler's fame has entirely overshadowed that of his master, and his name occurs as that of the best-known, if not the best, German, and perhaps European, mystic of the closing Middle Age. The impression of greatness left by this monk on the minds of his countrymen is reflected in the title of the first printed edition of his sermons, which begins as follows: " *Sermon des grossgelarten in gnaden erleuchteten Doctoris Johannis Tauleri predigerr ordens, weisende,*" &c. As has been observed in the case of Fra Giordano, Tauler did not write his sermons, which were taken down by certain of his hearers, and may have been modified, in some degree, by editors. Unlike Fra Giordano, however, Tauler did not neglect composition, and his writings include, what is perhaps the most interesting of them all, an *Imitatio Christi*, or, to quote the more significant German title, *Nachfolgung des armen Lebens Christi*. His works have been translated into High German, Latin, Dutch, and Italian —a circumstance which attests, as it contributed to spread, his fame.

The spirit of poetry and romance as revealed in Seuse spent itself in the relations betwixt himself *Heinrich von* and his Maker, Elsbeth Stagel being little *Nördlingen.* else than reverent disciple and amanuensis. It was otherwise with Heinrich von Nördlingen, who, suitably as may be thought to his quality of secular priest, did not disdain earthly, and even feminine, attachments, in which respect he may be compared to that eminent moralist, Samuel Richardson. Nördlingen, however, in his dealings with *Gottesfreundinnen,* appears to have cultivated a somewhat warmer style of address than Richardson would probably have deemed advisable. His chief friends were Christina and Margareta Ebner, who have also bequeathed to us accounts of their spiritual experiences ; and of the two, Margareta, younger by fourteen years than her sister, was the favourite. He calls her " the dearest treasure of his heart given him by Christ "; and it is in the emotional epistles addressed to her by Nördlingen that we can best discern the nature of such companionships, as well as the aims and ideals of the sect to which both belonged. Finally, Heinrich von Nördlingen imparted to the *Offenbarungen* of Mechtild von Magdeburg the High German setting in which they alone survive.

Having treated of Rulman Merswin, I shall perhaps have exhausted the various categories to which individual mystics can be referred. Hitherto, *An impostor?* the worst fault imputed to any of them has been, in thought or action, a tendency to run into extremes. But hypocrisy always dogs the steps of genuine enthusiasm ; and Rulman Merswin, a layman, is not exempt from the suspicion of having imposed on the simplicity of his co-religionists. A well-to-do citizen of Strasburg, and god-child of Tauler, he was on friendly terms with Heinrich von Nördlingen and Margareta Ebner ; and having founded a house for the Knights of St John in his native city, forsook the world and devoted himself to the care of his new institution. Merswin was the author of two works discovered after his death — a spiritual autobiography, and a *Book of the Nine Rocks* (or degrees), expressing essentially the same idea as Dante's *Purgatorio*, but in a style how different ! Indeed, as literature, these works are by no means on a par with those of his fellow-mystics, and are interesting chiefly as specimens of the theological culture attainable in that age by laymen. Nothing, however, can atone for his systematic abuse of the authority of Tauler, or, at the very least, his invention of a Great

Unknown, with whom that renowned teacher has been generally identified.[1]

In France the great days of mediæval preaching were now past.   The preceding age had produced men

French preachers. of mark—*e.g.*, Jacques de Vitry, Robert de Sorbon, Étienne de Bourbon; the four-teenth century, on the contrary, plagued with barren-ness, can show but one name of equal merit and distinction — Jean Gerson.   If we inquire into the cause of this sterility, it would appear to lie, partially at least, in the abundance of ready - made sermons easily procurable, and dissuading the common curate from exertions thus rendered unnecessary.

In Jean Gerson we encounter a man uniting in himself the virtues and accomplishments of a great

Jean Gerson. preacher, for he was learned, and eloquent, and talented, and permeated with the spirit of Christianity.   Masterpieces of method, his Latin ser-mons were collected and printed centuries ago; but his French discourses are, even now, in a large measure inedited.   However, it is with the latter that we have principally to do.   Gerson's French preaching divides into two epochs, of which the first extends from 1389 to 1397.   He was then quite a young man.   Born in 1363, in a vanished village of which he assumed the name, Jean Charlier had risen by rapid steps to be professor of the sacred sciences at the College of Navarre; and he was destined to still higher promo-

---

[1] On the German mystics see *Deutsche Mystiker des* 14 *Jahr hunderts* (ed. Pfeiffer: Leipzig, 1845-57) ; and W. Preger, *Geschichte der deutschen Mystik im Mittelalter :* Leipzig, 1874-81.

tion through the favour of Philip the Good, Duke of
Burgundy, who presented him with a living in
Flanders, gave him lodgings in his *hotel* at Paris,
and procured for him the title of Chancellor of the
University, and the honour of preaching before the
Court. Among the sermons which Gerson composed
at this time were some of those on the *Mystères,* and
a portion of his *Panégyriques des. Saints;* also discourses adapted to the chief festivals of the Church—
Whitsunday, Christmas, the Epiphany, Candlemas, &c.
In 1397, in consequence of political disturbances and
Court intrigues of which he was the object, Gerson
retired to his benefice in Flanders; but early in the
following century he was back again in Paris, addressing distinguished audiences in the principal
churches—St Paul, Notre Dame, St Séverin, and St
Antoine.

This second ministry was marked by a feature
absent from the first. The parish of St-Jean-en-
Grève, of which he had charge, contained a large
working-class population, and Gerson, somewhat in
the spirit of George Herbert (likewise an ex-courtier),
devoted his brilliant gifts to its spiritual edification,
initiating a course of systematic instruction in
Christian morals, which he developed during successive Lents and Advents. In 1414 he attended the
Council of Constance as delegate of the University of
Paris and representative of the king. During its
sessions he engaged in proceedings certain to draw
upon him the resentment of Jean sans Peur, and
barring his return to Paris. Accordingly, he with-

drew to the mountains of La Bavière, and afterwards
to the monastery of the Celestines at Lyon. His last
days were spent in catechising little children and
writing books of devotion. He died in 1429, the
memorable year wherein Joan of Arc defeated the
English at Patay, and delivered France.

"'Twas a great matter at Paris," says a chronicler
of 1400, "when Maistre Jehan Gerson, Maistre
Eustache de Pavilly, Frère Jacques le
Grand, and other doctors and clerks, used
to preach so many excellent sermons." The doctor
and clerk in Gerson's composition is certainly not
hard of perception. The rhythm even of his popular
discourses may be traced to the rhetorical periods
of those learned models he had studied from youth.
His erudition is paraded without scruple, and in
such a way as to lead one to wonder what his less
educated disciples could make of his allusions.
Moses and Mercury, Christ and Jupiter, Aristotle
and Augustine—such are the personages that Gerson
associates, apparently without any thought of incongruity.   Equally strange to modern ideas is his
use, or rather abuse, of allegory. Vices become
cavaliers, virtues "damoiselles."   Prayer is "the
chamber-maid of the soul."   The Holy Ghost is a
good curé, and the soul is his parishioner.   These
characteristics belong to his earlier manner, and the
days when he addressed the Court. In his discourses
to the people he strikes a different note, and exhibits
a sympathetic feeling which rises sometimes to
vehemence and passion, so that we instinctively recall

Doctor and clerk.

Jean de Varennes, driven to madness by the miseries and corruptions of the age.[1]

Gerson's career has many points of resemblance to that of John Wiclif, the "morning-star of the Re-

John Wiclif. formation." Yorkshire "full of knights" never produced a more chivalrous character than this learned and discreet, but also bold and resolute clerk. For some years Master of Balliol, he became head of Canterbury Hall, afterwards incorporated with Christ Church. In 1367 he was removed from this post by Archbishop Langham, a prelate of strong monkish sympathies. The phrase *clericus peculiaris regis* applied to him warrants the belief that Wiclif was chaplain to the king. As an author he was known to a select few for his Latin tractates, especially his logic, in which the examples are culled from Holy Scripture.

In the quarrel between the king and Pope Urban V., in which he was now to participate, Wiclif, instead

Politics. of replying to his challenger directly, set forth the various aspects of the subject in a dialogue between seven lords of Parliament— in fact, in a regular debate. In the end the cause of patriotism wins a complete triumph. Encouraged by his success on this occasion, Wiclif became more and more the mouthpiece of a large and influential party bent on limiting the authority of the Pope.

---

[1] Gerson, however, was no friend to the mystics; indeed, he distinguished himself by opposing the recognition of St Bridget, the enthusiastic Swedish nun. It is to be regretted that his own writings are still largely inaccessible.

When, in 1372, Arnold Garnier, a French Dominican, arrived as papal nuncio and receiver of dues, Wiclif drew up a pamphlet showing precisely how these exactions operated. Again, in October 1377, on the assembling of the first Parliament under Richard II., when the question was raised whether it was right for England, in defiance of the Pope's orders and his threat of ecclesiastical penalties, to restrain the outflow of national treasures to foreign shores, Wiclif supported the affirmative.

Meanwhile he had been busy defining for himself and for others the principles upon which his actions *Principles.* were based. These are revealed in a work entitled *Summa in Theologia,* in which the nature of authority is discussed in all its bearings. Wiclif's conception of the Church, as here presented to us, is simple in the extreme. Like Marsilio, he rejects the hierarchical system as a thing which had been grafted on the plain teaching of the Gospel, and slights the distinction between clerk and layman, between priest and bishop. Also the office of the Pope is accepted with considerable reserves. The idea of papal infallibility was not then in the air, and Wiclif boldly affirms that the Pontiff's decrees are binding only in so far as they harmonise with the laws of Christ. Consistently with this avowal, in all his subsequent course he manifests an ever-lessening regard for the papacy and an ever-increasing reverence for the Bible. Nor did he shrink from giving, as far as possible, full practical effect to his convictions.

Influenced it may be by the appearance in its complete and final form of *Piers Ploughman*, Wiclif began to employ the popular speech for *"Pore preestes."* sermons, for controversial pamphlets, for moral and didactic tracts, thus inviting the attention of the laity to points of doctrine hitherto reserved for the clergy. Not content with written addresses, the circulation of which, in that age of ignorance, would have been too limited, he founded an order of itinerant preachers, who travelled from place to place with a staff in their hands, and arrayed in long crimson robes of coarse wool. These persons were commonly known as " pore preestes," but they gradually came to include many who were not ordained. Like the first disciples, they were, for the most part, " unlearned and ignorant men." Wiclif, however, made up for their defects by putting into their hands model discourses, and, often enough, sketches of the sermons they afterwards preached to the multitude. Herein he was probably assisted by a circle of devoted Oxford friends, both old and young, who had been persuaded to adopt his opinions. These deliverances, in their piquant satire, their direct and forcible style, their homely images, are not altogether unlike those of Latimer in the time of the great Reformation.

Even this did not suffice. The " pore preeste," unlettered as he generally was, could never be fully *Translation of* equipped whilst the Bible remained, to *the Bible.* so large an extent, a sealed book. The special views Wiclif held as to the unique authority of Scripture and the right of the laity to a richer participation in the life of the Church, marked him out as, beyond all others, the man best fitted for this difficult, and, in many ways, novel task. In order to ensure its completion he drew to his side a collaborator, Dr Nicholas of Hereford, to whom he entrusted the Englishing of the Old Testament, while he reserved to himself the translation of the New. Wiclif's personal contribution was successfully made, and a similar remark will apply to the Canonical books of the Old Testament. With reference to the Apocrypha, Hereford had arrived at Baruch iii. 20, when, his life being in danger, he suddenly vanished. With this exception Wiclif might claim the proud distinction of being the originator, and in part author, of the first complete version of the Bible in the English tongue. This was a great achievement; but, as might be anticipated in a first attempt, the work was not in all respects satisfactory. Its prime defect, which Wiclif considered perhaps its chief virtue, lay in the circumstance that the translator's hand was too plainly revealed. The grand principle, apparently, which influenced both Wiclif and Hereford, was scrupulous fidelity to the Vulgate, and if greater experience in the composition of English rendered Wiclif's version less awkward and stiff than those of his yoke-fellow, it did not prevent even his style from swarming with Latinisms. His translation, completed about 1380, was revised and much modernised by John Purvey no later than 1388.

Little more can be said as to Wiclif's public proceedings; his permanent breach with the mendicant

orders, on whose iniquities he poured the whole wealth
of his sarcasm; his rejection of the doctrine of tran-
substantiation; and the *odium theologicum* these things
brought upon him. The general effect of his conduct
was to defeat, or, at least, to postpone, the realisation
of his hopes. The authorities were alarmed, and
adopted vigorous measures for repressing the new
heresy. Wiclif himself was fain to retire to his
Leicestershire living, where he spent the remainder
of his days, peacefully enough, in ministering to his
flock and writing fresh sermons and treatises.[1] He
died, from a stroke of apoplexy, on St Sylvester's day,
1384.

[1] See *Select English Works of John Wyclif*, ed. T. Arnold, M.A.:
Oxford, 1871, with the supplement of F. D. Matthew (E.E.T.S.,
1880). A good edition of Wiclif's translation of the Bible is that of
J. Forshall and Sir F. Madden (4 vols.: Oxford University Press,
1850), entitled, *The Holy Bible in the Earliest English Versions made
from the Latin Vulgate, by John Wycliffe and his Followers.*

CHAPTER IX.

CONCLUSION.

ALTHOUGH such a process necessarily involves repetition, it is desirable, before closing the record, to "tabulate" the results obtained in the preceding pages —in other words, to exhibit, without special regard to authors or countries, the qualities characterising the period as a whole. The fourteenth century differs from earlier ages in being a time of great personalities. For centuries there had been no commanding name —no Homer, no Virgil even—to bespeak the homage of contemporaries and successors. Dante, it is true, speaks in high terms of Arnaut Daniel, but such compliments show the nakedness of the land, and Dante, moreover, knew nothing of Walther von der Vogelweide, sweetest and freshest of lyrical poets. Even Walther, however, though he carols charmingly, rises as the lark rises. He does not tower above his fellows by virtue of his own bulk; and, again, while his note is sweet, his plumage is plain. Perchance, in another age, he might have grown to larger proportions and attired himself in brighter vesture. There is something magical about the fourteenth century. Dante himself, whilst confined within the limits of the thirteenth century, is still a follower of Guido Guinicelli; but the moment he crosses the threshold of the fourteenth century, all is changed. In the year 1300 A.D. comes the wondrous vision, and the *Divina Commedia*, impossible before, becomes possible now.

But Dante, though incomparably the greatest man of his time, is not a solitary figure. Single reputations of the highest, or all but the highest, distinction were achieved in Italy by Petrarch and Boccaccio, in France by Froissart, in England by Chaucer. What is the explanation? Is it a simple accident that five of the world's greatest writers lived and laboured in the same age? Doubtless accident played some—and, indeed, an important—part in this, as in all human affairs, but there may have been other elements. Dante's example, for instance, proving that literary excellence was in no sense the prerogative of antiquity, exercised a powerful influence over the best minds of the succeeding generation. They could not indeed repeat his performance; but the memory of what he had accomplished stimulated them to fresh effort, and kept ambition in them awake. Boccaccio and Chaucer openly acknowledge Dante as their master, and if Petrarch long strove against his mastery, the final capitulation is for that reason all the more striking.

The fourteenth century is remarkable as an epoch of harvestings, of vast consummations. Dante sums up the whole of the Middle Age—theological, philo-

sophical, economic, social, artistic; it is all there, in
his great poem. In this sense the nearest parallels to
the *Commedia* are the *Decameron* and the *Canterbury
Tales*. In them we find the same variety, the same
juxtaposition of old and new, domestic and foreign,
the same universality. Neither the one nor the other,
however, possesses the same organic perfection. In
the case of both later works, the relation of the parts
to the whole is looser, less necessary, and the connection might be dissolved without fatal consequences.
This circumstance might be interpreted as a sign of
inferiority on the part of the writers, as it is certainly
a proof of inferiority in the compositions themselves.
But all three works are alike in their material genesis.
They have been formed out of a pre-existing chaos
of heterogeneous elements. They are alike, too, in
their artistic ripeness. Where the past could show
only half-hearted attempts, unfinished *abbozzi*, the
products of Dante's, of Boccaccio's, of Chaucer's old
age display firm outlines, contrasts of light and shade,
and plenitude of detail.

The vital connection between politics and literature
is a topic which in these days hardly needs
emphasising; but, if emphasis be needed, it may be in
some sort vicariously provided in Professor Fenini's
brief *Letteratura Italiana*, based on the absolute recognition of the principle. The "system of actions
and reactions" is capable of easy exemplification in
the history, political and literary, of the fourteenth
century. Thus the grand ideas of which the Guelf-
Ghibelline riots were the caricature are worthily

reflected in the breadth and majesty of the *Commedia,* while the fact that the poem was written in a tongue "understanded of the people" attests the influence and freedom of the people in the Italian commonwealths. The absence of literary pretence and literary frippery, in so far as it is not attributable to the nobility of the writer, is due to the same cause. A generation passes; commonwealths are supplanted by despotisms, and the new style in politics is kept, as it were, in countenance by new fashions in literature. The wide sweep of the *Commedia,* with its *remissus et humilis modus loquendi,* gives place to the soliloquies of the *Canzoniere,* or the proud aloofness of the *Secretum.* Boccaccio, it is true, seems cast in a more popular mould, but the pomp of his period is symptomatic of a tendency which culminated, politically, in pinchbeck Cæsarism.

A political and economic fact of the first importance is the prosperity of the middle-class. This fact has been already insisted on in the opening chapters, and incidentally throughout the work. A few remarks, however, may be permitted by way of "apology." Deliberately to assail the middle-class, in a country of which it is popularly supposed to be the backbone, would argue a temerity of which the writer is guiltless, and he has no desire to bring a swarm of hornets about his ears by representing, as some wretches have done, the sober and salutary middle-class as of essence vulgar and unpoetical. If anything is assailed, it is not the middle-class, at any rate *per se,* but monopoly and limitation. All true

literature is a protest against the undue predominance
of the sentiment of class.   The best and highest
literature appeals, not to a party, but, fully and
frankly, to mankind.   Were it not for this necessary
qualification, I should not scruple to describe the
Commedia as a splendid expression of middle-class
feeling; but Dante does not address his poem to the
middle-class—he is not prejudiced against the barons,
poor fellows—and so there is a difference.   Literature
addressed to a stratum of humanity is bound to suffer
for its favouritism.   The line of section, if it is to be
drawn at all, must be drawn vertically, and delimit,
not a class, but a nation.

Dante is middle-class by virtue of the purity of his
moral sentiment, by virtue of his "ecclesiastical-
mindedness."   In the region of art it seems fair to
associate with the prevalence of the middle-class the
spread and triumph of allegory, of which, of course,
the *Commedia* is the supreme example.   Although
Dante in his later years espoused the cause of the
Ghibellines, he was never Ghibelline, as it were, out-
and-out.   He was Guelf by inheritance, and the whole
bias of his nature was towards Guelfism.   It was his
instinct to sympathise with the clerisy, not with the
secular nobility.   Indeed, he was a clerk himself.
Now the abstract, the allegorical—"the evidence of
things not seen"—was essentially the field of the
clerks, condemned to live for the most part at second-
hand, and to postpone their enjoyments to beyond the
tomb.   Courtiers and worldlings might invade this
field, either for convenience or for disport, but the

clerisy held, so to speak, the original deed ; and they were both the spiritual guides and the intellectual sponsors of the middle-class. Wherever and whenever the middle-class became important, and, as at Florence, was strong enough to disfranchise the nobility, and affect a literature of its own, the doctrine and dialect of the clerisy grafted themselves on the new lyric and the new prose, and even bore fruit in vast poetical efficacy. The phenomenon is not quite confined to Italy — the Apocalypse and the Old Testament prophecies were in tolerably wide diffusion — but Italy was mistress of the literary art, and the Meistersingers were theologians first, and poets, by a long, long way, last.

The fourteenth century was distinctively an age of tolerance. This quality might be illustrated in a variety of ways. Boccaccio's bold attacks on the clergy, notably in his tale of the conversion of Abraham the Jew, would have been wholly impossible a century or two later, when his works were subjected to official censure and expurgation. Abraham's change of religion was due to a candid study of facts. He had been to Rome and failed to discern in churchmen any sign of goodness. How was he to account for the continued existence of Christianity ? There was only one method of accounting for it, and that was that the Holy Ghost himself, the Hand of God, sustained the fabric of the Church, which would otherwise have collapsed in ruin. This selection of a Jew as critic of the established religion — and it may be worth recalling that he is substituted in this *rôle* for the noble Saladin—is indeed notable. When we think of the mediæval Jew in relation to literature, we are apt to remember the tragedy of Lincoln, as rehearsed in the *Canterbury Tales*, to brand in our imagination the unholy Israelite as the incarnation of all that is bad—the black beast of a black time. In the Middle Age, however, literature owed much to the Jew. On this subject let me quote the sentence of an able French scholar, M. Adolphe de Puibusque : " Les services rendus par d'autres Israélites sont inappréciable. Ces hommes sans patrie ont rempli l'office d'agents de communication entre toutes les nations de l'ancien monde ; ils ont suppléé par leur activité à l'inertie des populations musulmanes et devancé le mouvement propagateur de l'imprimerie ; après avoir fait circuler de proche en proche les traditions antiques dans les littératures orientales, ils les ont introduites en Occident par des versions soit en latin soit en langue vulgaire." [1] Incidentally, in the first chapter of this work, has been mentioned the co-operation of a Jew in the *Erweiterung* of *Parzival*, but such humble and obscure service in the building of European literature is naturally forgotten in after-ages. Not so the splendid achievements of the Jewish moralists in Spain, in the fourteenth century the most liberal country in Europe. Nor was Spanish courtesy confined to the Jew. It was shared in equal measure by the hereditary but now vanquished enemy, the Moor. A curious monument of the intercourse between the

[1] See Preface to his translation of *El Conde Lucanor*, p. 136.

two races has been preserved in the manuscript of *Josef*, a Castilian poem written in Arabic characters. The rise of a whole national literature, as in England, is a yet more striking proof of tolerance, but, *au bout du compte*, the most striking of all possible proofs is Messer Giovanni Boccaccio. How many a poor wretch has been hanged by the neck, or burnt at the stake, for daring immeasurably less than he ! But to deform is often safer than to reform, though, in regard of learning, the mocker was reformer too.

From a strictly literary, and at the same time broadly European, point of view, the most salient feature of the age is the forfeiture of the primacy, in matters intellectual, by France. Amidst the distractions of endless unlucky wars it would have been nothing short of a miracle had Frenchmen been able to revenge their national calamities by perpetuating their spiritual empire. At any rate this consolation was refused them, and the French now looked, not indeed to England, which had been intellectually a province of their own, but to Italy, for the supply of fresh models. It was not that Italy could offer much new material. The material was, on the whole, the joint-stock of all European nations, and France herself might claim a considerable part on the ground of invention, or prescription, or first effectual use. But the Italians had studied more profoundly the art of expression, and by discarding the fresh utterances of the old French school for more of form and method, had succeeded in elevating themselves to the position of classics. This excessive attention to form, especially

metrical form, as seen, for example, in the German
Meistersingers and the French lyric poets, is a
symptom not altogether favourable, since the practice tends to reverse the natural order of things.
Content should find its own form, and not *vice versa*.
There is something predestined in the metre of the
great masterpieces.

Closely allied with the end of French monopoly in
the lighter sorts of literature is the fall of Latin as the
sole, or nearly the sole, gate and garner of the fruits
of research and serious thought.   The fourteenth
century was indeed, for all the important as well as
some unimportant vernaculars, an era of complete enfranchisement; or if anything yet lacked of complete
enfranchisement, it was the fault less of external
opportunity than of inward unreadiness.   A folk-
tongue cannot pass in a moment into an apt and
artful vehicle of philosophic subtleties or social re-
finements.   Necessarily this is the work of time, and
the fourteenth century, notwithstanding laudable
efforts, never mastered the manifold possibilities of
prose.   A flexible prose-style comes not with observation, and to some languages, swaddled with syntactical
formulæ, comes not at all.   Prose, however, though
still unripe artistically, was constantly growing in
volume and encroaching on the domain of verse, with,
at least, this result, that a basis was formed for experiment.   In so far as it was not a copy, a blurred
reproduction of the past, there is the character of the
fourteenth century.   It was emphatically an age of
experiments.   The period was marked by no strong

general tendency except in the direction of symbolism, which, in spite of Dante, can hardly be accounted a merit. Were I in love with paradox, I should say of the fourteenth century that it was not, as regards literature, a great age, but that it was an age of great men. In order to be great, an epoch must be solid, homogeneous ; and the fourteenth century is a bundle of contradictions. But the greatness of individual writers — Dante, Petrarch, Boccaccio, Froissart, Chaucer—is beyond the reach of cavil and controversy, being indeed all the more appreciable by reason of the mediocrity, or less, that serves them for a background.

INDEX.

PRINTED BY WILLIAM BLACKWOOD AND SON.